BLACK

9/11

MONEY, MOTIVE & TECHNOLOGY

MARK H. GAFFNEY

Published by:
Trine Day LLC
PO Box 577
Walterville, OR 97489
1-800-556-2012
www.TrineDay.com
publisher@trineday.net

Library of Congress Control Number: 2012936843

Black 9/11: Money, Motive & Technology/Gaffney, Mark H.
—1st ed.
p. cm.
Includes bibliography.
Epub (ISBN-13) 978-1-936296-47-7 (ISBN-10) 1-936296-47-0
Kindle (ISBN-13) 978-1-936296-48-4 (ISBN-10) 1-936296-48-9
Print (ISBN-13) 978-1-936296-46-0 (ISBN-10) 1-936296-46-2
1. September 11 Terrorist Attacks, 2001. 2. United States -- Politics and government -- 2001-2009. 3. United States -- Politics and government -- 1945-2001. 4. Conspiracies -- United States -- History I. Title

FIRST EDITION
10 9 8 7 6 5 4 3 2 1

Printed in the USA
Distribution to the Trade by:
Independent Publishers Group (IPG)
814 North Franklin Street
Chicago, Illinois 60610
312.337.0747
www.ipgbook.com

Publisher's Foreword

Watching a coordinated, devastating attack on our country from an underground bunker at the White House can affect how you view your responsibilities.

We will, in fact, be greeted as liberators.

The people that were involved in some of those activities before 9/11 are still out there.

– Dick Cheney

Honestly, where are we headed? More of us are becoming aware of the criminality entrenched in our system, but while the image in the rear-view mirror gets clearer, our experience of our true heritage recedes. Quaint American notions: freedom, liberty and the pursuit of happiness have been rendered foggy mists. Wispy memories pushed into near extinction by economic, social and political chicanery, leaving us hoi polloi operating as mindless reactionaries, shills and pawns. A game is afoot and we the people aren't even in the race – even though we pay the bills.

Mark Gaffney's, *Black 911: Money, Motive and Technology* takes us on a journey of trying to understand the events of that fateful day in a different light. Showing us what was hidden; what was going on while our thoughts were diverted elsewhere. To help us comprehend the scope, and especially the *size* of the quasi-official "black funds" Mark gives some of the historical underpinnings to this massive deceit. A secret history of criminality and corruption beyond the wildest imagination of fiction.

Gaffney also treats us to investigations into secret technologies that may have played a major role in 9/11. He searches for the answers to questions such as: How did the inexperienced hijackers pull off such intense military-type aerial maneuvers? Was UAL 93 shot down in Shanksville? What did the eyewitness see in Shanksville? What does the radar data show? What happened to World Trade Center buildings 6 & 7? Was remote control of the airliners an operational option at the time of 9/11? And many more...

In the good old days, an honest politician was one who lied only when he had to. But now lies are becoming the accepted language of government at the highest levels, the theory being that sooner or later the people of the country will become so confused and disillusioned that they will just mind their own business, and leave governing to well-placed liars."

– Richard Reeves December 17, 1989

A little over a decade ago, our world changed. Or did it? From David R. Simon's *Elite Deviance*: "Between 1860 and 1920, the United States suffered only two major crises involving corruption on the federal level. This amounts to about one scandal every fifty years. However, beginning in 1963 with the investigation into the assassination of President Kennedy, the US government has experienced repeated scandals. The scandals themselves are serious social problems, causing all manner of social harm." And: "Many of the scandals that have occurred in the United States since 1963 have been fundamentally interrelated; that is, the same people and institutions have been involved in a number of scandals."

Black 911: Money, Motive and Technology gives us a framework on which to understand how a corrupting confluence of hidden cash, official secrecy and classified technology, may have engendered our horrendous national nightmare – leaving the last vestiges of our republic tattered and torn.

The ruling power elite have no illusions, as "Bush's brain" Karl Rove told Ron Suskind in 2004, "We're an empire now, and when we act, we create our own reality. And while you're studying that reality – judiciously, as you will – we'll act again, creating other new realities, which you can study too, and that's how things will sort out. We're history's actors ... and you, all of you, will be left to just study what we do."

With *Black 9/11* we do get to study what *they* have done.

Onward to the Utmost of Futures

Peace,
Kris Millegan
Publisher
TrineDay
April 8, 2012

This book is dedicated to all whistleblowers,
and to trail blazers like Gary Webb,
who instead of cursing the darkness lit a candle...

Acknowledgments

Wayne Anderson, Matt Walker, Thomas R. McInroy, Richard A. Grove, Steve DeNoo, Peggy and Sterling Seagrave, John Farmer, Bob Pinnacle, Kirk Oakes, Ken Jenkins, Richard A. Sharpstein, Jeremy Hammond, Daniele Ganser, Marcel Bernard, Ben Connor, Jim Fetzer, Frank Barnaby, Bill Deagle, Frank Legge, Miles Kara, Erik Larsen, Rob Balsamo, David Guyatt, William Bergman, Robert Schopmeyer, Russell Becker, Elizabeth Woodworth, and, last but not least, Ed Atkin.

Contents

National Transportation Safety Board

Washington, D.C. 20594

Office of the Managing Director

August 11, 2008

Mr. Aidan Monaghan

███████████████

Las Vegas, Nevada ███████

RE: Freedom of Information Act (FOIA) Appeal, Request No. 20080160A

Dear Mr. Monaghan:

   I write in response to your letter, which the Safety Board received on July 31, 2008, in which you appealed the response of the National Transportation Safety Board's FOIA Officer to your FOIA request for "copies of records revealing the process by which wreckage recovered from the aircraft used during the terrorist attacks of September 11, 2001, was positively identified as belonging to: American Airlines [flights 11 and 77], and United Airlines [flights 175 and 93]." Your request opined that the Safety Board must have utilized unique serial numbers of components from each of the four aircraft in order to identify the wreckage from each aircraft. The Safety Board's FOIA Officer responded to your original request on July 18, 2008, in which the FOIA Officer indicated that the Board did not have any records within the scope of your request.

   Your appeal asserts that the Safety Board's response was erroneous. In particular, your appeal states that Safety Board records mention the four aircraft "within numerous public NTSB records," and that Safety Board employees participated in the identification, collection, and examination of the wreckage of the aircraft, such as the flight data recorders and cockpit voice recorders. In addition, you assert that, "[p]hysical examination of the wreckage in question alone, cannot provide for a satisfactory basis for the affirmative determination made by the NTSB regarding the identities of the wreckage described herein," and that you believe that identification of the wreckage must have been based on "some tangible record provided to the NTSB, as allowed for by the NTSB's Quality of Information Disseminated by the National Transportation Safety Board: Guidelines for Ensuring and Maximizing the Quality of Information." With regard to your last assertion, you quote from the Safety Board's statement concerning information quality, which is available on the Board's website.

   I have carefully reviewed your appeal of the Safety Board's response to your FOIA request, and determined that the Board must deny your appeal. The Safety Board performed an adequate, reasonable search for any records within the scope of your request, in accordance with the provisions of the FOIA, and did not locate any records within the scope of your request. Oglesby v. Dep't of the Army, 920 F.2d 57, 68 (D.C. Cir. 1990); see also Campbell v. Dep't of Justice, 164 F.3d 20, 27 (D.C. Cir. 1998). The Safety Board does not have any records that "[reveal] the process by which wreckage was recovered from the aircraft used during the terrorist attacks of September 11, 2001." As you probably know, the Safety Board assisted the Federal

Bureau of Investigation (FBI) as the FBI investigated the circumstances under which the four aircraft crashed, pursuant to Congress's direction requiring the Board to relinquish its investigative priority to the FBI when the Safety Board and FBI determine that an intentional criminal act likely caused the accident at issue. 49 U.S.C. § 1131(a)(2)(B). As such, the Safety Board did not ensure that the owners of the aircraft completed wreckage release forms, as the Board typically does in investigations in which the Board has priority. See 49 C.F.R. § 831.12(b). Overall, the Safety Board does not have any records that describe the "process" by which the Board or the FBI identified wreckage.

   To the extent that you seek to inform the Safety Board of an error in its reports under Section 515 of the Treasury and General Government Appropriations Act for Fiscal Year 2001 (Public Law 106-554; H.R. 5658), and pursuant to government-wide guidelines issued by the Office of Management and Budget to assure the quality of information that Federal agencies disseminate, as described at 67 Fed. Reg. 8,452 (Feb. 22, 2002), submitting a FOIA appeal is not the appropriate mechanism. As described in the Board's Information Quality Guidelines, which, as you know, are listed on the Board's website at http://www.ntsb.gov/info/quality.htm, you must submit a request to Executive Secretariat/Information Quality, and include the following information:

1. Your name, telephone number, address and/or e-mail address;
2. Description and documentation as to how information is to be corrected, revised, or reviewed;
3. Explanation of how person submitting the request is affected by any information error;
4. Explanation of how the disseminated information failed the quality standards; and
5. Any pertinent attachments.

   Based on the foregoing, I have determined that your appeal must be denied. This response constitutes the final action from the National Transportation Safety Board on your appeal. The Freedom of Information Act, 5 U.S.C. § 552, provides for judicial review of this determination.

Two-page letter from the National Transportation Safety Board in response to Aidan Monaghan's FOIA appeal, affirming that it has no aircraft identification records.

Sincerely,

[signature]

Joseph G. Osterman
Managing Director

Plausibility of 9/11 Aircraft Attacks Generated by GPS-Guided Aircraft Autopilot Systems
— Part One —

by Aidan Monaghan (B.Sc., EET)

The flight performance of inexperienced terrorist pilots during the September 11, 2001 attacks has surprised knowledgeable observers. This is because the amateur pilots who are alleged to have committed the attacks showed great skill in operating complex flight control systems. Although less is known about the flight operations of the two planes that struck the World Trade Center (WTC), i.e., American Airlines Flight 11 (AA 11) and United Airlines Flight 175 (UAL 175), because the Flight Data Recorders (FDRs) for these aircraft were not recovered, both WTC impacts nonetheless showed a high level of piloting skill.

The points of impact also reveal a remarkable coincidence: each aircraft struck precisely the bottom portion of the only sections of each tower recently upgraded (between 1995 and 2000) with thermal insulation, to guard against building fires. The renovation of the North Tower (struck by AA 11 at floors 94-96) involved floor 92 and above. Similarly, the renovation of the South Tower (struck by UAL 175 at floor 78-81) involved floor 77 and above.[1]

The fact that work crews had recently been granted access to the very floors struck on 9/11 is suspicious, and raises questions about the true nature of the "upgrade." Could this explain why the collapse of each tower initiated very near the points of the visually spectacular impacts? As we know, largely for this reason, the collapses were attributed to structural failure. Yet, because of the "upgrades," the opportunity clearly existed for the clandestine planting of explosives in the critical floors of both towers.[2]

The Flight Data Recorders from the other two planes were recovered: American Airlines Flight 77 (AA 77), which hit the Pentagon, and United Airlines Flight 93 (UAL 93), which crashed in Pennsylvania. They indicate that in both cases the accused hijack pilots performed numerous complex autopilot mode changes.[3]

This has puzzled experts. Recently declassified 9/11 Commission records include interviews with United Airlines personnel who express skepticism that the accused hijack pilots could have performed flight operations involving this level of expertise. One said, "Entering changes to the autopilot is something that terrorist pilots probably would not have been trained or able to do. Even the United senior pilot who instructs on how to do that said that he always has to pause before he makes such corrections to make sure he remembered how to enter the change."[4]

The recovered FDRs from AA 77 and UAL 93 indicate multiple erratic changes in altitude, attitude, speed, and direction, which some have interpreted as evidence for human control. However, a chronological discrepancy in the chain of custody of AA 77's FDR suggests that data may have been altered or falsified.

AA 77's readout file was completed four hours and fifteen minutes before the FDR was even found.[5] This has never been explained.

Furthermore, the FDRs from AA 77 and UAL 93 are nearly the only ones during the previous twenty years of major National Transportation Safety Board (NTSB) US aviation mishap investigations for which unique inventory control serial numbers were not published.[6] Such serial numbers are required to facilitate FDR data readouts.[7] Indeed, when I contacted the NTSB, I was told that the agency possesses no records that positively identify the FDRs for either aircraft.[8]

We must therefore conclude that the official flight information documenting the alleged terrorist-pilot control of both these aircraft is unverifiable at best, and may be fraudulent.

9/11 HYPOTHESIS BASED ON EVIDENCE FOR PRECISE NAVIGATION

Juxtaposed to these unanswered questions is the rather compelling evidence for precision automated control of the allegedly hijacked aircraft on 9/11. Curiously, the flight paths of the commercial planes involved in the attack share common characteristics with the capabilities provided by precision automated flight control systems and related commercial aviation technology, all of which had emerged in the period just before 2001.

The following discussion supports a hypothesis involving the clandestine use of precise augmented GPS guided auto-pilot aircraft systems on 9/11.

Various US federal government and civil aviation industry publications describe the development and implementation, pre-September 11, 2001, of state-of-the-art systems capable of facilitating precise automated navigation of Boeing 757 and 767 aircraft to a given destination—the very same aircraft used in the 9/11 attacks. The navigational systems were developed in conjunction with Global Positioning System (GPS), a space-based radio-navigation system that generates accurate positioning, navigation and timing information for civilian use at no cost. The information signal is obtained through the use of GPS signal receiving equipment.[9]

Although GPS was originally developed for military use by the US Department of Defense, by the 1990s many civilian applications were emerging. These included navigational use by the Federal Aviation Administration (FAA) and commercial airlines. During this period, however, the US military continued to have priority, and for reasons of national security "selectively downgraded" the GPS signal available for civilian use.

This policy changed on May 1, 2000, with the announcement that the US would end the "selective availability" of GPS in order to promote transportation safety, as well as other scientific and commercial interests.[10] As a result of this decision, made by President Clinton, the US military partially lifted the "intentional degradation" of the GPS signal, whereupon its accuracy increased by a factor of ten. This shift, 16 months before 9/11, had powerful ramifications for commercial airline navigation.

Indeed, by the mid-1990s it had become evident that GPS was the navigation technology of the future. By this point, the FAA, assisted by companies such as Raytheon, was already making plans to eventually replace the older, more expensive ILS landing systems and VOR navigation systems with new augmented GPS signal service. Richard Armitage, a signatory of the "Project for the New

American Century," is known to have served on Raytheon's Special Advisory Board, although precisely when is unclear.[11]

AUGMENTED GPS

Augmented GPS was truly a quantum advance in airline navigation. The FAA announced its availability in August 2000, pending final approval by the FAA. This was just 13 months prior to 9/11. The new Wide Area Augmentation System (WAAS) was designed to further improve the accuracy of GPS. WAAS utilizes both satellites and precisely surveyed ground stations, which monitor the GPS satellite signal for errors.

Timing is crucial in GPS. The problem is that the GPS signal tends to be refracted, i.e., slows down, as it moves through the ionosphere toward earth, which causes errors in the system. The numerous ground stations correct these errors, then, relay the corrected GPS data to ground-based uplink stations, which transmit the corrected data to geostationary satellites. The satellites are the final link, broadcasting the corrected positional data.[12]

To understand the amazing improvement in accuracy, consider that in the days before GPS, conventional aviation navigation beacon signals provided placement information accurate to within one mile.[13] After GPS became available, accuracy improved to within 100 meters. Once the augmented GPS, i.e., WAAS, became available, accuracy of horizontal and vertical positional data radically improved again, to between 1 and 3 meters.

This level of accuracy made GPS-supported Category I precision aircraft runway approaches feasible throughout the contiguous United States.[14] The newly activated WAAS signal was even utilized to precisely survey the Ground Zero site in New York, following the September 11, 2001 terrorist attacks, according to Raytheon's director of satellite navigation systems.[15]

PERFORMANCE BASED NAVIGATION VIA WAYPOINTS

The availability of WAAS also improved the accuracy of another aircraft navigation and landing procedure system known as

"Required Navigation Performance" (RNP). First developed during the 1990s, RNP is a system for defining tolerances deemed necessary for navigational safety. The RNP system utilizes precisely constructed "highways in the sky" that can be navigated by the autopilot systems of aircraft like those involved in the terrorist attacks of September 11, 2001. Such routes "never vary more than 18 meters, half the wingspan of a Boeing 737".[16] WAAS-enabled RNP technology "pinpoints the location of a fast-moving jet to within yards".[17] Once the RNP system began to utilize the WAAS signal, pilots were "able to determine the airplane's vertical and horizontal position [to] within six or seven meters (about 20 to 23 feet)".[18]

The WAAS signal (horizontal and vertical position) accuracy of 1 to 3 meters was a significant improvement over the standard Instrument Landing System (ILS) technology then in general use at major US airports. The latter utilize antenna arrays that provide for aircraft centerline placement over the 150- to 200-foot wide runways; but are only accurate to 7.6 meters both vertically and horizontally at the middle marker.[19]

RNP "highway in the sky" routes provide for a containment accuracy within a virtual corridor, the dimensions of which are described in nautical miles. In 2003, Raytheon reported further improvement: the narrowing of WAAS-enabled corridors to just 243 feet (RNP 0.02). According to Raytheon, "WAAS ... supports required navigation performance (RNP) operations, providing a precision navigation capability down to RNP 0.02 (an accuracy of 0.02nm)," In plain English, WAAS is capable of maintaining an air corridor accurate to within .02 of a nautical-mile 95% of the time.[20]

In GPS navigation, a "waypoint" is defined as a three-dimensional location within the National Air Space, comprised of longitude, latitude and altitude coordinates.[21] RNP-supported flight paths and runway approach procedures are comprised of a series of waypoints.[22] Interestingly, the World Trade Center towers themselves are known to have occupied waypoint coordinates.[23]

Aircraft Flight Management Systems (FMS) facilitate precision instrument approach procedures that involve the interception of waypoint coordinates.[24] By substitution of WTC and Pentagon building waypoint coordinates for flight-leg terminating waypoint coordinates, a RNP-like waypoint intercept procedure under autopilot control could have accomplished the attacks on the Pentagon and WTC of September 11, 2001.

To be continued...

ENDNOTES

1   Nicholas J. Carino et al, "Federal Building and Fire Safety Investigation of the World Trade Center Disaster Passive Fire Protection," NIST NCSTAR 1-6A, P. 39, posted at http://wtc.nist.gov/NCSTAR1/PDF/NCSTAR%201-6A.pdf; Therese McAllister et al., "Chapter 1," World Trade Center Building Performance Study, p. 4, posted at http://www.fema.gov/pdf/library/fema403_ch1.pdf.

2   Kevin Ryan, "Another amazing coincidence related to the WTC," *9/11 Blogger*, January 6, 2008, posted at http://www.911blogger.com/node/13272.

3   John O'Callaghan and Daniel Bower, Ph.D, "Study of Autopilot, Navigation Equipment, and Fuel Consumption Activity Based on United Airlines Flight 93 and American Airlines Flight 77 Digital Flight Data Recorder Information," February 13, 2002, posted at http://www.ntsb.gov/info/autopilot_AA77_UA93_study.pdf.

4   Miles Kara, "COMMISSION SENSITIVE UNCLASSIFIED - MEMORANDUM FOR THE RECORD - Interviews of United Airlines and American Airlines personnel in key roles on September 11, 2001," November 2003, p. 2, posted at http://media.nara.gov/9-11/MFR/t-0148-911MFR-01098.pdf.

5   Aidan Monaghan, "NTSB Affirms Dubious Explanation For Pentagon "Black Box" Data File Time Stamp Discrepancy," *9/11 Blogger*, October 27, 2008, posted at http://www.911blogger.com/node/18294.

6   Aidan Monaghan, "Was Essential 9/11 Aircraft 'Blackbox' Identification Information Withheld From NTSB?" *9/11 Blogger*, June 13, 2008, posted at http://www.911blogger.com/node/16089.

7   "Flight Data Recorder Handbook for Aviation Accident Investigations," NTSB. Posted at http://www.scribd.com/doc/50836952/FDR-Handbook

8   Aidan Monaghan, "NTSB Elaborates On Absent Records Pertaining To Positively Identified 9/11 Aircraft Wreckage, Including 2 Flight Data Recorders," *9/11 Blogger*, August 14, 2008, posted at http://www.911blogger.com/node/17139.

9   "Global Positioning System," Wikipedia, posted at http://en.wikipedia.org/wiki/Gps.

10 "STATEMENT BY THE PRESIDENT REGARDING THE UNITED STATES' DECISION TO STOP DEGRADING GLOBAL POSITIONING SYSTEM ACCURACY," May 1, 2001, posted at http://ngs.woc.noaa.gov/FGCS/info/sans_SA/docs/statement.htm.

11 "The Making of U.S. Foreign Policy -- BIOGRAPHIES OF THE AUTHORS, AMBASSADOR RICHARD LEE ARMITAGE," posted at http://usinfo.state.gov/journals/itps/0900/ijpe/pj52bios.htm.

12 "Navigation Services - WAAS - How It Works," Federal Aviation Administration, August, 2010. Posted at http://www.faa.gov/about/office_org/headquarters_offices/ato/service_units/techops/navservices/gnss/waas/howitworks/

13 Mathew Brellis, "DIRECT FLIGHT NEW TECHNOLOGY WILL GUIDE PLANES," *Boston Globe*, October 7, 1999, posted at http://www.highbeam.com/doc/1P2-8569182.html.

14 "AMENDED VERSION: Wide Area Augmentation System Signal Now Available,"

Federal Aviation Administration, August 24, 2000, posted at http://www.faa.gov/news/press_releases/news_story.cfm?newsId=5249; "WAAS Fact Sheet," Federal Aviation Administration, posted at http://www.faa.gov/news/fact_sheets/news_story.cfm?newsId=6283.

15   David Johnson, "WAAS: Back in Step, Avionics Magazine," *Avionics Magazine*, February 1, 2002, posted at http://www.aviationtoday.com/av/categories/commercial/12571.html.

16   Domic Gates, "Kent company bringing a navigation revolution," *Seattle Times*, October 22, 2006, posted at http://seattletimes.nwsource.com/html/businesstechnology/2003316294_naverus22.html.

17   Michael Copeland, "A fuel-saving flight plan," *CNN Money*, July 9, 2008, posted at http://money.cnn.com/galleries/2008/fortune/0807/gallery.copeland_naverus.fortune/index.html.

18   Mathew Brellis, "DIRECT FLIGHT NEW TECHNOLOGY WILL GUIDE PLANES," Boston Globe, October 7, 1999, posted at http://www.highbeam.com/doc/1P2-8569182.html

19   "Replacing the ILS: the Wide-Area Augmentation System (WAAS) will provide ILS-like accuracy with GPS. Can it replace the familiar ground-based system on which we depend?" *Aviation Safety*, October 1, 2006, posted at http://www.highbeam.com/doc/1G1-157589720.html.

20   The math is straightforward: 1 nautical mile = 6,076 feet; RNP 0.02 = RNP (0.02 nautical mile radius) x 2 = RNP (121.5 foot radius) x 2 = a 243 foot wide corridor. "CRITERIA FOR APPROVAL OF CATEGORY III WEATHER MINIMA FOR TAKEOFF, LANDING, AND ROLLOUT," Federal Aviation Administration, posted at http://www.airweb.faa.gov/Regulatory_and_Guidance_Library/rgAdvisoryCircular.nsf/1ab39b4ed563b08985256a35006d56af/bbada17da0d0bbd1862569ba006f64d0/$FILE/AC120-28D.pdf.

Also see Graham Warwick, "UPS wins FAA certification for wide-area GPS receiver," *Flight International*, July 1, 2003, posted at http://www.flightglobal.com/articles/2003/01/07/159964/ups-wins-faa-certification-for-wide-area-gps-receiver.html.

21   "Waypoint," Wikipedia. Posted at http://en.wikipedia.org/wiki/Waypoint

22   "United States Standard For Required Navigation Performance (RNP) Approach Procedures With Special Aircraft And Aircrew Authorization Required (SAAAR)," Federal Aviation Administration, posted at http://www.faa.gov/documentLibrary/media/Order/ND/8260_52.pdf.

23   "The International GPS Global Positioning System Waypoint Registry TM," posted at http://www.waypoint.org/.

24   "FLIGHT MANAGEMENT SYSTEM (FMS) INSTRUMENT PROCEDURES DEVELOPMENT," Federal Aviation Administration, December 31, 1998, p. 6, posted at http://www.faa.gov/about/office_org/headquarters_offices/avs/offices/afs/afs400/afs420/policies_guidance/orders/media/826040B.pdf.

Prologue

The Day that Changed Everything

The events of September 11, 2001 fundamentally altered our world. It was as if all of humanity, in one horrifying day, passed through a portal into a different reality. The shift was such that modern history is now irrevocably split into "before" and "after," a bit like the traditional division of ancient history into BC and AD. Comparisons with the Japanese attack on Pearl Harbor, nearly sixty years before, are also apt, for just as the "date which will live in infamy" triggered the US entry in World War II, 9/11 likewise sparked a vastly expanded US military presence overseas, including a steep escalation of military force that continues to this day.

But it is a cruel truism to say that our nation was caught off-guard on 9/11. Yes, it is true, but not in the way that most people think. We humans are easily shocked and traumatized by sudden overwhelming violence, and respond in rather predictable ways to such an experience. Many people shut down and become passive; others fly into a blind rage. The point is that people who have been traumatized can be manipulated, quite easily, for some ulterior purpose.[1]

In the immediate aftermath of 9/11, I was among a minority of Americans deeply disturbed by the hysterical flag-waving and the jingoistic cries for war. Not because we did not care about our country, but because we sensed that our emotions and the distraught feelings of so many others were being exploited for nefarious ends. At the time, of course, and for years afterward, the tide of indignant patriotism ran so strongly that few dared to raise such concerns.

Today however, more than ten years after the attacks, it is clear that the skeptics were correct. Sadly, it is also apparent that most Americans still have not come to terms with the horrible events of that fateful day. Many people simply refuse to talk about it and have clearly pushed the experience into the backs of their minds, perhaps in an attempt to repress the pain. Typically, when asked, they insist that 9/11 is ancient history and that we must put it behind us and move on.

But we cannot move on because, as a nation, we are stuck in a vicious cycle. Too few Americans have consciously processed the mix of emotions associated with 9/11, and this is frustrating our collective capacity to think rationally about the future. Once again, we have failed to learn the lessons of history, and so are doomed to repeat them.

A well-known principle in psychotherapy goes like this: individuals who have been traumatized must face the pain in a conscious way to be free of the trauma's debilitating effects. Indeed, this is the goal of all therapy in these cases. It is no surprise that the principle also holds at the macro-level, that is, with regard to society as a whole. For what is society if not a collection of individuals? No wonder that in 2012 we as a nation are singularly unprepared for the future that is fast upon us.

America is probably the most propagandized country on earth, with the possible exception of totalitarian, backwater places like North Korea or Burma. Our countrymen have been systematically dumbed down, distracted and demoralized by our own government and its willing minions in the media and throughout much of academia. Here in the US, the dark arts of thought control have been elevated to a level of sophistication almost undreamed of by the Nazis and Soviets.

Many of our countrymen, succumbing to the twenty-four/seven drumbeat of hyped news and infotainment, have given up even trying to make sense of the world around them. When asked about some world event, they respond (if they respond at all) by regurgitating whatever they may have seen on FOX or CNN.

Given the reality of a largely disconnected public, it is hardly surprising that our nation is also bereft of any leadership worthy of the name. The success of democracy, as Jefferson wrote, requires an informed citizenry. Efforts by a small activist minority to reverse the trend and rein in our out-of-control war machine have so far been defeated at every turn. No wonder then that we are increasingly being overtaken by events beyond our control.

This is the common perception, and in this case the common perception happens to be correct. It is occurring internationally, but also here at home where we are experiencing the death of the American dream in the double whammy of economic decline and impending social breakdown. A poet friend hit the bulls-eye when he called America "the grave of rainbows."[2]

If this reasoning is accurate, our best, indeed perhaps our last, remaining shot to turn the tide is to revisit 9/11, not for the masochistic purpose of wallowing in pain for pain's sake, but for the therapeutic goal of honestly facing the key questions at their historical root: Was 9/11 simply a trigger pulled by al-Qaeda for jihad against the United States? Or did it hide deeper and even darker motives? The distinction is of enormous importance, because the correct answer makes all the difference.

For us, and for the world.

(ENDNOTES)

1   For more discussion of this phenomenon, see Naomi Klein, *The Shock Doctrine* (New York: Henry Holt, 2007).

2   Garrett Lambrev, *Dogstar and Poems from Other Planets* (Berkeley, CA: Beatitude Press, 2007).

"All the News That's Fit to Print"

The New York Times

Late Edition
New York: Today, sunny, a few afternoon clouds. High 77. Tonight, slightly more humid. Low 63. Tomorrow, sun then clouds. High 83. Yesterday, high 81, low 63. Weather map, Page C19.

VOL. CL .. No. 51,874   Copyright © 2001 The New York Times   NEW YORK, WEDNESDAY, SEPTEMBER 12, 2001   Beyond the greater New York metropolitan area   75 CENTS

U.S. ATTACKED

HIJACKED JETS DESTROY TWIN TOWERS AND HIT PENTAGON IN DAY OF TERROR

A CREEPING HORROR

Buildings Burn and Fall as Onlookers Search for Elusive Safety

By N. R. KLEINFIELD

It kept getting worse.

The horror arrived in episodic bursts of chilling disbelief, signified first by trembling floors, sharp explosions, cracked windows. There was the actual unfathomable realization of a gaping, flaming hole in first one of the tall towers, and then the same thing all over again in its twin. There was the merciless sight of bodies helplessly tumbling out, some of them in flames.

Finally, the mighty towers themselves were reduced to nothing. Dense plumes of smoke raced through the downtown avenues, coursing between the buildings, shaped like tornadoes on their sides.

Every sound was cause for alarm. A plane appeared overhead. Was another one coming? No, it was a fighter jet. But was it friend or enemy? People scrambled for their lives, but they didn't know where to go. Should they go north, south, east, west? Stay outside, go indoors? People but beneath cars and each other. Some contemplated jumping into the river.

For those trying to flee the very epicenter of the collapsing World Trade Center towers, the most horrible thought of all finally dawned on them: nowhere was safe.

For several panic-stricken hours yesterday morning, people in Lower Manhattan witnessed the inexpressible, the incomprehensible, the unthinkable. "I don't know what the gates of hell look like, but it's got to be like this," said John Maloney, a security director for an Internet firm in the trade center. "I'm a combat veteran, Vietnam, and I never saw anything like this."

The first warnings were small ones. Blocks away, Jim Farmer, a film composer, was having breakfast at a small restaurant on West Broadway. He heard the sound of a jet. An odd sound — too loud, it seemed, to be

Continued on Page A7

A Somber Bush Says Terrorism Cannot Prevail

By ELISABETH BUMILLER with DAVID E. SANGER

WASHINGTON, Sept. 11 — President Bush vowed tonight to retaliate against those responsible for the day's attacks on New York and Washington, declaring that he would "make no distinction between the terrorists who committed these acts and those who harbor them."

"These acts of mass murder were intended to frighten our nation into chaos and retreat, but they have failed," the president said in his first speech to the nation from the Oval Office. "Our country is strong. Terrorist acts can shake the foundation of our biggest buildings, but they cannot touch the foundation of America."

His speech came after a day of trauma that seems destined to define his presidency. Seeking to at once calm the nation and declare his determination to exact retribution, he told a country numbed by repeated scenes of carnage that "these acts shattered steel, but they cannot dent the steel of American resolve."

Mr. Bush spoke only hours after returning from a zigzag course across the country, as his Secret Service and military security teams moved him from Florida, where he woke up this morning expecting to press for his education bill, to command posts in Louisiana and Nebraska before it was determined the attacks had probably ended and he could safely return to the capital.

It was a sign of the catastrophic

Continued on Page A4

Steve Ludlum/The New York Times

President Vows to Exact Punishment for 'Evil'

By SERGE SCHMEMANN

Hijackers rammed jetliners into each of New York's World Trade Center towers yesterday, toppling both in a hellish storm of ash, glass, smoke and leaping victims, while a third jetliner crashed into the Pentagon in Virginia. There was no official count, but President Bush said thousands had perished, and in the immediate aftermath the calamity was already being ranked the worst and most audacious terror attack in American history.

The attacks seemed carefully coordinated. The hijacked planes were all en route to California, and therefore gorged with fuel, and their departures were spaced within an hour and 40 minutes. The first, American Airlines Flight 11, a Boeing 767 out of Boston for Los Angeles, crashed into the north tower at 8:48 a.m. Eighteen minutes later, United Airlines Flight 175, also headed from Boston to Los Angeles, plowed into the south tower.

Then an American Airlines Boeing 757, Flight 77, left Washington's Dulles International Airport bound for Los Angeles, but instead hit the western part of the Pentagon, the military headquarters where 24,000 people work, at 9:40 a.m. Finally, United Airlines Flight 93, a Boeing 757 flying from Newark to San Francisco, crashed near Pittsburgh, raising the possibility that its hijackers had failed in whatever their mission was.

Kelly Guenther for The New York Times
SECOND PLANE United Airlines Flight 175 nearing the trade center's south tower.

There were indications that the hijackers on at least two of the planes were armed with knives. Attorney General John Ashcroft told reporters in the evening that the suspects on Flight 11 were armed that way. And Barbara Olson, a television commentator who was traveling on American Flight 77, managed to reach her husband, Solicitor General Theodore Olson, by cell phone and to tell him that the hijackers were armed with knives and a box cutter.

In all, 266 people perished in the four planes and several score more were known dead elsewhere. Numerous firefighters, police officers and other rescue workers who responded to the initial disaster in Lower Manhattan were killed or injured when the buildings collapsed. Hundreds were treated for cuts, broken bones, burns and smoke inhalation.

But the real carnage was concealed for now by the twisted, smoking, ash-choked carcasses of the twin towers, in which thousands of people used to work on a weekday. The collapse of the towers caused another World Trade Center building to fall 7 hours later, and several

Continued on Page A14

Awaiting the Aftershocks

Washington and Nation Plunge Into Fight With Enemy Hard to Identify and Punish

By R. W. APPLE Jr.

WASHINGTON, Sept. 11 — Today's devastating and astonishingly well-coordinated attacks on the World Trade Center towers in New York and on the Pentagon outside of Washington plunged the nation into a warlike struggle against an enemy that will be hard to identify with certainty and hard to punish with precision.

The whole nation — to a degree the whole world — shook as hijacked airliners plunged into buildings that symbolize the financial and military might of the United States. The sense of security and self-confidence that Americans take as their birthright suffered a grievous blow, from which recovery will be slow. The aftershocks will be nearly as bad, as hundreds and possibly thousands of people discover that friends or relatives died awful, fiery deaths.

Scenes of chaos and destruction evocative of the nightmare world of Hieronymus Bosch, with smoke and debris blotting out the sun, were carried by television into homes and workplaces across the nation. Echoing Franklin D. Roosevelt's description of the attack on Pearl Harbor as an event "which will live in infamy," Gov. George E. Pataki of New York, a Republican, spoke of "an incredible outrage" and Senator Charles E. Schumer of New York, a Democrat, spoke of "a dastardly attack."

But mere words were inadequate vessels to contain the sense of shock and horror that people felt. As Washington struggled to regain

a sense of equilibrium, with warplanes and heavily armed helicopters crossing overhead, past and present national security officials earnestly debated the possibility of a Congressional declaration of war — but against precisely whom, and in what exact circumstances? War ships were maneuvering to protect New York and Washington. The North American Air Defense Command, which had seemed to many a relic of the cold war, adopted a posture

Continued on Page A24

MORE ON THE ATTACKS

RESCUERS BECOME VICTIMS Firefighters who rushed to the trade center were killed.
PAGE A7

SEARCH FOR SURVIVORS Some people trapped in the rubble but heard were rescued.
PAGE A5

OFFICIALS SUSPECT BIN LADEN Eavesdropping intercepts after the attacks were cited.
PAGE A6

TERRORISTS EXPLOIT WEAKNESS Investigators had criticized precautions against hijacking.
PAGE A5

CASUALTIES IN WASHINGTON Unknown number of people were killed at the Pentagon.
PAGE A10

Justin Lane for The New York Times

AMERICAN TARGETS A ball of fire exploded outward after the second of two jetliners slammed into the World Trade Center; less than two hours later, both of the 110-story towers were gone. Hijackers crashed a third airliner into the Pentagon, setting off a huge explosion and fire.

Ruth Fremson/The New York Times

Chapter 1

Crashes

O f the four allegedly hijacked airliners on September 11, United Airlines Flight 93 is the most intriguing. There are a number of reasons for this, but primarily because UAL 93 was the plane that went astray. It appears that, for whatever reason, this fourth aircraft was unable to complete its mission, whether to impact the US Capitol, as many believe, or perhaps to target World Trade Center Building 7, as some have suggested.

The 9/11 attacks involved an extremely complex set of operations, and because their success depended on timing, it is not surprising that problems would arise. The belated collapse of WTC-7, which was not impacted by an aircraft, is one likely example. Some believe the original plan was to drop WTC-7 immediately after the collapse of the North Tower, when the immense dust cloud would have provided concealment, obscuring what appeared to be a classic demolition.

Something went wrong however, which meant dropping this building in plain view shortly after 5 P.M. on the afternoon of September 11. The perpetrators got away with it by exercising near total control over the mainstream media, which kept the shocking collapse footage of WTC-7 out of the news.

Although UAL 93's intended target remains unknown, whatever went wrong in-flight evidently compelled the forces behind the curtain (possibly elements of the US intelligence community) to resort to a back-up contingency plan. If this reasoning is valid, it means they felt it necessary to take extraordinary measures that involved major risks to themselves. It follows that the crash of UAL 93 could hold one of the keys to exposing the plot.

UAL 93 was late departing from Newark International on the morning of September 11, 2001. The flight was scheduled to leave at 8 A.M. but was delayed on the runway for approximately 42 minutes. Some skeptics reject the "late factor" as too obvious to account for UAL 93's failure to reach its target. Surely, they argue, the plotters would have been well aware that flights out of Newark are subject to frequent delays. Some even believe they factored the delayed take-off into the attack plan.

But I seriously doubt this. UAL 93 departed Newark just minutes before American Airlines Flight 11 impacted the North Tower. If the flight had been delayed much longer, UAL 93 might have been grounded before it could leave. This ought to tell us that the delay was not part of the planning. It is hard to escape the conclusion that Newark was simply a poor choice in an attack plan where everything depended on timing.

So, why Newark? I suggest that the masterminds of the attack did not exercise control over every planning decision. The selection of Newark may indicate that Mohamed Atta & company not only hijacked the planes, but were actively involved in planning various details of the operation.

If they were being used in someone else's larger plan, it would nonetheless be essential for the hijackers to believe that they were in total control of the operation. They had to be free to make some of the planning decisions, at the risk of making bad ones.

With regard to UAL 93's failure to reach a target: something may have gone wrong, requiring a drastic "clean up" intervention. We do not know what happened, but the case may illustrate just how ill-prepared the terrorist pilots were, when left to their own devices.

According to the official story, five hijackers boarded flights AA 11, UAL 175, and AA 77, but only four boarded UAL 93. Were the terrorists undermanned on the last flight? Perhaps, and if so this supports the likelihood that heroic passengers may indeed have taken matters into their own hands in the flight's last minutes.

Nearly everyone knows the story of heroism aboard United Flight 93, how, in the plane's last desperate moments, passengers stormed the cockpit in an attempt to wrest control from the hijackers. The narrative is familiar because, within days of September 11, the government and the media began to spin the UAL 93 tragedy into a national legend. In 2006, two Hollywood productions, *United 93* for theaters and *Flight 93* for television, played upon our collective pain, grief and loss, while helping to deliver continued popular support for President Bush's so-called War on Terror. The script for *that* production included blank checks for war-without-end against an almost invisible adversary.

While it is right to celebrate the heroism of our fellow Americans, there is good reason to doubt the official explanation, which is that hijack pilot Ziad Jarrah crashed the plane before the passengers could gain control of the cockpit.

Before examining the UAL 93 story in further detail, however, other anomalies deserve consideration.

WHAT HAPPENED, AND WHERE?

It is not surprising that so many Americans initially questioned whether UAL 93 actually crashed at Shanksville, in western Pennsylvania. Even as the 9/11 attacks were unfolding, *CBS News* reported that UAL 93 had crashed near Camp David, Maryland, which is located about 90 miles east of Shanksville.[1]

The network identified the source as an FBI official in Washington. In its report, CBS also noted the significance of the timing and the presumed target. Camp David is the presidential retreat where, *on September 11, 1978*, Israeli Prime Minister Menachem Begin and Egyptian President Anwar Sadat signed the historic Camp David Peace Accords, ending decades of on-and-off warfare between the two states. Yet, even if the network was wrong about the presumed target, the date chosen for the attacks signaled the jihadists' disdain for that agreement.

It is also noteworthy that the CBS report about Camp David aired immediately *after* the network reported that "a large plane crashed in western Pennsylvania, at Somerset," not far from Shanksville, which is in Somerset County. The ambiguous coverage reflected the day's fluid state of affairs, as Americans, including journalists, attempted to piece together what was happening in real time. Another network, CNN, likewise briefly mentioned a crash at Camp David during its coverage of rescue efforts at the collapsed World Trade Center.[2]

Bush administration officials also referred to a Camp David crash. During a midair press briefing as he flew to Washington from Peru, Secretary of State Colin Powell told journalists, "One [plane] crashed near Camp David and the other crashed out in western Pennsylvania."[3] Powell's wording resembles the ambiguous CBS report, which suggests that Powell may have been watching the CBS coverage of 9/11 while en route and simply repeated what he had heard from a source presumed to be reliable.

Former White House press secretary Ari Fleischer also mentioned a Camp David crash, while participating in a 9/11 commemoration event on September 11, 2006. Fleischer had been with President Bush in Sarasota, Florida on the morning of 9/11. At the commemoration, responding to a question from CNN anchor Soledad O'Brien, he reminisced about his experience: "We heard about the Pentagon on the way to Air Force One in the motorcade. We boarded Air Force One and went straight into the president's cabinet to start taking notes. That's when we heard about the fourth plane. The first report being ... *it went down near Camp David* [my emphasis]. That was the first report the president got."[4]

In the confusion there was also a false report that UAL 93 had landed in Cleveland. On September 11, WCPO TV, an ABC-affiliated television station based in Cincinnati, Ohio, reported that "a Boeing 767 out of Boston" landed in Cleveland amidst concerns about a possible bomb on board. According to the WCPO report: "United identified the plane as UAL 93."[5] As you may already have noticed, the report includes other incorrect information: UAL 93 was a Boeing 757, not a 767, and was out of Newark, not Boston. Later in the day, *USA Today* correctly identified the aircraft that landed at Cleveland as Delta Flight 1989.[6]

Nonetheless, as a result of such reports, and because of the paucity of wreckage at the alleged UAL 93 crash site, many Americans remained skeptical about the official version of events. Nor was the matter resolved in 2002 when the National Transportation Safety Board released the transcript of UAL 93's cockpit voice recorder (CVR), along with its own official flight path study of UAL 93, based on the aircraft's recovered flight data recorder. Serious questions have lingered about the authenticity of this evidence.

This book, of course, will not resolve all outstanding issues. But Freedom of Information Act requests have led to the release of some highly relevant information. The release of the RADES (Radar Evaluation Squadron) 9/11 radar data in October 2007 and the subsequent release of many air traffic control (ATC) audiotapes from 9/11 have made it possible to resolve some of the important issues without relying either upon the plane's CVR or a possibly dubious NTSB study.

First and foremost: The radar data and ATC tapes confirm that UAL 93 crashed near Shanksville. Multiple radar towers tracked UAL 93 continuously from the moment the flight departed Newark, and the radar tracks end several miles north of Shanksville. Also, the readily available ATC tapes from 9/11 now make it possible for anyone to review what happened, and to follow the air traffic controllers as they grappled with a midair disaster.[7] The radar data and the ATC tapes are mutually corroborative, and both strongly support a crash near Shanksville.[8]

Even so, I must confess, I was not fully convinced myself until I paid a visit in March 2011 to the crash site in western Pennsylvania. The surrounding countryside is quite beautiful, at least where the land has not been ruined by strip mining. The little burgh of Shanksville is both a blue-collar town and picturesque, with a fine river running through it. I was reminded of postcards of New England.

I was no less impressed by the residents, who without exception were friendly and helpful. Fortunately, many were also willing to talk about 9/11, including Nevin Lambert, whom I interviewed at his farm overlooking the UAL 93 crash site, presently administered by the US Park Service.

Lambert has lived and worked in the area all of his life. A local country road and a nearby borough bear his family's name. He told me how, on the morning of 9/11, he was shoveling coal outside his home when he heard the roar of jet engines. Lambert looked up and chanced to witness the death throes of UAL 93. He said the wings tipped back and forth several times just before the airliner plunged nose-down into a field about a quarter mile from where we stood.

The horrendous impact scattered debris across his farm. As I listened, Lambert fell silent and struggled with his feelings. When he spoke again about the people who died, his voice cracked. The man has no doubt recounted the same story numerous times over the years. But the trauma of that fateful day was still an open wound. Before my trip, I had read an account by Lambert on the Internet. But it is a very different thing to meet a witness in the flesh and hear about it firsthand. Nothing had prepared me for the depth of his emotions.

Incident at Camp David?

Of course, the fact that UAL 93 crashed at Shanksville does not rule out the possibility of another separate incident at Camp David. It is not a matter of either/or.

In fact, there is substantial evidence that something *did* occur in the vicinity of Catoctin Mountain Park, where Camp David is located. In addition to the press reports and official statements already cited, the *Northwestern Chronicle,* a campus newspaper associated with Northwestern University, also posted a story about Camp David on September 11.

The brief text reads as follows: "Air Force officials say an airliner has been forced down by F-16 fighter jets near Camp David."[9]

A glance at the link shows that the reporter at *Northwestern Chronicle* posted his story at 10:50 A.M. on September 11, 2001. The timing is significant, because a dossier of Secret Service files from 9/11 made public in 2010 includes a timeline document stating that a "plane crashed at Camp David" at 10:38 A.M.[10] This tallies closely with the news report, as it is quite plausible that a crash occurring at 10:38 would be reported at 10:50. The two pieces of data are quite compatible. Judging from this, it would appear that *something* did happen at Camp David on 9/11. The question is, What?

On September 12, however, the *Baltimore Daily Record* printed a "correction" under the headline "Camp David crash rumor proves false": "Early reports that an airliner had crashed on or near Camp David, the presidential retreat in Western Maryland's Catoctin Mountains, proved unfounded." The paper cited J. Mel Poole, the Catoctin Park superintendent, who flatly denied that there had been any crash.

Yet the article also contains other contradictory information which to my knowledge has not been reported anywhere else and which challenges the *apparently* blanket denial in the *Record.* As we will later see, here the devil is indeed in the details.

The article quoted a restaurant manager in Thurmont, Maryland, who "heard that a plane went down ... in the Catoctin Mountain Park," which is about three miles east of Thurmont. This would place the crash at, or very close to, Camp David. The same source told the paper that first responders were on the scene: "Lots of fire trucks were on the road," she said on September 11, "and no one can get up there." Park superintendent Poole, however, was insistent: "All the [fire] trucks here in the park are still in station."[11]

With the passage of time, this story was almost forgotten. But there is, in fact, another excellent reason to believe the restaurant manager's account. Surprisingly, *The 9/11 Commission Report* of 2004 also makes reference to a crash at Camp David, in an excerpt from an exchange between an FAA official in Washington DC and someone at the North American Aerospace Defense Command's Northeast Air Defense Sector (NEADS) headquarters in Rome, New York:

> NEADS: I also want to give you a heads-up, Washington.
> FAA (DC): Go ahead.
> NEADS: United nine three, have you got information on that yet?
> FAA: Yeah, he's down.
> NEADS: He's down?
> FAA: Yes.
> NEADS: When did he land? 'Cause we have got confirmation-
> FAA: He did not land.
> NEADS: Oh, he's down? Down?
> FAA: Yes. *Somewhere up northeast of Camp David* [my emphasis].
> NEADS: Northeast of Camp David.
> FAA: That's the last report. They don't know exactly where.[12]

The phrase "somewhere northeast of Camp David" is telling, because this is the wrong direction. Shanksville is located about 90 miles *west* and slightly north of Camp David, not to the northeast. It seems that whoever made the decision to include this transcript in the Commission's report was unfamiliar with the actual geography of the region, and may also have been unaware of the several reports of a crash at Camp David.

If this reasoning is correct, it could indicate that the authorities hushed up the reports of a Camp David incident so thoroughly that not even the 9/11 Commission and its staff knew about them. The matter is made even more mysterious because when radar expert John Farmer checked the 9/11 radar data in his computer at my request, he found that no airliners or military aircraft were anywhere near Camp David during the relevant timeframe.[13] The radar coverage in the area is excellent, so there is no chance that an incident occurred below radar. (# #)

I first learned about an "incident at Camp David" from Ken Jenkins, a well-known 9/11 activist (and video producer) who heard about it from a close friend who lived in Maryland at the time of the attacks. The friend was acquainted with a man who claimed to have witnessed a midair explosion near Camp David that morning. As the story goes, the man was working on his roof with several helpers when they saw a plane explode high above. Although I succeeded in contacting this witness, he declined to be interviewed.

To sum up, we are left with multiple reports of an air disaster, including a possible sighting, yet no radar evidence that any aircraft was in the vicinity. If something did happen on 9/11 at Camp David, authorities somehow covered it up.

Before I offer my thoughts about what that "something" may have been, some other relevant matters that may seem unrelated to the events of 9/11 need discussion.

(ENDNOTES)

1　The CBS footage may be viewed at Youtube, as a part of a skeptical analysis. Whether one agrees with the editorializing or not, the raw CBS footage speaks for itself. It is posted at http://www.youtube.com/watch?v=bqh2aof6W80.

2　"FBI targets Florida sites in terrorist search; Survivors may be still in Trade Center rubble," CNN, September 11, 2001, posted at http://edition.cnn.com/2001/US/09/11/america.under.attack/.

3　Attack on America, Secretary Colin L. Powell Press Briefing on Board Plane En Route Washington, DC; September 11, 2001, posted at http://avalon.law.yale.edu/sept11/powell_brief03.asp.

4　"AMERICAN MORNING: 9/11: The World Remembers; United Airlines Flight Diverted," CNN, September 11, 2006, posted at http://transcripts.cnn.com/TRANSCRIPTS/0609/11/ltm.04.html

5　Nine News staff, "Plane Lands in Cleveland: Bomb Feared Aboard," WCPO.com News, September 11, 2001, posted at http://web.archive.org/web/20021109040132/http://wcpo.com/specials/2001/americaattacked/news_local/story14.html.

6　Marilyn Adams, "Part II: No one was sure if hijackers were on board," *USA Today*, August 13, 2002, posted at http://www.usatoday.com/travel/news/2002/2002-08-13-clear-skies.htm.

7　The air traffic control tapes are available on the Internet: http://www.megaupload.com/?d=LJ2ZSSX7.　http://www.megaupload.com/?d=NYOUXJ71.　http://www.megaupload.com/?d=HLSYOY9G.　http://www.megaupload.com/?d=K8T8RED9.　http://www.megaupload.com/?d=NOW6ND57.　http://www.megaupload.com/?d=68LC77OP.

8　The group Pilots for 9/11 Truth has taken the position that UAL 93 did not crash at Shanksville, based on a single FAA document released in 2009. The pilots refer to it as an air-traffic-control document, and they imply that it is a transcript based on "real time" air traffic control audiotapes. However, this is incorrect. The document is actually a compilation put together after the fact, from phone conversations be-

No mention of NASA hanger extension of this story

tween the FAA facility at Herndon (near Dulles IAP) and FAA traffic control in Cleveland. The fact that it is not a "real time" record makes it a secondary (and less reliable) source. FAA staff in Herndon never spoke with the pilot or copilot of UAL 93 on 9/11. The primary ATC sources, with regard to UAL 93, are the audiotapes of the real time conversations of controllers in Cleveland sector and the transcripts of these tapes. These tapes and transcripts are consistent with the 9/11 radar data indicating that UAL 93 crashed at Shanksville. Here is the post by Pilots: http://pilotsfor911truth.org/store.html. Here is the FAA transcript: http://www.scribd.com/doc/14141827/NYC-B1-NTMO-East-Position-3-Fdr-Transcript. *debatable point*

9   Michael Hoes, "Fighters force down airliner near Camp David," *Northwestern Chronicle*, September 11, 2001, 10:50 A.M., posted at http://www.chron.org/tools/viewart.php?artid=77.

10   The Secret Service files were released in April 2010 thanks to a FOIA request filed by Aidan Monaghan, who subsequently posted them at 9/11 Blogger: http://911blogger.com/node/23269. The Secret Service files may also be downloaded here: http://www.mediafire.com/?vydb4nxdmyy. Information about the 10:38 A.M. crash can be found on page 13.

11   Peter Geier, "Camp David crash rumor proves false," *Baltimore Daily Record*, September 12, 2001, posted at http://findarticles.com/p/articles/mi_qn4183/is_20010912/ai_n10048109/?tag=content;col1.

12   *The 9/11 Commission Report* (New York: W.W. Norton, 2004), p. 31.

13   At around 9:30 A.M., two fighters from the 111th Air National Guard Fighter Wing were circling over Lebanon, PA, which is about 70 miles northeast of Camp David. They remained aloft until until 9:38 A.M., when they returned to base at the Willow Grove Naval Air Station. The fighters never flew near Camp David. In any event, they had returned to base before the reported crash. No other fighters were in the area. Emails from John Farmer, March 17 & 18, 2011.

Maurice Greenberg

Chapter 2

Forewarnings

For many years, bankrupt Cold War policies have crippled our nation's capacity to play a positive role on the world stage. Many foreigners no longer view the United States with admiration and respect, but increasingly with fear and loathing. But here, US elites seem oblivious to such concerns. They do not care, and they are quite candid about what they view as the CIA's pragmatic "need" to associate with unsavory individuals and criminals in the interest of furthering US foreign-policy goals. Their true colors can be identified between the lines of the policy papers.

Take, for instance, a 1996 intelligence report prepared by AIG CEO Maurice Greenberg for the Council on Foreign Relations, which earned Greenberg a nomination to replace John Deutch as director of the CIA. Greenberg states that the capability to undertake covert operations "constitutes an important national security tool." In a section titled "Intelligence and Law Enforcement," he is clear about the subordinate place of law enforcement under *realpolitik*:

> Foreign policy ought to take precedence over law enforcement when it comes to overseas operations. The bulk of US intelligence efforts overseas is devoted to traditional national security concerns; as a result, law enforcement must ordinarily be a secondary concern. FBI and Drug Enforcement Agency agents operating abroad should not be allowed to act independently of either the ambassador or the CIA lest pursuit of evidence or individuals for prosecution cause major foreign policy problems or complicate ongoing intelligence and diplomatic activities.[1]

This of course means that when criminals are judged to be intelligence assets they are to be granted protection from prosecution for narcotrafficking, money laundering, extortion, rape, even terrorism and murder. Such has been our de facto policy since at least the final days of World War II. And in 1982, the CIA and the US Department of Justice apparently even worked out a secret agreement to this effect.[2] The deal exempted the CIA from having to report drug trafficking by CIA assets, which made a mockery of then-presidential wife Nancy Reagan's much ballyhooed "just say no" anti-drug campaign.

At the time, most Americans trusted Ronald Reagan and believed that his administration was serious about the so-called War on Drugs. But hindsight shows clearly that the Reagan White House badly abused the public's good faith.

The foreign policy outlined by Maurice Greenberg is in large part responsible for the drug-related violence on the streets of our cities, and for the epidemic of drug addiction among our children – sacrificed to the false god of national security. Nor is the social carnage limited to the United States. Drug addiction in Muslim Iraq was almost unknown prior to the US invasion in 2003; it has since become a major problem. A similar explosion of heroin use has occurred in Iran, right next door to Afghanistan, where the poppies are grown with the blessing of the CIA.

Such foreign policies are evil, a scourge upon the planet, yet are intimately associated with US empire building. Time and again, the same historic pattern has played out: US military intervention, whether in Southeast Asia, Central America or, since 2001, Afghanistan and Iraq, has been accompanied by a sharp increase in narcotrafficking, with all of the attendant evils.

Quite simply, a US power elite has followed in the footsteps of the British and French, who in their day also exploited the immensely profitable opium and heroin trade.

The CIA's secret collusion with/domination of the Department of Justice gave it veto power over law enforcement, effectively blunting the capacity of US law-enforcement agencies to interdict the flow of illegal drugs into the US. The timing seems no accident. The deal of 1982 coincided with the start of the CIA's Contra war in Central America, and would explain why, in 1983, the Drug Enforcement Agency under pressure from the Pentagon closed its office in Tegucigalpa, Honduras.[3]

The flow of drugs through Honduras had not diminished, just the opposite. For years, the country had been a transfer point for illegal drug smuggling into the US, a reality that Contra leaders readily exploited to finance their war against the Nicaraguan Sandinistas, and they did so with the full knowledge and approval of the CIA. For many years after, a CIA veto blocked legitimate efforts by US law enforcement to curb the illicit drug trade.[4]

Meanwhile, the American people were kept in the dark about the policy and its effects at every point in the chain, from the formulation of the policy, to its implementation, to its phony packaging for mass consumption. In fact, our knowledge about this corruption is primarily thanks to a courageous journalist named Gary Webb. In 1996, Webb produced a series of groundbreaking articles for the *San Jose Mercury News* exposing Contra links and CIA complicity in the crack cocaine epidemic that had ravaged the black communities of Los Angeles in the 1980s.[5]

The series, appropriately titled "Dark Alliance," was one of the first big news stories to be carried on the Internet. Later, Webb expanded it into an important book by the same name, in which he laid out the voluminous evidence in stark detail. But it was Webb's series of articles in 1996 that initially focused media attention on CIA complicity in the drug trade and compelled Agency director John Deutch to announce an internal investigation. Meanwhile, the CIA also simultaneously launched a disinformation campaign to discredit Webb, whom it viewed as a serious threat.

The campaign against Gary Webb has been called "one of the most venomous and factually inane assaults on a professional journalist's competence in living memory."[6] The mainstream press, seemingly always eager to do the bidding of authorities, appeared to take pleasure in savaging the messenger, even while tacitly conceding that his facts were basically correct.

One of the low points occurred on live TV on November 15, 1996, when NBC's Andrea Mitchell, wife of Federal Reserve chairman Alan Greenspan, referred to Webb's exhaustively documented expose as "a conspiracy theory," the kiss of death for any serious journalist.[7] At this same time, of course, Greenspan was busily (dare we say "conspiratorially"?) engineering the deregulation of Wall Street, setting the stage for the eventual financial meltdown of the global economy. As we will see, this deregulation may have also had a part in 9/11 itself.

CIA Inspector General Frederick Hitz led the Agency's internal probe, and even though his conclusions later confirmed Webb's main thesis, the CIA suppressed Hitz's report, even while leaking a denial of the allegations. The CIA's minions in the press corps did the rest. On December 19, 1997, an article by Tim Weiner in the *New York Times* and another by Walter Pincus in the *Washington Post* cited "unnamed sources," who insisted that Hitz had found no "direct or indirect" links between the CIA and cocaine traffickers. This was a blatant lie, indeed a breathtaking example of CIA deception. But it had its intended effect: neither reporter bothered to ask why Hitz's report was still under wraps.

How could the mainstream press fumble so badly? Probably because in the 1990s the issue of CIA complicity in the drug trade was politically out of bounds, simply unthinkable, beyond the realm of the possible. Today, things are a little different.

After the onset of the war in Afghanistan, the CIA's support for Afghan drug lords moved out of the closet. By 2009, even the major US papers were reporting on it.[8] However, the political climate of the 1990s simply would not allow an honest airing of the CIA-drug issue, much as a real investigation of 9/11 remains taboo, to this day. Webb's newspaper publisher ultimately caved under pressure and threw his Pulitzer Prize-winning reporter under the bus, even as Webb was turning up fresh evidence that indicated he had, if anything, understated the case against the CIA.[9]

When CIA Inspector General Fred Hitz finally testified before the House Intelligence Committee, in March 1998, he admitted it was all true: "Let me be frank about what we are finding. There are instances where CIA did not, in an expeditious or consistent fashion, cut off relationships with individuals supporting the Contra program who were alleged to have engaged in drug trafficking activity."[10]

On hearing this, Congressman Norman Dicks of Washington button-holed Hitz with the obvious next question: "Did any of these allegations involve trafficking in the United States?"

"Yes," Hitz replied, and went on to discuss the CIA's secret arrangement with the Department of Justice. According to Webb, who was in attendance, at that point a murmur swept through a shocked hearing room as the meaning of Hitz's testimony sank in.[11]

Of course, by this time Webb's career as a journalist had been destroyed. The CIA's vilification campaign had achieved the intended result, and the next day, the *Washington Post* buried its story about

Hitz's testimony deep inside the paper, along with its own culpability in helping to trash the reputation of one of America's finest investigative journalists.

Gary Webb was marginalized at the *San Jose Mercury News*, which he left to write his award-winning book, *Dark Alliance*. It appeared in 1999, to both acclaim and, predictably, still more press bashing. Webb subsequently worked as an investigator for the California legislature, and later took a position (at a steep pay cut) for the *Sacramento News and Review*. But the press attacks, his unemployability as an investigative writer, and deepening financial troubles took a toll on Webb, who had always been prone to bouts of depression. By 2004 the writer was in a downward spiral that was quite apparent to his friends and family.

His body was discovered on December 10, 2004, along with a note and other evidence of suicide. Because Webb had been shot twice in the head—evidently not as rare in suicide as might be presumed—many skeptics continue to believe that he was murdered. But even if Webb died by his own tragic hand, and the evidence indicates he did, does that exonerate those who drove him to it?

How can such a miscarriage happen in a nation that prides itself on being a free and open society? The answer is that complicity with narcotrafficking has exerted an insidious corrupting influence on our government, just as it did in the cases of Britain and France during their colonial periods, indeed as it did in the days of Rome. Government officials are not immune to the temptations of the drug trade, which is now the most profitable business on the planet by a wide margin. Arms smuggling, by comparison, comes in a distant second.

The outcome of a secret policy of complicity was entirely predictable: the possibilities for abuse are as unlimited as the criminal imagination. But I must admit to shock at learning just how far up the food chain the rot extends.

(ENDNOTES)

1   Maurice Greenberg, "Making Intelligence Smarter. The Future of US Intelligence," Council on Foreign Relations, 1996. Posted at http://www.fas.org/irp/cfr.html.

2   Gary Webb, *Dark Alliance* (New York: Seven Stories Press, 1998), p. 482.

3   Peter Dale Scott and Jonathan Marshall, *Cocaine Politics* (Berkeley: University of California Press, 1991), p 57.

4   The CIA's policy of protecting drug traffickers did not start with its secret deal with the US Justice Department. The policy had been a longstanding problem for US law enforcement agencies: "In south Florida, by the 1970s, police could scarcely arrest a dope dealer or illegal weapons trafficker without encountering the claim, often true, that the suspect had CIA connections. Perhaps the largest narcotics investigation of the decade, the World Finance Corporation case, involving scores of federal and state agents, had to be scrapped after a year because the CIA complained to the Justice Department that a dozen top criminals were 'of interest' to it." Jonathan Kwitny, *The Crimes of Patriots* (New York: W.W. Norton, 1987), p. 96.

5   Gary Webb, "Dark Alliance: The Story Behind the Crack Explosion," *San Jose Mercury News*, August 1996; the series is archived at http://www.narconews.com/ darkalliance/drugs/start.htm.

6   Alexander Cockburn and Jeffrey St. Clair, *Whiteout* (New York: Verso, 1998), p. 29.

7   Ibid., p. 31.

8   See, for example, Dexter Filkins, Mark Mazetti and James Risen, "Brother of Afghan Leader Said to Be Paid by C.I.A.," *New York Times*, October 27, 2009, posted at http://www.nytimes.com/2009/10/28/world/asia/28intel. html?adxnnl=1&adxnnlx=1301436779-la8vOSwZTeQilE0VwwLONQ.

9   Gary Webb, note 1, pp. 471-72.

10 Statement of Frederick P. Hitz, Inspector General CIA before the Permanent Select Committee on Intelligence, US House of Representatives, regarding investigation of allegations of connections between CIA and the Contras in drug trafficking to the US, March 16, 1998, posted at http://www.fas.org/irp/congress/1998_hr/980316-ps.htm.

11 Gary Webb, note 1, p 482.

Chapter 3

A Walk on the Dark Side

On September 10, 2001, the eve of the worst terrorist attack in US history, Secretary of Defense Donald Rumsfeld acknowledged during a press conference that the Department of Defense could not account for $2.3 trillion of the massive Pentagon budget.[1] At the time, I thought this number so large as to be almost incomprehensible.

But in the course of my 9/11 research, as you will see, I have had to comprehend even larger sums. For example, *merely the gold* of a secret treasure hoard falling, albeit incomplete and piecemeal, into the "unofficial" coffers of the US geopolitical establishment would be worth *well over $5 trillion* with gold at a "mere" $1000 per ounce, a price it has been far above recently. That mind-boggling hoard also included diamonds, sapphires, emeralds, etc.; platinum and other strategic metals; as well as "priceless" art and artifacts; all collected by looting various Asian nations over a fifty year period. Most of the treasure was carefully inventoried.

The piracy was then carefully covered up by agents of the US government, for reasons that may have seemed sound in the aftermath of World War II, but which cannot be justified, today. For, indeed, the legacies of these initiatives currently threaten our system of representative democracy.

According to the late Chalmers Johnson, a longtime expert on Japan, East Asia and US foreign policy, as much as 40% of the Pentagon budget is "black," meaning hidden from public scrutiny.[2] If his figure is even approximately correct, and I believe it is, this means that democratic oversight of US military research and development has become all but impossible. In which case, our democratic values and way of life are now at risk: not from without—no foreign enemy can subvert the US Constitution—but from within.

At 9:38 A.M. on the morning after Rumsfeld's press conference, the nascent investigation of the missing money was derailed even before it could get underway, when the west wing of the Pentagon exploded in flames and smoke, the target of a terrorist strike. And with the attack also died any remaining hope that the US military might still get its budgetary house in order. Curiously, the exact point of impact was the Department of Defense accounting offices on the first floor.

The odds against this being a coincidence, given the Pentagon's enormous size, prompted skeptics of the official story to read a dark design into the attack. The surgical destruction of the Department of Defense's records and staff, nearly all of whom died in the rubble, leads to important questions about who benefited from 9/11. The answers suggest that Deep Throat's famous dictum during the Watergate revelations—"follow the money"—may be no less important to a deep understanding of 9/11.

Was the destruction of the Pentagon accounting office one of the diabolical objectives of the attack? And if so, why would anti-American Islamic jihadists pick such a target over others that surely had much greater military significance?

Without question, the Pentagon's west wing presented a much more challenging target than the east wing. Targeting the west wing required a difficult approach over the Arlington skyline. The final approach was especially dicey and amounted to a downhill obstacle course, skirting apartments and a large complex of buildings about a quarter-mile from the Pentagon known as the Naval Annex, which sits atop a hill rising from the flat ground along the Potomac River.

In April 2008, I interviewed Army Brigadier General Clyde Vaughn, a credible witness to the events of that morning. Vaughn explained over the telephone that on 9/11 he was on his way to work at the Pentagon via the Henry G. Shirley Memorial Highway (I-395) when the strike occurred. The general told me the hijacked aircraft (presumably American Airlines Flight 77) just missed the Naval Annex and that it would have hit the 270-feet-tall US Air Force memorial presently occupying the site.[3] The new memorial was constructed and dedicated in 2006.

Why did the terrorists not take the easy approach up the Potomac River? The river approach would have afforded a reasonably good chance to crash the offices of Secretary of Defense Rumsfeld and the Joint Chiefs of Staff, which were located on the opposite side of the building, in the middle of the outer "E" ring. The location of their offices was no secret. Surely terrorists would have been more interested in decapitating the command structure of the US war machine than going after a bunch of accounting clerks.

There were other striking anomalies that morning. The crash of American Airlines Flight 11 into the North Tower of the World Trade Center at 8:46 A.M. should also have raised red flags, because the point of impact at the 95th and 96th floors was another remarkable happenstance. Both floors were occupied by Marsh & McLennan, one of the world's largest insurance brokerages, with ties to the private intelligence firm Kroll Associates, which held the security contract at the World Trade Center. Indeed, the network of corporate ties here is so entangled that tracing all the links would fill this entire volume, but the most salient connections can be enumerated.

The CEO of Marsh & McLennan on 9/11 was Jeffrey Greenberg, son of Maurice "Hank" Greenberg, owner of AIG, the world's largest insurance conglomerate (or second largest, depending on the source). Greenberg's other son, Evan, was CEO of Ace Limited, another large insurance company. Maurice Greenberg had been a director of the New York Federal Reserve Bank for many years, and in 1994-95 served as its chairman. Greenberg was also vice-chairman of the Council on Foreign Relations, which, as already noted, sponsored his 1996 report, "Making Intelligence Smarter: The future of U.S. Intelligence." As a result of that report, Senator Arlen Specter floated Greenberg's name as a candidate for the directorship of the CIA.[4]

Although George Tenet eventually got the job, the mere fact that Greenberg was in the running shows the extent of his influence. In 1993, Greenberg's huge insurance conglomerate AIG reportedly bankrolled the Wall Street spy firm, Kroll Associates, saving it from bankruptcy. Thereafter, Kroll became an AIG subsidiary. After the 1993 World Trade Center bombing, Kroll acquired the contract from the Port Authority of New York to upgrade security at the World Trade Center, in the process beating out two other firms.[5] Kroll continued with the WTC security contract through the period leading up to the September 11 attacks. One of Kroll's directors, Jerome Hauer, also managed New York mayor Rudolph Giuliani's Office of Emergency Management, which was located on the 23rd floor of WTC-7, which was also destroyed on September 11.[6] Kroll's contract gave it unfettered access to all of the buildings destroyed in New York on 9/11.

Nor was this all. In 1998, AIG invested $1.35 billion in the Blackstone Group, a private New York merchant bank.[7] According to the *New York Times,* the two companies had worked together for many years. Indeed, Maurice Greenberg had served on Blackstone's advisory board since 1989. The connection is of special interest because in October 2000, Blackstone Real Estate Advisors, the real estate management arm of Blackstone Group, purchased the mortgage secured by WTC-7.[8]

This startling string of coincidences should have been reason enough for the 9/11 Commission to investigate both the Blackstone Group and Kroll's shady background as well as their relations with AIG, Ace Limited, and Marsh & McLennan. The Commission was armed with subpoena authority and could have probed deeply enough to learn the truth. Unfortunately, the official investigators were not interested in connecting the dots. *The 9/11 Commission Report*, released in 2004, was *at best* shamefully inadequate, as will become apparent in the course of this narrative.

Important evidence continued to appear, nonetheless. In 2006, a whistleblower named Richard A. Grove went public with stunning testimony about his involvement with the Greenberg empire: an up-close-and-personal experience, Grove says, that nearly cost him his life.[9] During the period leading up to 9/11, Grove worked as a salesman for Silverstream Software, a firm marketing designer solutions to a number of Wall Street institutions, including Merrill Lynch, Deutsche Bank, Bankers Trust, Alex Brown, and Morgan Stanley. According to Grove, Silverstream "built Internet transactional and trading platforms," designed "to Web-enable the critical business functions of Fortune 500 companies, basically integrating and making available on the Web the disparate legacy applications and mainframes while simultaneously streamlining workflow and traditional paper processes." The "end result [was] a lower cost of operation and more efficient transactions because inefficiencies such as people were being taken out of the loop."[10]

Grove was so successful as a salesman, that he earned over a million dollars before the age of thirty. He only realized later that the software he sold might have enabled fraudulent trading in the hours before, and possibly during, the 9/11 attacks. The most advanced software of all went to Marsh & McLennan, which, he says, placed an order in 2000 for a technological solution "beyond what we had done for any of the above-named companies; insofar as it would be used to electronically connect Marsh to its major business partners via Internet portals, for the purpose of creating 'paperless transactions' and expediting revenue and renewal cycles."

Grove inked the software deal with Marsh & McLennan in October 2000, and Silverstream stationed a team of thirty to forty technicians in the client's offices in WTC-1, led by several software developers who proceeded to design and build the software package "from the ground up." During this period, Grove served as liaison between Silverstream and Marsh, to insure that the software would perform as specified. The team worked around-the-clock, seven days a week, to meet Marsh's July 2001 deadline. The end result was "a specific type of connectivity that was used to link AIG and Marsh & McLennan, the first two commercial companies on the planet to employ this type of transaction."[11]

Grove says he had first noticed fiscal irregularities in October 2000, when he and a colleague helped "identify about $10,000,000 in suspicious purchase orders." Marsh's chief information officer, Gary Lasko, later confirmed that "certain vendors were deceiving Marsh ...selling ... large quantities of hardware that were not necessary" for the project. But Grove did not worry too much about this at the time, nor did he run into personal trouble until the spring of 2001, when he learned, while negotiating a license renewal contract with Lasko, that his own employer (Silverstream) had been overbilling Marsh "to the tune of $7 million, or more."

Grove brought the matter to the attention of Silverstream executives, but was told to keep quiet and mind his own business. A Marsh executive advised him to do the same. By this point, a number of Marsh employees had earned Grove's trust, and when he shared his concerns with them, they agreed that "something untoward was going on." Grove names these honest employees in his testimonial, who in addition to Gary Lasko, included Kathryn Lee, Ken Rice, Richard Breuhardt and John Ueltzhoeffer. According to Grove, all of these individuals perished on 9/11, and a quick check confirmed that their names do indeed appear on the fatality list of World Trade Center victims.[12]

The proverbial manure hit the fan on June 5, 2001, the day after Grove sent an email to his sales team informing them that "Silverstream was billing Marsh millions above and beyond the numbers we were being paid commissions on ..." There seemed only two possibilities: either the members of his team were being cheated out of their rightful commissions, or Silverstream was defrauding Marsh & McLennan.

Later that day, Grove received word from Gary Lasko that Marsh had decided to retain Silverstream for the next phase of the project. He immediately informed his boss of the good news. Grove was personally delighted because his rightful commission "would have been a payday worth well over a million dollars." He never collected it however, because the next morning Grove was summoned to his boss's office and abruptly terminated.

This is not the end of the story. Several weeks later, Grove suffered a medical emergency that required hospitalization, emergency surgery and weeks of recovery. In August 2001, while still bedridden, he was contacted by Silverstream's Chief Financial Officer and offered $9,999 in cash plus an extension of his medical benefits if he would agree never to talk about the work he did for the company. Grove needed the continuing medical coverage and agreed to Silverstream's terms. During his convalescence however, he became suspicious about the secrecy agreement and decided that, at the very least, he should maintain contact with the honest employees at Marsh, several of whom had become close friends.

Shortly thereafter, one of them arranged for Grove to attend a meeting they had arranged at the offices of Marsh & McLennan, where they planned to "openly question the suspiciously unconcerned executive who seemed to be at the center of the controversial secrecy." That executive had agreed to participate via a telephone-conference link from his apartment in uptown Manhattan. This was the same individual who, months before, had warned Grove to look the other way.

Grove claimed to be in possession of documents proving illicit activity, and he planned to produce them at the meeting. On the day of the showdown however, he ran late, delayed by heavy Manhattan traffic. Grove says he was on Vesey Street, between Buildings 6 and 7 of the WTC complex, when the South Tower exploded, apparently from the impact of UAL 175. By then, all or most of his friends in the North Tower were already dead or trapped on the upper floors. All told, some three hundred or more Marsh employees perished that morning, the victims of terrorists.

Endnotes

1   http://www.cbsnews.com/stories/2002/01/29/eveningnews/main325985.shtml.

2   Chalmers Johnson, *Nemesis: The Last Days of the American Republic* (New York: Henry Holt, 2006), pp. 9, 115. This is the final installment of an impressive trilogy discussing American foreign policy; it was preceded by *Blowback: The Costs and Consequences of American Empire* and *The Sorrows of Empire: Militarism Secrecy and the End of the Republic*.

3   Vaughn's testimony is intriguing because it does not conform in all respects to the official narrative. Vaughn told CNN: "There wasn't anything in the air, except for one airplane, and it looked like it was loitering over Georgetown, in a high, left-hand bank," he said. "That may have been the plane. I have never seen one on that (flight) pattern." The aircraft described by Vaughn has never been identified. Ian Christopher McCaleb, "Three-star general may be among Pentagon dead," CNN, September 13, 2001, posted at http://edition.cnn.com/2001/US/09/13/pentagon.terrorism/.

4   Maurice Greenberg, "Making Intelligence Smarter. The Future of US Intelligence," Council on Foreign Relations, 1996. Posted at http://www.fas.org/irp/cfr.html.

5   Douglas Frantz, "A Midlife Crisis at Kroll Associates," *New York Times*, September 1, 1994, posted at http://query.nytimes.com/gst/fullpage.html?res=9401EEDC1738F932A3575AC0A962958260&sec=&spon=&pagewanted=all.

6   http://en.wikipedia.org/wiki/Jerome_Hauer.

7   Peter Truell, "AIG Will Put $1.35 Billion Into Blackstone," *New York Times*, July 31, 1998. Posted at http://www.nytimes.com/1998/07/31/business/aig-will-put-1.35-billion-into-blackstone.html

8   October 17, 2000, Press release: Blackstone Acquires Debt on 7 World Trade Center, posted at http://www.blackstone.com/news/details/blackstone-acquires-debt-on-7-world-trade-center

9   http://www.freewebs.com/abigsecret/Grove.html.

10   Ibid.

11   Ibid.

12   http://www.foxnews.com/story/0,2933,62151,00.html#wtc.

Richard Grove

Chapter 4

Insiders Trade

R ichard Grove believes that "hundreds of billions in fraudulent transactions" occurred just prior to 9/11 in addition to the transfers perpetrated by Marsh and AIG.[1] He points to the evidence for insider trading reported by the press in the first days and weeks after 9/11, when many suspected that al-Qaeda had profited from the attacks. Grove's estimate may be off, but he is right about the evidence for informed, or insider, trading, which from the first appeared to be a worldwide phenomenon. The list of affected nations was long, and included the US, Germany, Japan, France Luxembourg, the UK, Switzerland and Spain; Hong Kong was also targeted.[2] One consultant, Jonathan Winer, told ABC, "It's absolutely unprecedented to see cases of insider trading covering the entire world from Japan to the US to North America to Europe."[3]

Soon, independent investigations were underway on three continents, in the belief that the paper trail would lead to the terrorists. Press statements by leading figures in the international banking community left little doubt that the evidence was compelling. Ernst Welteke, President of the German Deutsche Bundesbank, was among the believers. According to the *Miami Herald*, "A preliminary review by German regulators and bank researchers showed there were highly suspicious sales of shares in airlines and insurance companies, along with major trades in gold and oil markets, before September 11 that suggest ... advance knowledge of the attacks. Welteke said that his researchers came across ... almost irrefutable proof of insider trading." Welteke himself was blunt: "If you look at the movements in markets before and after the attacks, it really makes your brow furrow.... What we found makes us sure that people connected to the terrorists must have been trying to profit from this tragedy."[4]

In the UK, London City regulators investigated a flurry of suspicious sales processed just before the attack. A Financial Services Authority (FSA) spokesperson confirmed that market regulators in Germany, Japan and the US had received information about short selling of insurance company shares and airline stocks, which fell sharply as a result of the attacks. The FSA had been "drawn into the investigation because it had a transaction monitoring department that checks suspicious share movements." Richard Crossley, a London analyst, "said that he had tracked suspicious short selling and share dumping in a swath of stocks badly affected by the terrorist attacks."[5]

Among the WTC tenants were dozens of banks and insurance companies, including several that were now going to have to pay out billions to cover heavy losses from the attacks. Assuming nefarious individuals were armed with foreknowledge, they stood to make a windfall by dumping stock and selling competitors short, not to mention vast potential profits from last-minute electronic money laundering via computers which, the perpetrators had to know, would be destroyed within hours.

CBS reported a sharp upsurge in purchases of put options on both United and American Airlines. A put option is a contract that allows the holder to sell a stock at a set price during a specified time period, which can reap huge profits should the stock plummet. The uptick had occurred in the days prior to 9/11.

Sources on Wall Street told CBS that they had never before seen that kind of trading imbalance. The only airlines affected were United and American, the two involved in the attack. American Airlines stock dropped 39% in a single day. United Airlines stock fell even more, a whopping 44%.[6]

Although many stocks tumbled, there were also big winners, especially in the military sector. Contractors like L-3 Communications, Alliant Techsystems and Northrop Grumman all reported large gains. The biggest winner, though, was Raytheon, which manufactures Tomahawk missiles. In the trading week of September 17-21, 2001, Raytheon stock climbed by an astounding 37%.[7] On the day prior to 9/11, the purchase of call options for Raytheon had suspiciously surged by 600%.[8]

The sale of five-year US Treasury Notes also spiked just before 9/11, as reported by the *Wall Street Journal.* Among the purchases was a single $5 billion transaction, which pointed to large investors: "Five-year Treasury notes are among the best investments in the event of a world crisis, especially one that hits the US. The notes are prized for their safety and their backing by the US government, and usually rally when investors flee riskier investments, such as stocks." According to a Wall Street bond-market strategist: "If they were going to do something like this they would do it in the five-year part of the market. [Because] It's extremely liquid, and the tracks would be hard to spot." The article noted that the value of those notes had risen sharply in the three weeks since the events of September 11.[9]

Suspect Stocks	Industry	Suspect Stocks	Industry
American	Airline	Marsh & McLennan	Finance
Continental	Airline	Morgan Stanley	Finance
Northwest	Airline	XL Capital Ltd.	Finance
Southwest	Airline	Am. Intl. Group (AIG)	Insurance
United	Airline	AXA	Insurance
US Airways	Airline	Chubb Group	Insurance
W.R. Grace	Chemicals	Cigna Group	Insurance
Carnival Corp.	Cruise Line	MetLife	Insurance
Royal Caribbean Cruises	Cruise Line	Progressive Corp	Insurance
American Express	Finance	Royal & Sun Alliance	Insurance
Bank of America	Finance	Boeing	Military
Bank of New York	Finance	General Motors	Military
Bank One	Finance	Hercules Inc.	Military
Bear Stearns	Finance	Lockheed Martin	Military
Citigroup	Finance	Raytheon	Military
CNA Financial	Finance	Lone Star Technologies	Oil & Gas
Dean Witter	Finance	Vornado Reality Trust	Real Estate
John Hancock Financial	Finance	L-3 Communications	Security tech
Lehman Brothers	Finance	LTV Corporation	Steel

The Securities and Exchange Commission (SEC) led the US government probe of allegations of insider trading.[10] For weeks, the SEC remained close-mouthed about the scope of its investigation; then it sent out a request to securities firms around the world for more information on trading in thirty-eight different stocks.[11] SEC Chairman Harvey Pitt told the House Financial Services Committee, "We will do everything in our power to track those people down and bring them to justice."[12] By this time, however, the fix was apparently in.

The *San Francisco Chronicle* reported that the SEC took the unprecedented step of deputizing "hundreds, if not thousands, of key players in the private sector." Wrote the *Chronicle*, "In a two-page statement issued to 'all securities-related entities' nationwide, the SEC asked companies to designate senior personnel who appreciate 'the sensitive nature' of the case and can be relied upon to 'exercise appropriate discretion' as 'point' people linking government investigators and the industry." The requested information was to be held in strictest confidence. The SEC statement included the following passage: "We ask that you disseminate the information within your institution *only on a need-to-know basis* [my emphasis]."[13]

In his book *Crossing the Rubicon,* former LAPD detective Michael Ruppert described the SEC's unprecedented move to deputize: "What happens when you deputize someone in a national security or criminal investigation is that you make it illegal for them to disclose publicly what they know ... In effect, they become government agents and are controlled by government regulations rather than their own conscience. In fact, they can be thrown in jail without a hearing if they talk publicly. I have seen this implied threat time and again with federal investigations, intelligence agents, and even members of the United States Congress who are bound so tightly by secrecy oaths and agreements that they are not even able to disclose criminal activities inside the government for fear of incarceration ... members of congressional intelligence committees ... sign even more draconian secrecy agreements in order to get their assignments."[14]

All this surely means that al-Qaeda had nothing to do with the insider trading.[15] When the evidentiary trail led back to Wall Street, the SEC moved quickly to control the evidence and muzzle potential witnesses. Despite the best efforts of the SEC, however, a few details did leak to the world press. In mid-October 2001, *The Independent* (UK) reported, "To the embarrassment of investigators, it has ... emerged that the firm used to buy many of the 'put' options – where a trader, in effect, bets on a share price fall – on United Airlines stock was headed until 1998 by Alvin 'Buzzy' Krongard, now executive director of the CIA."[16]

The evidence of malfeasance was buttressed by the fact that in one case the purchaser failed to collect what would have been $2.5 million in profits made from the collapsing price of UAL shares.[17] The only plausible explanation was that a person or persons at the purchasing institution feared exposure and subsequent arrest.

For the most part, the US press failed to pick up the story, which appeared to link Wall Street and the US intelligence community to the 9/11 attacks. Indeed, the *New York Times* apparently led the disinformation campaign.[18]

George Tenet notes in his memoirs that in February 1998 he recruited Buzzy Krongard to become his Councilor,[19] in which capacity Krongard probably served as Tenet's personal liaison to Wall Street. Krongard had already been a consultant to CIA director James Woolsey in the mid-1990s. Then Krongard became chairman of America's oldest investment banking firm, Alex Brown and Sons, Inc., which was acquired by Bankers Trust in 1997. In 1999, BT Alex Brown was in turn purchased by Deutsche Bank, the firm which placed most of the UAL put options.

In 1998, BT Alex Brown refused to cooperate with a Senate subcommittee that was conducting hearings on the involvement of US banks in money-laundering activities.[20] At the time, BT Alex Brown, like other large US financial institutions, was in the business of private banking, meaning that it catered to unnamed wealthy clients, often for the sole purpose of setting up shell companies in foreign jurisdictions, such as on the Isle of Jersey, where effective bank regulation and oversight are nonexistent. According to Michael Ruppert, Krongard's last job at Alex Brown was to oversee "private client relations,"[21] meaning that Krongard personally arranged confidential transactions and transfers for the bank's unnamed wealthy clientele.

Private banks typically offer a range of services to their clients for the purpose of shielding them from oversight. Private banks set up multiple offshore accounts in multiple locations under multiple names. They also facilitate the quick, confidential and hard-to-trace transfer of money across jurisdictional boundaries. In many such cases, the private banks do not even know who owns the account, which, of course, means that not even the bankers can follow the transactions with "due diligence." Many private banks do not even try, for fear of scaring away business, especially from foreign clients. Even though private bankers are responsible for enforcing legal controls against money laundering, where such laws exist, in practice oversight is typically weak or nonexistent.

You may be surprised to learn that although it is illegal for US banks to launder ill-gotten money originating within the United States, it is not illegal for them to accept dirty money from elsewhere. Thus, many US banks openly solicit business from Central American drug lords, arms merchants and other shady entities.

Computer technology has also introduced a new level of anonymity, in the form of faceless transactions that do not require the intermediation of a financial institution. Internet money transfers and new payment technologies such as "e-cash," electronic purses and other electronic payment systems have created new ways to disguise the source and ownership of illicit money, as discussed in a US Treasury report of September 2001 on money laundering.[22]

It is therefore little wonder that law enforcement has failed to stem the growing international proliferation of laundered drug money and other illicit assets over the last several decades. The failure has been spectacular.

In 1999, a consensus of experts in Germany, Switzerland and at the US Treasury agreed that 99.9% of laundered money routinely escapes detection. The experts estimated that the annual total was between $500 billion and a trillion dollars, a mind-boggling number, about half of which is washed into the US economy, the rest into Europe.[23] Unfortunately, the failure of law enforcement has another important component: the complicity of the US intelligence community in the international drug trade.

After Buzzy Krongard's departure to the CIA, his successor at BT Alex Brown was his former deputy Mayo Shattuck III, who had worked at the bank for many years. In 1997, Shattuck helped Krongard engineer the merger with Bankers Trust, and he stayed on after Deutsche Bank acquired BT Alex Brown in 1999.[24]

According to the *New York Times,* Bankers Trust was "one of the most loosely managed [banks] on Wall Street," and during the 1990s was repeatedly rocked by scandal. In 1994, clients and regulators accused the bank "of misleading customers about its risky derivative products." The case went viral when tape recordings were made public that showed bank salesmen snickering about ripping off naïve customers.

In 1999, BT Alex Brown pled guilty to criminal conspiracy charges, after it was revealed that top-level executives had created a slush fund out of at least $20 million in unclaimed funds.[25] The firm had to pay a $63 million fine and would have been forced to close its doors but for the fact that it was acquired, just at this time, by Deutsche Bank, Europe's largest. According to the *New York Times,* Mayo Shattuck III had been made "co-head of investment banking in January [2001], overseeing Deutsche Bank's 400 brokers who cater to wealthy clients."[26] His sudden resignation on September 12, 2001 must be therefor viewed as highly suspicious.

Careful readers of *The 9/11 Commission Report* know that many of its most important details are buried in the endnotes. This is also true of its discussion of the insider-trading flap. The text of the report itself casts no light on the subject, beyond pronouncing government investigations as "exhaustive" and exonerating of al-Qaeda (*9/11 Commision Report,* pp. 171-72):

> There also have been claims that al-Qaeda financed itself through manipulation of the stock market based on its advance knowledge of the 9/11 attacks. Exhaustive investigations by the Securities and Exchange Commission, FBI, and other agencies have uncovered no evidence that anyone with advance knowledge of the attacks profited through securities transactions.[130]

This endnote 130 is more interesting, but only slightly more revealing (p. 499). It mentions that a "single U.S.-based institutional investor with no conceivable ties to al-Qaeda purchased 95 percent of the UAL puts," a likely reference to Mayo Shattuck III:

> 130. Highly publicized allegations of insider trading in advance of 9/11 generally rest on reports of unusual pre-9/11 trading activity in companies whose stock plummeted after the attacks. Some unusual trading did in fact occur, but each such trade proved to have an innocuous explanation. For example, the volume of

put options—investments that pay off only when a stock drops in price—surged in the parent companies of United Airlines on September 6 and American Airlines on September 10—highly suspicious trading on its face. Yet, further investigation has revealed that the trading had no connection with 9/11. A single U.S.-based institutional investor with no conceivable ties to al Qaeda purchased 95 percent of the UAL puts on September 6 as part of a trading strategy that also included buying 115,000 shares of American on September 10 [Commission's emphasis]. Similarly, much of the seemingly suspicious trading in American on September 10 was traced to a specific U.S.-based options trading newsletter, faxed to its subscribers on Sunday, September 9, which recommended these trades. These examples typify the evidence examined by the investigation. The SEC and the FBI, aided by other agencies and the securities industry, devoted enormous resources to investigating this issue, including securing the cooperation of many foreign governments. These investigators have found that the apparently suspicious consistently proved innocuous [my emphasis]. Joseph Cella interview (Sept. 16, 2003; May 7, 2004; May 10-11, 2004); FBI briefing (Aug. 15, 2003); SEC memo, Division of Enforcement to SEC Chair and Commissioners, "Pre-September 11, 2001 Trading Review," May 15, 2002; Ken Breen interview (Apr. 23, 2004); Ed G. interview (Feb. 3, 2004).

Evidently, we are supposed to presume that "American" means American Airlines. But here it could just as easily refer to American Express, which was also on the SEC's suspect list. If the major trading of the unnamed "US-based institutional investor with no conceivable ties to al Qaeda" was truly hedged as *The 9/11 Commission Report* describes, this would clearly exonerate it of "informed" or insider trading here. However, without more information, it is impossible to establish the facts regarding *even this one particular investing institution.*

As we know that thirty-eight firms were under investigation, the Commission's token nod at the issue is thoroughly unconvincing. What about the pre-9/11 surge in call options for Raytheon, for instance, or the spike in put options for the behemoth Morgan Stanley, which had offices in the South Tower? And what of the Greenberg insurance firm, Marsh & McLennan (also on the list, along with AIG), which saw the second highest spike in pre-9/11 put option activity, second only to United Airlines?[27] One will search

The 9/11 Commission Report in vain for any discussion of these or other suspect stocks. The truth, we must conclude, is to be found between the lines, in the *Report*'s conspicuous skirting of the whole insider-trading issue.

The case for insider trading is supported by two published statistical studies, both of which confirmed an unusual volume in options trading for United and American Airlines in the days before 9/11. The first study concluded that the data were "consistent with investors trading on advance knowledge of the attacks."[28] The second paper, by the Swiss Banking Institute, reached the same conclusion.[29] A third study looked at the Standard & Poor's 500 Index and found "abnormal trading volumes" in both put options and call options in the days before the attacks. The authors concluded that there was "credible circumstantial evidence to support the insider trading claim."[30]

Indeed, if the trading was truly "innocuous," a word used twice in the endnote, then why did the SEC muzzle potential whistleblowers by deputizing everyone involved with its investigation? The likely answer is that so many players on Wall Street were involved that the SEC could not risk an open process, for fear of exposing the unthinkable. This would explain why the SEC limited the flow of information to those with a "need to know," which, of course, means that very few participants in the SEC investigation had the full picture. It would also explain why the SEC ultimately named no names.

All of this hints at the probable frightening extent of criminal activity on Wall Street in the days and hours before (and during?) 9/11. The SEC was like a surgeon who opens a patient on the operating room table to remove a tumor only to sew him back up again after finding that the cancer has metastasized throughout the body.

At an early stage of its investigation, perhaps before SEC officials were fully aware of the implications, the SEC *did* recommend that the FBI investigate two suspicious transactions. We know about this thanks to a 9/11 Commission memorandum declassified in May 2009, which summarizes an August 2003 meeting at which FBI agents briefed the Commission on the insider-trading issue. The document indicates that the SEC passed the information about the suspicious trading to the FBI on September 21, 2001, just ten days after the attacks.[31]

Although the names in both cases are censored from the declassified document, thanks to some nice detective work by Kevin Ryan we know whom (in one case) the SEC was referring to. Ryan was able to fill in the blanks because, fortunately, the government censor was not 100% efficient, and inadvertently left enough details in the document to infer the name of the suspicious trader. His identity, it turns out, is a stunner and should have been prime-time news on every television network, world-wide.[32]

The trader was none other than Wirt Walker III, a distant cousin to then-President G.W. Bush. Several days before 9/11, Walker and his wife Sally purchased 56,000 shares of stock in Stratesec, one of the companies that provided security at the World Trade Center up until the day of the attacks. Notably, Stratesec also provided security at Dulles International Airport, where AA 77 took off on 9/11, and also security for United Airlines, which owned two of the four allegedly hijacked aircraft. At the time, Walker was a director of Stratesec. Bush's brother Marvin was also on the board. Walker's investment paid off handsomely, gaining $50,000 in value in a matter of days. Given the links to the World Trade Center and the Bush family, the SEC lead should have sparked an intensive FBI investigation. Yet, incredibly, in a mind-boggling example of criminal malfeasance, the FBI concluded that because Walker and his wife had "no ties to terrorism....there was no reason to pursue the investigation." The FBI did not conduct a single interview.

The 9/11 Commission Report also fails to mention other compelling evidence for insider trading: the approximately four hundred computer hard drives found by workmen in the ruins of the WTC. In December 2001, Reuters and CNN reported that US credit card, telecommunications and accounting firms had hired a German company named Convar to recoup data from the damaged hard drives. Convar got the contract because it had developed a method for recovering data using a cutting-edge laser scanning technology. Richard Wagner, a data-retrieval expert at Convar, told CNN that the new laser process made it "possible to read the individual drive surfaces and then create a virtual drive." Convar had already examined thirty-nine hard drives and in most cases had succeeded in recovering 100% of the data; at least sixty-two more were in line for processing.[33]

By searching for encryption keys, indicating a financial record, Convar found evidence stored on the drives of an "unexplained surge" in financial transactions prior to the attacks. According to Reuters: "Unusually large sums of money, perhaps more than $100 million, were rushed through the computers as the disaster unfolded."

Convar director Peter Henshel elaborated:

> The suspicion is that insider information about the attack was used to send financial transaction commands and authorizations in the belief that amidst all the chaos the criminals would have, at the very least, a good head start ... Of course, it's possible that Americans went on an absolute shopping binge, that Tuesday morning. But at this point there are many transactions that cannot be accounted for. Not only the volume but the size of the transactions was far higher than usual for a day like that. There is a suspicion that these were possibly planned to take advantage of the chaos.[34]

After this initial reporting by Reuters and CNN, the issue of the WTC hard drives disappeared from the news, and nothing has been heard since. Although reports on the Internet that Kroll has meanwhile purchased Convar remain unsubstantiated, it is nonetheless clear that someone made the story (and the evidence?) go away.[35] But why would anyone wish to do that unless the initial indications from Convar of insider trading were correct?

Further evidence for insider trading was later provided in chilling fashion by a Deutsche Bank New York branch employee who survived the attacks. The whistleblower, who insisted on remaining anonymous for his own protection, told Mike Ruppert that "about *five minutes before the attack* the entire Deutsche Bank computer system had been *taken over by something external* that no one in the office recognized, and every file was downloaded at lightening speed to an *unknown location* [my emphases]."[36]

Chilling indeed.

ENDNOTES

1   http://www.freewebs.com/abigsecret/Grove.html.

2   Dave Eberhart, "Still Silence From 9-11 Stock Speculation Probe", *NewsMax*, June 3, 2002, http://www.newsmax.com/archives/articles/2002/6/2/62018.shtml.

3   *World News Tonight*, September 20, 2001.

4   William Drozdiak, "'Insider trading' by terrorists is suspected in Europe," *Miami Herald*, September 24, 2001, http://web.archive.org/web/20011109160700/www.miami.com/herald/special/news/worldtrade/digdocs/099922.htm.

5   James Doran, "Insider Trading Apparently Based on Foreknowledge of 9/11 Attacks," *London Times*, September 18, 2001, archived at http://911research.wtc7.net/cache/sept11/londontimes_insidertrading.html.

6   "Profiting from Disaster," *CBS Evening News*, September 19, 2001, archived at http://www.cbsnews.com/stories/2001/09/19/eveningnews/main311834.shtml.

7   Less than a month after the attacks, *Bloomberg News* reported suspicious imbalances in a number of sectors: "Bank of America among 38 stocks in SEC's attack probe," *Bloomberg News*, October 3, 2001, archived at http://911research.wtc7.net/cache/sept11/bloombberg_BAamong38.html. By September 2002, it was clear who the big winners were: Michelle Ciarrocca, "Post-9/11 Economic Windfalls for Arms Manufacturers," *Foreign Policy in Focus*, September 2002, posted at http://old.911digitalarchive.org/objects/50.pdf.

8   "Bank of America among 38 stocks in SEC's attack probe," *Bloomberg News*, Wednesday, October 3, 2001.

9   Charles Gasparino and Gregory Zuckerman, "Treasury Bonds Enter Purview Of U.S. Inquiry Into Attack Gains," *Wall Street Journal*, October 2, 2001. p. C.1

10   According to a 9/11 Commission staff document, the SEC agreed to play the lead role at a multi-agency meeting held on September 17, 2001: John Roth, Douglas Greenburg, and Serena Wille, National Commission on Terrorist Attacks Upon the United States, Monograph on Terrorist Financing, Staff Report to the Commission. Although the document is undated, it probably was completed in 2004.

11   The list included six airline stocks: American, United, Continental, Northwest, Southwest and US Airways, as well as Martin, Boeing, Lockheed Martin Corp., AIG, American Express Corp, American International Group, AMR Corporation, Axa SA, Bank of America Corp, Bank of New York Corp, Bank One Corp, Cigna Group, CNA Financial, Carnival Corp, Chubb Group, John Hancock Financial Services, Hercules Inc, L-3 Communications Holdings, Inc., LTV Corporation, Marsh & McLennan Cos. Inc., MetLife, Progressive Corp., General Motors, Raytheon, W.R. Grace, Royal Caribbean Cruises, Ltd., Lone Star Technologies, American Express, the Citigroup Inc., Royal & Sun Alliance, Lehman Brothers Holdings, Inc., Vornado Reality Trust, Morgan Stanley, Dean Witter & Co., XL Capital Ltd., and Bear Stearns; "Bank of America among 38 stocks in SEC's attack probe," Bloomberg News, October 3, 2001, see note 7.

12   Erin E. Arvedlund, "Follow The Money: Terrorist Conspirators Could Have Profited More From Fall Of Entire Market Than Single Stocks," *Barron's* (Dow Jones and Company), October 6, 2001.

13   Scott Winokur, "SEC wants data-sharing system," *San Francisco Chronicle*, October 19, 2001, posted at http://www.sfgate.com/cgi-bin/article.cgi?file=/chronicle/archive/2001/10/19/BU142745.DTL.

14   Michael Ruppert, *Crossing the Rubicon* (New Society Publishers, 2004), p. 243.

15   According to *Bloomberg*, the FBI reached the same conclusion. Although the September 2003 newswire is no longer posted on the Internet, the text is archived at http://s15.invisionfree.com/Loose_Change_Forum/ar/t1699.htm.

16   Chris Blackhurst, "Mystery of terror 'insider dealers'," *The Independent* (UK), October 14, 2001.

17   Ibid.; Christian Berthelsen, Scott Winokur, "Suspicious profits sit uncollected," *San Francisco Chronicle*, September 29, 2001, archived at http://www.sfgate.com/cgi-bin/article.cgi?file=/chronicle/archive/2001/09/29/MN186128.DTL.

18   "Whether advance knowledge of U.S. attacks was used for profit," *New York Times*, October 1, 2001, archived at http://www.hinduonnet.com/2001/10/01/stories/06010006.htm.

19   George Tenet, *At the Center of the Storm* (New York: Harper Collins, 2007), p. 19.

20   Hearings before the Permanent Subcommittee on Investigations, 106th Congress, November 9 and 10, 1999, p. 87, posted at http://frwebgate.access.gpo.gov/cgi-bin/getdoc.cgi?dbname=106_senate_hearings&docid=f:61699.pdf.

21   http://www.fromthewilderness.com/free/ww3/10_09_01_krongard.html.

22   "The 2001 National Money Laundering Strategy," prepared by the Office of Enforcement, US Department of the Treasury, in consultation with the US Department of Justice, September 2001; p. 29 and note 19.

23   Raymond W. Baker, "The Biggest Loophole in the Free Market System," *Washington Quarterly*, Autumn 1999, p. 29, posted at (see p. 1061) http://frwebgate.access.gpo.gov/cgi-bin/getdoc.cgi?dbname=106_senate_hearings&docid=f:61699.pdf.

24   "Chief Steps Down At Alex Brown," *New York Times*, September 15, 2001.

25   Timothy L. O'Brien, "The Deep Slush at Bankers Trust," *New York Times*, May 30, 1999, posted at http://www.nytimes.com/1999/05/30/business/the-deep-slush-at-bankers-trust.html?src=pm.

26   "Chief Steps Down At Alex Brown," *New York Times*, September 15, 2001.

27   Kyle F. Hence, "Massive pre-attack 'insider trading' offers authorities hottest trail to accomplices," *Global Research*, April 21, 2002. Posted at http://globalresearch.ca/articles/HEN204B.html

     Also see http://nsarchive.files.wordpress.com/2010/04/9-11-sec-report.pdf

28   Allen M. Poteshman, "Unusual Option Market Activity and the Terrorist Attacks of September 11, 2001," *Journal of Business*, 2006, vol. 79, no. 4, http://www.journals.uchicago.edu/doi/abs/10.1086/503645.

29   Marc Chesney, et al., "Detecting Informed Trading Activities in the Options Markets," Social Sciences Research Network, 13 January 2010, http://papers.ssrn.com/sol3/papers.cfm?abstract_id=1522157.

30   Wing-Keung Wong, et al, "Was there Abnormal Trading in the S&P 500 Index Options Prior to the September 11 Attacks?" Social Sciences Research Network, April 2010, http://papers.ssrn.com/sol3/papers.cfm?abstract_id=1588523.

31   9/11 Commission memorandum entitled "FBI Briefing on Trading", prepared by Doug Greenburg, 18 August 2003, p. 4-5. Posted at http://media.nara.gov/9-11/MFR/t-0148-911MFR-00269.pdf.

32   Kevin Ryan, "Evidence for Informed Trading on the Attacks of September 11," *Foreign Policy Journal*, November 18, 2010. Posted at http://www.foreignpolicyjournal.com/2010/11/18/evidence-for-informed-trading-on-the-attacks-of-september-11/all/1/

33   Rick Perera, "Computer disk drives from WTC could yield clues," CNN, December 20, 2001, posted at http://archives.cnn.com/2001/TECH/industry/12/20/wtc.harddrives.idg/.

34   "German firm probes final World Trade Center deals," Reuters, December 17, 2001, posted at http://www.rediff.com/money/2001/dec/17wtc.htm.

35   Michael Fury, "The Ghost in the Machines: Evidence of Foreknowledge in the WTC Hard Drive Recoveries," *Journal of 9/11 Studies*, December 2008, posted at http://www.journalof911studies.com/volume/2008/GhostWTC.pdf.

36   Michael Ruppert, see note 14, p. 244.

AIG's Shanghai Office

Chapter 5

American International Group

Before we proceed further, let us briefly review what we have already learned. In addition to the suspicious coincidences surrounding Kroll, the Blackstone Group, and the World Trade Center, there is also the extraordinarily heavy pre-9/11 put option activity in the case of the Greenberg-run Marsh & McLennan, which no doubt prompted the SEC to place M & M on its list of 38 suspect companies. Additionally, we have the testimony of Richard Grove and the 1996 national security paper by Maurice Greenberg in which the AIG chief explicitly endorsed a policy of harboring drug traffickers, money launderers, even murderers, in the ill-conceived interests of national security. To this evidence I would add a relevant factoid: Although in 2001 the US insurance industry as a whole suffered through one of its worst years on record, AIG's immense profitability continued and hardly lost a beat. Whereas the rest of the industry paid out some $40 billion in insurance settlements as a result of the 9/11 attacks, AIG reported a handsome $5.36 billion profit for the year; which was only a slight decline from the $5.64 billion profit AIG posted 2000.[1] Even subtracting Marsh & McLennan's $126 million in losses, the Greenberg family beat the trends in 2001. All of the above, I would argue, calls for a closer look at Maurice Greenberg and AIG. Although the following discussion will range beyond 9/11, I believe the digression is justified by the overwhelming evidence for criminality, which further supports our darkest suspicions about 9/11.

AIG has always been an American-owned company, though it had its origins in China. Cornelius V. Starr founded American Asiatic Underwriters in Shanghai in 1919 (though it was also American International Underwriters before assuming its current name), the first western insurance firm in the Far East. From the start, the company's international scope of operations was ideally suited for intelligence gathering. In 1939, the Japanese invasion of China compelled Starr to relocate to New York, where in 1943 he joined with Office of Strategic Services chief William "Wild Bill" Donovan to form a special insurance unit to gather war-time intelligence about Nazi Germany and Japan. During the war, the OSS actually shared Starr's offices in New York City.

The special unit used Starr's connections in China, including his Shanghai newspaper, as a spy network. Meanwhile, the agents back in New York sifted through mountains of insurance documents for blueprints of enemy bomb plants, the design of the Tokyo water supply, timetables for tide changes, and other details about shipping and manufacturing which aided the Allied war effort. As World War II drew to a close, the special unit investigated how the Nazis might try to launder their assets via phony insurance policies.[2]

Maurice Greenberg's father had begun as Cornelius Starr's chauffeur in Shanghai, which explains the younger Greenberg's entry into the Starr empire. Cornelius recognized Maurice's promise from an early age, paid for his education, and later brought him into the business. In 1962, Starr picked Maurice Greenberg to manage AIG's holdings in the US, which were not doing well at the time. Greenberg administered a quick turnaround, and in 1968 he succeeded Starr as head of AIG.[3] The next year, Maurice issued a public stock offering and began to expand the company.

According to various sources, Greenberg was a longtime confidant of Ronald Reagan's CIA Director William Casey, who had headed up the Securities and Exchange Commission under Richard Nixon. After his appointment, Casey attempted to recruit Greenberg to be his deputy at CIA, but Greenberg declined, preferring to remain at AIG.[4] Once, in a *New York Times* interview, Casey mentioned Greenberg as one of the few individuals outside of government whom he relied on for advice.[5]

Henry Kissinger was another friend and client. In 1987, Greenberg appointed Kissinger as chairman of AIG's advisory board.[6] For years, both men lobbied China's leaders to open the country to western investment, though Kissinger's role is of course more

widely known. In 1980, the Chinese finally granted Greenberg a
license to sell insurance in Beijing, and in 1996 AIG reoccupied the
same Shanghai offices originally used by Cornelius Starr.[7]

Under Greenberg's leadership, AIG generated profits at a rate
that blew away the competition. Over a ten-year period, from 1988
to 1998, AIG's earnings compounded at an average rate of 14%, an
impressive figure in a business that tends to be cyclical. While the
rest of the insurance industry suffered periodic ups and downs,
AIG behaved more like a "growth" company. Its consistently high
earnings wowed investors.

Some compared AIG to a perpetual money-making machine. In
a column, David Schiff, publisher of an insurance industry newsletter, wrote that, "AIG is to the insurance business what the Yankees
are to baseball."[8] The comparison was based on more than whimsy.
Rumor had it that Maurice "Hank" Greenberg drew his nickname
from the first Jewish superstar of American professional sports:
baseball's "Hammerin' Hank" Greenberg, a native New Yorker
whom the Yankee's had recruited in 1929, before deciding on another first baseman named Lou Gehrig. Hammerin' Hank ended up
playing for the Detroit Tigers.

How did AIG beat the trends? Writing in 1998, Schiff opined,
"No one quite knows the answer. Some who follow AIG have told
us they can't really analyze it."[9] Many investors did not bother to
try. They simply accepted the fact that Greenberg was brilliant,
and that AIG was somehow unique. The view expressed in 2002 by
Morgan Stanley analyst Alice Shroeder was typical: "What investors really want is for Hank to become immortal."[10]

Many also felt that way about Bernie Madoff, but there were significant differences: AIG was no Ponzi scheme. Yet, whereas other
large insurance firms like State Farm were fairly simple to understand, AIG, by comparison, was "fabulously complex," virtually im-
penetrable from the outside. The reason: AIG had hundreds of af-
filiates spread among one hundred thirty countries, and did most
of its business offshore, beyond the scrutiny of US regulators. The
Wall Street Journal once referred to AIG as a "black box" (likewise
characterizing Enron). This probably helps to explain why Greenberg and AIG remained untouchable for so long.

AIG was not solely an insurance firm. By the 1990s, Greenberg
had diversified into other areas, such as derivatives trading, private

banking, financial services and asset management. Another division boasted the world's largest airline rental company. But AIG achieved its lofty reputation by succeeding where others failed.

Most traditional insurance companies lose money underwriting policies. They manage to turn a profit by shrewdly investing the premiums. AIG was different. It had a reputation for actually *making money* writing insurance policies. Or so people thought.

In the spring of 2005, when the dust finally settled, it had become clear that AIG also lost money in the insurance business, but had obscured the fact through a myriad of creative accounting schemes which transformed AIG's underwriting (business) losses to investment (capital) losses, a slick way to enhance its corporate balance sheets. Insiders recalled one of Greenberg's favorite expressions: "All I want in life is an unfair advantage."[11]

After 9/11, however, it gradually became clear that not even AIG insiders were privy to some of the decisions being made at the top. In 2002, an internal audit committee reported that AIG's financial accounting was suspect.[12] Later that year, the Securities and Exchange Commission uncovered evidence of securities fraud. In 2000, AIG had marketed an insurance product that enabled a company named Brightpoint Inc. to conceal $11.9 million in losses.[13] When the case was settled, the SEC doubled AIG's fine to $10 million because CEO Maurice Greenberg refused to cooperate.

One of Greenberg's tactics was to stall the investigation by delaying the transfer of subpoenaed documents, including one internal whitepaper that "completely contradicted everything they'd been saying about how this was just the fault of one guy who wasn't getting supervised."[14] Such scams were evidently company policy.

In subsequent weeks, even as AIG sought to portray the Brightpoint case as an isolated incident, federal investigators uncovered another phony transaction that enabled a subsidiary of PNC Financial Services to remove problem loans and assets from its balance sheet, thus enhancing its financial position. AIG paid a $115 million fine.

But this was only the beginning. Soon, both AIG and Marsh & McLennan were in the crosshairs of a state probe launched by New York Attorney General Elliot Spitzer. In October 2004, Spitzer sued Marsh for bid rigging and numerous other fraudulent accounting practices. As the investigation widened, several other insurance companies were also named, including Ace Limited (run by Green-berg's son Evan) and Hartford.[15] Spitzer pointedly refused to ne-gotiate with Marsh's CEO, Jeffrey Greenberg, whom the attorney general accused of stonewalling. The apple, as they say, falls close to the tree. In the end, the younger Greenberg was forced to step down, and Marsh paid $850 million in restitution. Two AIG execu-tives pled guilty to criminal charges.

It is notable that Marsh & McLennan purchased Kroll from AIG for $1.9 billion in July 2004, several months *before* Spitzer's lawsuit. At the time, Kroll's CEO was Michael Cherkasky, who years earlier had been Spitzer's boss at the Manhattan district attorney's office.[16] Cherkasky joined Kroll in 1994, became CEO in 2001, and replaced Jeffrey Greenberg as CEO of Marsh when the younger Greenberg was forced out in late 2004.[17] Thus, it was Cherkasky who negoti-ated the final settlement with Spitzer.

Did AIG pass Kroll on to Marsh to better shield the spy firm from Spitzer's investigation, as Richard Grove has suggested? Possibly. It certainly appears that Cherkasky was named to lead Marsh be-cause of his previous supervisory relationship with Spitzer.

Spitzer, whose reputation was squeaky-clean at the time, went on to become governor of New York; but was himself forced to resign in disgrace in March 2008 after being outed as a regular client of a prostitution escort service. The investigation into Spitzer, a married father of three, began when his bank informed the US Treasury De-partment about suspicious activity in one of his personal accounts. When investigators examined the transactions, they learned that the recipients were apparent shell companies associated with the escort service, to which Spitzer evidently had subscribed since his days as Attorney General.[18]

The timing of the bust was curious and appears to have been re-taliation. Just weeks earlier, governor Spitzer had attacked the Bush administration for actively assisting US banking institutions that were engaging in predatory lending practices.[19]

By early 2005, separate SEC and Department of Justice investiga-tions were closing in on Maurice Greenberg. By this point, the AIG board was also pressuring Greenberg to name a successor and step down. But Greenberg, who was approaching his 80th birthday, had no intention of relinquishing control of the company he had domi-nated for thirty-seven years. Hank had always viewed regulators with disdain, and over the course of his long career he had generally succeeded in intimidating them, one way or another.

In 1996, for instance, when the state of Delaware launched an investigation of AIG's bizarre relationship with a Barbados-based reinsurance company named Coral Re, instead of cooperating Greenberg rang up the Delaware insurance commissioner and gave her a tongue-lashing over the telephone. Greenberg also apparently sent Kroll detectives to harass the state regulators.

The get-tough strategy produced the intended result. Even though state laws had been broken, Delaware had no stomach for a fight, and the regulators drew back. In the end, AIG got off with a mildly worded reprimand, and was not even required to pay a fine. When Coral Re was dissolved, as per the settlement, AIG shifted its business to several new shell companies molded upon the form of the defunct reinsurer.

Greenberg also resorted to Kroll after AIG's general counsel Michael Joye resigned in 1992 to protest fraudulent accounting practices. Joye kept the facts secret for many years, but here is the gist: In the early 1990s Joye was evidently shocked to learn that AIG was cheating several states, including New York, out of tens of millions in workers' compensation funds. Moreover, it was happening with the full knowledge and consent of CEO Greenberg. After conducting his own internal investigation, Joye sent Greenberg a bluntly worded memo informing him that AIG's "intentional violations" could lead to "criminal fraud and racketeering charges," in addition to exposing the company to astronomical civil penalties.[20]

Joye determined that for AIG to comply with regulations, the company "would have to hire about forty new people to do filings properly. It would also have to charge clients more and pay 'much higher' assessment fees." But according to the *New York Times*, Greenberg was not interested. When the issue came up in a meeting, Greenberg asked, "Are we legal?" An employee responded, "If we were legal we wouldn't be in business." Hearing this, "M.R.G. [Greenberg] began laughing and that was the end of it."[21] After Joye tended his resignation, Greenberg sent Kroll a copy of Joye's personnel file. It is not known what Kroll operatives did with it, but the case illustrates Greenberg's temperament and autocratic style.

By early 2005, AIG's directors were pursuing their own internal investigation, which eventually led offshore to several Greenberg-controlled corporations that were a part of the AIG empire. One was the Starr Investment Corporation (SICO), a mysterious holding company which dated to AIG's original founding by Cornelius Starr. The other firm, C.V. Starr (also named after the founder, whose original Dutch surname was Van der Starr), was no less mysterious. Both were based in Bermuda, which is famous for having no corporate income tax, one of two reasons why the island is a boon for insurance companies. Bermuda's other draw is the absence of regulation.

Both SICO and C.V. Starr held substantial amounts of AIG stock, and were used by Greenberg to reward top AIG executives. But C.V. Starr was also reserved for an inner circle who received lavish compensation.[22] The inner group included Howard Smith, AIG's chief financial officer, and Mike Murphy, SICO's treasurer. Smith had previously worked for PricewaterhouseCoopers, the accounting giant that for many years conducted AIG's annual audits.

The final showdown began on March 23, 2005, when a team of AIG lawyers arrived in Bermuda to examine SICO records and conduct interviews. The same facility housed both SICO and AIG employees. Martin Sullivan had already replaced Greenberg as AIG's CEO; though Greenberg still remained as chairman. By this point, a rift was developing between Greenberg's supporters and the rest of the board, all of whom wanted the public relations disaster simply to end. The plot thickened when the directors issued a company-wide order to cooperate with regulators.

The next day, AIG employees in the company's Dublin, Ireland office (also shared with SICO) seized a SICO computer and placed it under lock and key. Things quickly escalated. Mike Murphy, a Greenberg loyalist with a passkey, led a group of SICO employees into the Bermuda office under cover of night, and hustled eighty-two boxes of SICO documents out of the building to a separate location. SICO was incorporated in Panama, a major money-laundering center, and there was concern that Murphy was about to move evidence beyond the reach of US law enforcement. The next day, an SEC official in New York received a message: "Looks like they're destroying documents in Bermuda."[23] It was the last straw.

When word reached New York, Attorney General Spitzer issued a stern warning to CEO Sullivan and also subpoenaed the SICO and AIG records. Sullivan personally flew to Bermuda, summarily fired Mike Murphy, and took possession of the documents. The AIG board, now under threat of criminal prosecution, had no choice but to demand Greenberg's immediate resignation.

In subsequent months, the court proceedings played out in the press. The details gradually emerged about AIG's largest deception: a $500 million deal "in which various AIG insiders staged an elaborate artificial transaction with the Gen Re Corporation," a major reinsurer owned by Warren Buffet. AIG ostensibly bought $600 million in reinsurance from Gen Re for a $500 premium, indicating a risk of $100 million.[24] However, because Greenberg wanted no risk exposure, the deal's "purported terms were all undone" by his staff "in undisclosed side agreements" that rendered the transaction "a sham," according to the SEC, which claimed that papers had been altered to distort the nature of the transaction.[25]

Buffet's company provided records to Spitzer documenting everything. The records showed that AIG's purpose had been to generate a large tax write-off in order to make the company look more prosperous than it was. The documents also proved Greenberg's personal involvement.[26] One of the investigators told the *New York Times* that the intent may have been "to mask the activities of murky offshore entities that AIG used extensively during Mr. Greenberg's tenure at the company."

In 2006, AIG reached a $1.6 billion settlement with state and federal authorities: the largest fine ever paid by any financial services company in US history.[27] In February 2008, four former executives of Gen Re, and one from AIG, were convicted of conspiracy, securities fraud, mail fraud and making false statements to the SEC.[28]

It is important to understand that Maurice Greenberg is not some run-of-the-mill hoodlum. As noted, he served as chairman of the Federal Reserve Bank of New York, is a director of the New York Stock Exchange, is the vice-chairman of the Council on Foreign Relations, and is a member of the Trilateral Commission. He also served as vice-chairman of the Center for Strategic and International Studies, and is the Director of the Institute for International Economics, is the Director of the US-China Business Council, the vice-chairman of the US-ASEAN Business Council, the Director of Project Hope, founding chairman of the US-Philippine Business Committee, and, until his forced retirement, was a Trustee of the Asia Society. Nor does this pretend to be a comprehensive list of Greenberg's bona fides.

After Hank's departure from AIG, the new CEO Martin Sullivan told the press that the insurance giant would now prosper "with the right controls and checks and balances in place, and the right level of compliance."[29] As we know, however, things turned out rather differently. By 2008, AIG was in dire financial straits, largely because of the company's exposure to the sub-prime mortgage crisis, the predictable outcome of no regulation of derivatives. By September 16, 2008, AIG stock had fallen by more than 95%: from a high of $70.13 to just $1.25/share. For the year, AIG reported a $99 billion loss, and received a controversial $85 billion bailout.[30]

Greenberg pointed an accusatory finger at the current directors, and told the press that AIG's sales of credit default swaps had exploded after he left. Sullivan denied this, insisting that AIG actually stopped writing credit default swaps in 2005. By March 2009, AIG's federal bailout had expanded to $150 billion, making it the largest single bailout by far in US history. AIG also set another dubious record when it posted a $61.7 billion loss for the final three months of 2008, the largest quarterly loss in corporate history.[31] That same month, AIG announced that it would disperse $1.2 billion in bonus packages to its employees, seventy-three of whom would receive checks of at least $1 million.[32]

Not surprisingly, the bonus announcement stirred public outrage. But the press failed to ask the really important questions. The investigations of the Greenberg empire showed that AIG was not that different from the rest of the industry: AIG also lost money, at times, in the insurance business. Given that AIG managed its risks by ceding as much as 70% of its premiums to various reinsurers, this means that most of AIG's insurance revenue was unavailable for investment. Nor can the remaining 30% account for AIG's impressive earnings over many years.[33]

So, how did Maurice Greenberg manage for so long to produce a silk purse from a sow's ear? Did Greenberg succumb to the temptations of the powerful, and step over the line? What is clear is that AIG's offshore dealings were key to the company's profitability, even during the downturns that affected the rest of the industry but to which AIG seemed largely immune. David Schiff, a Greenberg admirer, put it this way: "AIG's unique global franchise obscured the reality of the company's financial condition."[34]

Former LAPD narcotics detective Michael Ruppert arrived at a different conclusion. In August 2001, just weeks before 9/11, Ruppert posted an article exploring possible AIG involvement in the drug trade.[35] Ruppert was astounded to learn that Coral Talavera Baca, the wife (or girlfriend, it is not clear which) of Medellin drug lord Carlos Lehder was at the time employed at AIG's San Francisco office, ostensibly as a legal consultant, a position for which Talavera had neither the requisite training nor the credentials. What was she doing there?

Incredibly, as it turns out, Coral Talavera Baca was the very woman who in 1995 supplied investigative reporter Gary Webb with the initial lead that resulted in his groundbreaking series of articles in the *San Jose Mercury News* about CIA links to Latin American drug traffickers.[36]

Talavera's husband, Carlos Lehder, was one of the central figures in the notorious Medellin drug cartel led by Pablo Escobar, which in the mid-1980s grew into the world's largest cocaine-smuggling ring. Shortly after Lehder's 1987 arrest in a Columbian jungle, he reportedly cut a deal with US officials that allowed him to keep much of his estimated $2.5 billion fortune amassed from the drug trade.[37] Lehder was extradited to the US where he entered a witness protection program.

But why would the US government negotiate with a man who had been "public enemy number one"? Lehder and his cohorts in Medellin are believed to have ordered the assassination of numerous Columbian officials, newspaper editors, journalists, informants, as well as six hundred policemen. But the cartel is perhaps best known for the grisly attack on the country's Palace of Justice in November 1985 that left nearly one hundred people dead, including eleven of Columbia's supreme court justices. No mistake, Lehder was a bad apple.

According to the *Pittsburgh Post-Gazette*, it was none other than Vice President George H.W. Bush who negotiated the deal with Lehder.[38] I was initially surprised by this, until I remembered that in 1982 President Reagan had named Bush to head up his "War on Drugs."

Although Lehder testified for US prosecutors at the 1992 trial of Panamanian dictator Manuel Noriega, his testimony proved of little value to the prosecution. According to knowledgeable sources, Noriega's conviction was a foregone conclusion. Some wondered why the US was so interested in Noriega in the first place, since Lehder was a much bigger fish in the drug world. Alfred McCoy, a respected historian of the drug trade, believes that the US prosecution of Noriega had nothing to do with curbing the drug trade and everything to do with projecting US power in Central America. Noriega's crime was that he had turned nationalist, developed his own power base, and was pursuing an independent path for Panama, much like his predecessor General Omar Torrijos, who died in a mysterious plane crash possibly orchestrated by the CIA.[39]

But there is also more to the story. George H.W. Bush probably ordered the December 1989 invasion of Panama and the arrest of Noriega to clean up his *own* mess, that is, to protect his own political rear. It was Bush as CIA director who had first put Noriega on the Agency payroll. According to investigator Joseph Trento, Noriega was in possession of highly compromising information about the Bush-led CIA's first attempt to finance covert operations in this hemisphere with profits from the drug trade, just as it had done in Southeast Asia many years before.

For instance, Noriega knew all about Operation Watchtower, a highly illegal mission in 1975-76 involving US Special Forces teams that were sent into the jungles of northern Columbia to set up transmitters enabling dozens of aircraft loaded with narcotics to fly from Bogota into Panama undetected by radar. The drug money was then laundered through Panamanian banks and the cash used to arm factions in Columbia deemed friendly to the CIA. Once in custody, Noriega's chances of damaging Bush were nil.

At his trial, Noriega's only defense was that he had been working for the CIA. He claimed that he had been paid $10 million for his services. But the judge ruled that "information about the content of the discrete [CIA] operations in which Noriega had engaged in exchange for the alleged payments was irrelevant to his defense" and would only "confuse the issues before the jury."[40]

The US soldiers who had participated in the Watchtower missions fared even worse than Noriega. According to Trento, one individual who gave an affidavit in 1980, and a score of others, later died "under circumstances that would stretch the credulity of even the most devout conspiracy theorist."[41]

Three years after the Noriega trial, Lehder complained in a letter to US District Judge William Hoeveler of Miami that he had been double-crossed by the US government. Weeks later, according to eyewitnesses, Lehder was whisked away in the dead of night from the witness protection center at Mesa, Arizona. He was not seen again for ten years, when he appeared in a Florida courtroom in 2005 to appeal his life-plus-135-years prison sentence. The judge dismissed his appeal out of hand. No surprise there.

But what about the $2.5 billion in assets that Lehder reportedly retained? Nearly eleven years after 9/11, the questions raised on the eve of the attack by Mike Ruppert about Baca's connections with AIG, and AIG's possible involvement in the drug trade, remain unanswered. But the Baca connection is not the only evidence of illicit activity. Consider the strange case of Coral Re.

CORAL RE

It is curious that Maurice Greenberg chose to expand AIG into financial services in 1987, the year of Lehder's arrest in Columbia. The timing corresponds with a sharp upsurge in the revenues of the international drug trade at this time, which by the late 1980s exceeded an estimated trillion dollars a year.[42] That same year, AIG also entered into the strange relationship with Barbados-based Coral Re. The details, as I have noted, came to light in the mid-1990s when Delaware state regulators discovered that AIG secretly controlled Coral Re.

In the insurance world, companies often reduce their exposure to underwriting losses by passing on a percentage of the risk to insurance wholesalers, also known as reinsurance companies. As payment, the reinsurance companies receive a percentage of the premiums. Wholesalers are generally based offshore in places like Bermuda, Barbados, the Cayman Islands and Luxembourg, where taxes are minimal or nonexistent and accounting records can legally be kept secret. Although state laws in the US require insurance companies to keep a certain amount of capital in reserve to cover losses, the amount is less if a company has reinsurance. AIG was a major user of reinsurance because it specialized in high-risk policies.

US law, however, requires that both parties to such a transaction, i.e., the insurer and reinsurer, must be independent of one another, for obvious reasons. If the two are affiliated, then reinsurance provides no true risk reduction. This was the issue with Coral Re, and what had attracted state regulators in the first place, because despite persistent denials by AIG, Coral Re turned out to be a shell company, created by AIG for reasons that were never made clear and seem doubly suspicious in retrospect.

At the time that Coral Re was established, the Wall Street firm Goldman Sachs sent around a confidential memo cautioning those involved to keep the whole business secret. Indeed, the memo stipulated that all copies of the memo were to be returned to Goldman Sachs. When Delaware state regulators nevertheless managed to obtain a copy, they were incredulous. The dozen or so "investors" who lent their names to the enterprise put up no money of their own, yet were guaranteed a profit, a sweet deal if ever there was one.[43]

Within days of its creation, Coral Re recorded $475 million in losses, which soon topped $1 billion. Between 1987-1993 AIG ceded $1.6 billion of insurance premiums to the new reinsurer. Yet, Coral Re's total equity capital never exceeded $52 million.[44] In addition to being severely under-capitalized, the new company had no actual offices of its own; it was managed by a subsidiary of AIG. Coral Re's board of directors made no decisions and conducted no business.

At the time of the dubious memo, the CEO of Goldman Sachs was Robert Rubin, who later served as Secretary of the Treasury under Bill Clinton, where he led the push to deregulate the financial services industry.

Rubin's main "achievement" during his tenure at Treasury was persuading President Bill Clinton to support repeal of the 1933 Glass-Steagall Act, a key part of Franklin Delano Roosevelt's New Deal program. Glass-Steagall had created a regulatory firewall between commercial and investment banking, for the soundest of reasons: to prevent conflicts of interest and other abuses within the banking system. But Robert Rubin, Alan Greenspan and others on Wall Street viewed the New Deal as an aberration, and in 1999 they brought Clinton around.[45]

The previous year, Rubin had joined with Greenspan in blocking attempts by Brooksley Born, chairman of the Commodities Futures Trading Commission, to regulate commodities derivatives, which

MEMORANDUM NO.____
NAME _____

1,000 Shares

CORAL REINSURANCE COMPANY LTD.

Common Stock

THIS PRIVATE PLACEMENT MEMORANDUM HAS BEEN PREPARED SOLELY FOR THE BENEFIT OF SELECTED ACCREDITED INVESTORS IN CONNECTION WITH THE PRIVATE PLACEMENT OF 1,000 SHARES OF COMMON STOCK (THE "COMMON STOCK") OF CORAL REINSURANCE COMPANY LTD. ("CORAL" OR THE "COMPANY"). THE RECIPIENT OF THIS MEMORANDUM ACKNOWLEDGES THAT IN CONNECTION WITH HIS OR ITS INVESTIGATION OF THE COMPANY HE OR IT WILL RECEIVE CONFIDENTIAL INFORMATION. SUCH RECIPIENT BY ACCEPTING A COPY OF THIS MEMORANDUM AGREES THAT NEITHER HE OR IT NOR ANY OF HIS OR ITS EMPLOYEES SHALL USE FOR ANY PURPOSE OR DIVULGE TO ANY PARTY ANY SUCH INFORMATION AND SHALL RETURN THIS MEMORANDUM AND ALL COPIES OF THIS MEMORANDUM AND SUCH INFORMATION TO GOLDMAN, SACHS & CO. (THE "SELLING AGENT") PROMPTLY UPON REQUEST. THIS MEMORANDUM IS NOT TO BE REPRODUCED OR REDISTRIBUTED.

THESE SECURITIES HAVE NOT BEEN REGISTERED UNDER THE SECURITIES ACT OF 1933, AS AMENDED (THE "ACT"), OR APPROVED BY THE SECURITIES AND EXCHANGE COMMISSION OR THE REGULATORY AUTHORITY OF ANY STATE NOR HAS SUCH COMMISSION OR ANY REGULATORY AUTHORITY PASSED ON THE ACCURACY OR ADEQUACY OF THIS MEMORANDUM. ACCORDINGLY, THE SECURITIES ARE OFFERED ONLY IN TRANSACTIONS EXEMPT FROM REGISTRATION REQUIREMENTS UNDER THE ACT. THIS MEMORANDUM DOES NOT CONSTITUTE AN OFFER IN ANY JURISDICTION IN WHICH AN OFFER IS NOT AUTHORIZED.

"AIG's interest in creating [Coral] is to create a reinsurance facility which will permit its U.S. companies to write more U.S. premiums..."

THE INFORMATION CONTAINED IN THIS MEMORANDUM HAS BEEN OBTAINED FROM THE COMPANY AND AMERICAN INTERNATIONAL GROUP, INC. ("AIG"). NO REPRESENTATION OR WARRANTY IS MADE, HOWEVER, AS TO THE ACCURACY OR COMPLETENESS OF SUCH INFORMATION, AND NOTHING CONTAINED IN THE MEMORANDUM IS, OR SHALL BE RELIED UPON AS A PROMISE OR REPRESENTATION AS TO THE FUTURE. CERTAIN PROJECTIONS ARE PRESENTED IN THIS MEMORANDUM AND, ALTHOUGH IT IS BELIEVED SUCH PROJECTIONS ARE REALISTIC, NO REPRESENTATION CAN BE MADE AS TO THEIR ATTAINABILITY.

GOLDMAN, SACHS & CO.

DECEMBER 1, 1987

Born and others correctly saw as a threat to the stability of financial markets.[46] The defeat of every attempt to regulate derivatives, together with the repeal of Glass-Steagall, opened the floodgates to the wild speculation of the G.W. Bush years, and is responsible for the real estate bubble, collateral debt obligations, sub-primes, credit default swaps, legalized skimming rackets and, ultimately, the 2008 global financial meltdown.

After Rubin departed from Treasury in July 1999, he joined the board of Citigroup, the largest US bank, which had recently been rocked by several huge money-laundering scandals. One was on the order of a $100 million, and involved the brother of Mexican President Carlos Salinas. Yet, in 2001, under Rubin's tutelage, Citigroup paid $12 billion to acquire the second largest bank in Mexico, Banamex, whose owner Roberto Hernandez Ramirez was known to be deeply involved in the international drug trade.

In December 1998, the daily *Por Esto!*, Mexico's third largest newspaper, reported that Ramirez's estate on the coast of Yucatan was a regular transshipment point for tons of South American cocaine. According to local fishermen, the coke arrived by boat during the night and, after being offloaded, was sent to the US via small planes operating out of a private airstrip on Ramirez's sizable estate. The property is located on the tip of Punta Pajaros: "Bird Point."[47] So flagrant was the trafficking that local people dubbed it "la peninsula de la coca": the cocaine peninsula.

When Ramirez sued *Por Esto!* for libel, a Mexican court threw out the case after determining that the evidence for narcotrafficking was genuine.[48] A succession of Mexican presidents, including Ernesto Zedillo and Vicente Fox, reportedly vacationed with the drug lord-banker at his lavish estate, as did President Bill Clinton in February 1999.[49]

Citigroup evidently acquired Banamex to gain easy access to drug money, which many US banks now depend on for liquidity. In 2009, Antonia Maria Costa, head of the UN Office on Drugs and Crime, told the press that billions of dollars of laundered drug money had saved the US financial system during the 2008 meltdown on Wall Street.[50]

But not even laundered drug money could save Citigroup. The bank suffered enormous losses due to its sub-prime exposure, and at the height of the crisis "required" a $45 billion transfusion from the Federal Reserve, the second largest bailout after AIG's. By December 2008, Citigroup's stock had plummeted to $8/share from a high of $55 in 2006. Angry shareholders filed a lawsuit charging that Robert Rubin and other insiders not only deceived them about the bank's losses, but had also cashed out, selling their own inflated stock options *before* the collapse.

Later, the SEC agreed with shareholders that Rubin and other bank officials knew about the losses. This, of course, would mean that they are guilty of both defrauding investors and insider trading.[51] At last report, however, no one had been indicted, although one bank officer was fined $100,000, a hand-slap that is almost laughable given Rubin's reported earnings of $120 million while at Citigroup.[52]

Citigroup may be the largest, but it is not the only big US bank involved in narcotrafficking. Others evidently include Bank of America, American Express Bank, Wells Fargo and Wachovia. Recently, *Bloomberg* reporter Michael Smith learned why US authorities have failed to crack down harder on the big banks' profiting from the drug trade when he interviewed Jack Blum, a legendary US Senate investigator.[53] Said Blum: "There's no capacity to regulate or punish them [the big banks] because they are too big to be threatened with failure.... They seem ... willing to do anything that improves their bottom line, until they're caught." Blum called their too-big-to-fail status "a get-out-of-jail-free-card for big banks."[54]

However, banks do not become money laundering institutions merely by chance, but thanks to the complicitous involvement of regulators, elements of the US intelligence community, and corrupt US government officials – often at the highest level. As we are about to discover, Hank Greenberg's decision in 1987 to expand AIG into financial services also corresponds with other developments half-way around the world, namely, the ouster of Philippine dictator Ferdinand Marcos, whose fabulous wealth, like AIG's bottom line between 1988-2000, has stirred considerable speculation.

ENDNOTES

1   The figures for 2001 are posted at http://www.behindtheheadlines.info/teaching911/the-economic-impact-of-911-industry-loss-estimates.php

and http://www.fundinguniverse.com/company-histories/American-International-Group-Inc-company-History.html

Dave Thomas, "9/11 Impact on Marsh & McLennan Cos. Nothing Short of Devastation," *Insurance Journal*, September 10, 2004. Posted at http://www.insurancejournal.com/news/national/2004/09/10/45707.htm

2   Mark Fritz, "The Secret (Insurance) Agent Men," *Los Angeles Times*, September 22, 2000.

3   David Schiff, "AIG's Relationship with Three Starr Entities," *Schiff's Insurance Observer*, March 30, 2005.

4   http://spitfirelist.com/for-the-record/ftr-531-interview-with-lucy-komisar-about-offshore/.

5   Ronald Shelp, *Fallen Giant* (Hoboken, NJ: John Wiley & Sons, 2006), p.10.

6   Walter Isaacson, *Kissinger: A Biography* (New York: Simon & Schuster, 2005), pp. 739-40.

7   http://investmentwatchblog.com/some-history-of-aig-maybe-china-would-like-to-see-the-aig-bailout-continue/.

8   David Schiff, "A Darkness on the Edge of Town," *Schiff's Insurance Observer*, October 1998.

9   Ibid.

10   Devon Leonard, "All I Want In Life is an Unfair Advantage," *Fortune*, August 8, 2005; posted at http://money.cnn.com/magazines/fortune/fortune_archive/2005/08/08/8267642/index.htm.

11   Ibid.

12   David Schiff, "AIG, Audit Committees, Legends, and P/E Ratios," Schiff's Insurance Observer, July 25, 2002; also see Carrie Johnson and Dean Starkman, "Accountants Missed AIG Group's Red Flags," *Washington Post*, May 26, 2005.

13   Kurt Eichenwald and Jenny Anderson, "How a Titan of Insurance Ran Afoul of the Government," *New York Times*, April 4, 2005.

14   Devon Leonard, see note 19.

15   David Schiff, "Spitzer sues Marsh: Bid Rigging, Fraud, Collusion," *Schiff's Insurance Observer*, October 15, 2004. Also see AG Spitzer's press release, posted at http://www.ins.state.ny.us/press/2005/p0501311.htm.

16   Peter Lattman and Anupreeta Das, "Marsh & McLennan Sells Kroll for $1.3 Billion," *Wall Street Journal*, June 8, 2010.

17   http://www.altegrityrisk.com/management/cherkasky.

18   Keith B. Richburg, Susan Schmidt and Carrie Johnson, "FBI Watched Spitzer Before February Incident," *Washington Post*, March 12, 2008, posted at http://www.washingtonpost.com/wp-dyn/content/article/2008/03/11/AR2008031100380_pf.html

19   Eliot Spitzer, "Predatory Lenders' Partner in Crime," *Washington Post*, February 14, 2008.

20   Devon Leonard, see note 19.

21   "Excerpts From Complaint Against A.I.G. by New York," *New York Times*, May 27, 2005; posted at http://query.nytimes.com/gst/fullpage.html?res=9A07E3D61039F934A15756C0A9639C8B63.

22   Ibid.

23   Ibid.

24   http://www.delawarelitigation.com/uploads/file/int8B.PDF.

25   Timothy O'Brien and Jenny Anderson, "AIG Documents Said to be Altered," *New*

York Times, April 8, 2005.

26   Devon Leonard, see note 19.

27   Ron Shelp, *Fallen Giant* (Hoboken, NJ: John Wiley & Sons, 2006), p.173.

28   http://lawprofessors.typepad.com/whitecollarcrime_blog/aig/.

29   Devon Leonard, see note 19.

30   Andrew Simpson, "Greenberg: AIG's Risky Subprime Activity 'Exploded' After He Left," *Insurance Journal*, October 10, 2008.

31   http://news.bbc.co.uk/2/hi/business/7918643.stm.

32   Elizabeth MacDonald, "American Inconscionable Group," *FOX Business*, March 17, 2009., posted at http://www.foxbusiness.com/markets/2009/03/17/american-inconscionable-group/.

33   Devon Leonard, see note 19.

34   David Schiff, "AIG and the Art of Financial Prestidigitation," *Schiff's Insurance Observer*, April 4, 2005, p. 3.

35   http://www.fromthewilderness.com/free/ciadrugs/part_2.html.

36   Gary Webb, see note 1.

37   Bill Moushey, "Protected Witness," *Pittsburgh Post-Gazette*, June 15, 1996; posted at http://www.fear.org/carlos1.html.

38   Ibid.

39   McCoy also pointed out in the same interview that Panama, once part of Columbia, is home to a miniature version of Wall Street. Panama City has a number of large banks, whose primary purpose is to launder money for Columbia drug lords. In short, the replacement of Noriega was an administrative move. The flow of drugs and drug money through Panama hardly paused, and may even have increased. See

      "An Interview with Alfred McCoy by David Barsamian, conducted at University of Wisconsin-Madison, February 17,1990," posted at http://www.druglibrary.org/schaffer/heroin/McCoy2.htm.

40   UNITED STATES of America, Plaintiff-Appellee, v. Manuel Antonio NORIEGA, Defendant-Appellant, United States Court of Appeals, Eleventh Circuit, July 7, 1997, see paragraph 30; posted at http://ftp.resource.org/courts.gov/c/F3/117/117.F3d.1206.92-4687.96-4471.html.

41   Joseph Trento, *Prelude to Terror* (New York: Carroll & Graf, 2005), pp. 83-86.

42   William Engdahl, *Gods of Money* (Wiesbaden, Germany: Engdahl Press, 2009), p. 272.

43   To view a copy of the memo go to David Schiff, "Have We Got a Deal for You," Emerson, Reid's, March 1996, p. 7, posted at http://www.insuranceobserver.com/PDF/1996/030196.pdf.

44   David Schiff, "Coral Re: AIG's $1-Billion Secret," *Emerson, Reid's*, July 1996, pp. 10-13.

45   The 1999 repeal legislation was known as the Gramm-Leach-Bliley Act.

46   Matthew Leising and Roger Runningen, "Brooksley Born `Vindicated' as Swap Rules Take Shape," Bloomberg, November 13, 2008, posted at http://www.bloomberg.com/apps/news?pid=newsarchive&sid=aVYf8XDXiSZM&refer=home.

47   http://www.narconews.com/newboss1.html.

48   Mike Ruppert, *Crossing the Rubicon* (Gabriola Island, BC: New Society Publishers, 2004), p. 79.

49   Bill Clinton was no innocent bystander when he hobnobbed with drug lord and

banker Roberto Hernandez Ramirez in Yucatan. By that time, the US president had his own dark history. Clinton's complicity with the international drug trade began during his Arkansas governorship. For it so happens that one of the original investors in AIG's shell entity, Coral Re, was the Arkansas Development and Finance Authority (ADFA), created in 1985 by then-governor Bill Clinton to promote job creation in the state; but which is known to have laundered hundreds of millions of dollars of drug money during Ronald Reagan's Contra war against the Nicaraguan Sandinistas.

The story of the CIA's arms pipeline through the small town of Mena in western Arkansas is no secret and has been public knowledge for many years. The fact that the vast majority of Americans still know nothing about it is an indictment of our so-called free press, which has regularly failed to inform on many issues vital to our democracy. Although this operation was but a small part of the broader Contra war effort, the Mena story was, and continues to be, political dynamite because of its direct linkage to Clinton and also George H.W. Bush. Terry Reed and John Cummings, *Compromised* (Landham, MD: Clandestine Publishing, 1995).

The Mena operation came about as a result of 1982's so-called Boland amendment, passed by a Democratically controlled Congress. It was actually a series of amendments intended to tie President Reagan's hands: laws blocking him from supporting the counter-revolutionary Contra war in Nicaragua. Frustrated by Congress, the Reagan administration resorted to other means. In 1984-85, CIA flight instructors trained Contra pilots at a secret airstrip in the Ouachita National Forest, located about twelve miles north of Mena, Arkansas.

Meanwhile, CIA pilots, including William Cooper and Barry Seal, airlifted arms out of Mena to Contra bases in Central America. They flew planes owned by Southern Air Transport, the largest of several CIA proprietary airlines. The pilots returned with duffel bags full of cash, which they air-dropped at night at a ranch outside of Little Rock. Some of the cash may have originated from the sale of arms, but most of it came from the drug trade.

Clinton cronies retrieved the duffel bags and washed the dirty money through the ADFA with the assistance of another Clinton confidante, Dan Lasater, who ran a local bonding agency. Lasater's personal chauffeur was none other than Roger Clinton, the governor's brother. Just to show how closely-knit the Clinton political machine was, much of ADFA's legal work was handled by the Rose Law Firm, which employed Hillary Clinton. At that time. Arkansas-style politics was one big happy family. Ibid., p. 67.

Some of the millions washed through ADFA probably financed new industries that created jobs benefiting the people of Arkansas. But much of it went as "preferred loans" to arms manufacturers involved in the Contra resupply effort. According to whistleblower author Terry Reed, one of the CIA flight instructors, Marine Lt. Col. Oliver North orchestrated the Mena operation out of the White House "basement." At the time, however, Reed knew him only as "John Cathey." In his remarkable memoir, *Compromised*, published in 1995, Reed writes that he was shocked to learn that his friend and fellow pilot, Barry Seal, was bringing in planeloads of cocaine, some of which ended up in the hands of Roger Clinton, later convicted of narcotrafficking.

Seal was a legendary figure, and is believed to have personally smuggled somewhere between $3 billion and $5 billion worth of drugs into the US, making him the largest drug smuggler in US history. Yet, Seal was no thug. By all accounts he was a likable, if haunted, individual. This is according to a 1986 letter from the Louisiana attorney general to then-US Attorney General Edwin Meese; quoted in Sally Denton and Roger Morris, "The Crimes of Mena," *Penthouse*, July 1995. This exposé was to have appeared in the *Washington Post*, but was pulled at the last minute.

Seal was certainly a highly skilled pilot. He was flying Boeing 747s for TWA at the tender age of 26, that is, until the authorities caught him smuggling explosives to anti-Castro groups operating in Mexico. In 1984, Seal faced jail time after a drug-smuggling conviction, but he stayed out of prison by turning informant. Subsequently, he helped the Drug Enforcement Agency prosecute several cases of narcotrafficking. Seal also provided evidence leading to the indictment of Medellin drug lords Carlos Lehder, Pablo Escobar, Jorge Ochoa and Jose Gonzalo Rodriguez Gacha. Meanwhile, he flew arms out of Mena for the CIA. "The Drug War and Cold War Collide," *Frontline*, July 17, 1984.

But Seal's flying days came to an abrupt end on February 19, 1986, outside a federal halfway house in Baton Rouge, Louisiana. Seal was sitting in his car, when two hit-men from the Medellin drug cartel sprayed him with automatic weapons fire. In 1985, Seal had participated in a sting operation purportedly linking the leftist Sandinistas to Columbian cocaine traffickers, part of Ronald Reagan's ideological war against the Communists. Daniel Hopsicker, *Barry and the Boys* (Eugene, OR: Madcow Press, 2001).

Seal's cover was blown when the White House leaked details to exploit the sting's propaganda value. Claiming he was acting on orders, Oliver North told *Frontline* that he briefed a US Senator, who passed the information to the press, thus masking the White House as the source of the leak. http://www.pbs.org/wgbh/pages/frontline/shows/drugs/special/north.html (Kerry?)

Seal's attorney Lewis Unglesby believes that a federal judge effectively set his client up for the hit by confining him to the halfway house, which made Seal an easy target. Unglesby says he was with Seal shortly before his murder when Seal make a direct call to Vice President George "Poppy" Bush; Seal was irate because the Internal Revenue Service had just seized his property. According to Unglesby, Seal told Bush, "If you don't get these IRS assholes off my back, I'm going to blow the whistle on the Contra scheme." The details were confirmed in a phone conversation with me on January 28, 2011, by Richard A. Sharpstein, the lawyer who defended Miguel Velez, one of the Columbian hit-men. Also see *Barry and the Boys*, p. 442.

One week later, a federal judge ordered Seal confined to the halfway house. Within days, he was dead. Unglesby's view is supported by evidence obtained by New Orleans attorney Sam Dalton, legal counsel to the Columbian hit-men who murdered Seal. Dalton suspected CIA complicity in the hit, and later subpoenaed two boxes of Seal's personal effects, which had been in the trunk of the car at the time of the murder but were seized by the FBI. Dalton took possession of the boxes only after an extended legal battle, whereupon he found something the FBI had perhaps missed: Vice President Bush's unlisted telephone number. Ibid., p. 3. For the details go to http://www.spartacus.schoolnet.co.uk/JFKseal.htm.

When I spoke with attorney Richard A. Sharpstein, he confirmed all of the above and told me something more. According to Sharpstein, the assassins claimed to have spoken to a US military officer who not only approved the hit, but actually gave them the address of the halfway house. Sharpstein is convinced that Barry Seal was about to go public with the evidence in the boxes, more than enough to incriminate both Vice President Bush and Governor Clinton. Phone conversation with Richard Sharpstein, January 28, 2011

50   Rajeev Syal, "Drug money saved banks in global crisis, claims UN advisor," *Guardian* (UK), December 13, 2009, posted at http://www.guardian.co.uk/global/2009/dec/13/drug-money-banks-saved-un-cfief-claims.

51   Joshua Gallu and Donal Griffin, "SEC Says Prince, Rubin Knew of Losses on Assets at Suit's Focus," *Bloomberg*, September 9, 2008, posted at http://www.bloomberg.com/news/2010-09-09/prince-rubin-knew-assets-at-focus-of-sec-claim-fueled-losses-agency-says.html.

The "military officer" was identified by Sharpstein to Hopsicker as Oliver North.

52   Martha Graybow, "Investors accuse Citi execs of 'suspicious' trades," Reuters, December 3, 2008, posted at http://www.reuters.com/article/idUSTRE4B-26JN20081203. Also see Zach Carter, "Why Robert Rubin and Citibank Execs Should Be in Deep Trouble," *Alternet*, September 9, 2010.

53   Blum was a part of the team led by Senator John Kerry that investigated the corrupt money laundering Bank of Credit and Commerce International (BCCI). Later, Blum also worked with Manhattan DA Robert M. Morgenthau in the prosecution of insider Clark Clifford, and his protege Robert Altman. Peter Truell and Larry Gurwin, *False Profits* (Boston: Houghton Mifflin, 1992).

54   Michael Smith, "Banks Financing Mexico Gangs Admitted in Wells Fargo Deal," *Bloomberg*, June 28, 2010, posted at http://www.bloomberg.com/news/2010-06-29/banks-financing-mexico-s-drug-cartels-admitted-in-wells-fargo-s-u-s-deal.html.

George Tenet

Chapter 6

Collateral Damage

When criminals evade justice should we not expect their criminal activities to burgeon, over time, and become ever more audacious? Yes, of course. The logic is obvious and straightforward. When society fails to hold wicked men accountable, what is to stop them from proliferating their criminal behavior, even to the point of undermining an entire nation? All the more so when the criminals in question are captains of industry, finance, and government.

It is a fact that despite the unprecedented security failures on September 11, 2001, *none* of the officials responsible, at the time, for protecting the US were subsequently held accountable. None were disciplined, sacked, nor even reprimanded. The only "just deserts" meted out after 9/11 were awards and promotions. One prime example was CIA Director George Tenet who, despite having presided over the greatest security failure in US history, was awarded the nation's highest honor, the Presidential Medal of Freedom.

Another important CIA player in the systematic failure that day, Richard Blee, chief of the Bin Laden unit (who had been charged with keeping Tenet briefed), was subsequently made station chief in Kabul, an important post where he promptly launched a regime of renditions and torture.[1] These are examples of accountability-in-reverse, a phenomenon that is more than suspicious and, in my opinion, constitutes prima facie evidence for collusion in the attacks.

Although such a possibility ought to be obvious, it has continued to be politically out-of-bounds here in the US. Throughout the decade after 9/11, the journalists and talking heads who dominate political discourse in the "land of the free" were strangely reticent to ask the key questions. How do we account for their reluctance? Again, the same blunt answer flies back in our face: the most rational explanation is that the prime suspects include highly placed members of the US political establishment and the US financial and corporate elite, men whom the press view as untouchable. But this need not deter us here. We have already ventured far out of bounds in our walk on the dark side. Why stop now?

WHY 9/11?

One researcher has proposed an intriguing answer to the deepest question of all: "Why 9/11?"

Instead of viewing 9/11 through the standard lens, i.e., as a terrorist attack, E.P. Heidner chose to study that horrible day as a detective would in the investigation of a crime. In this, Heidner took his cue from several skeptics who had suggested that the attacks were staged to cover up financial criminality. After conducting his own six-year investigation, Heidner posted the results in 2008: a heavily documented 57-page paper titled "Collateral Damage," in which he argues that the skeptics basically had it right.[2]

Heidner's research convinced him that a number of individuals who had escaped justice for Iran Contragate in the mid 1980s became emboldened, and hatched an even more outrageous plot at the end of the Cold War for the purpose of eliminating Russia, once and for all, as a potential future challenger to the sole remaining global superpower.

Heidner argues that in 1991 a cabal of bankers and intelligence spooks led by H.W. Bush financed this clandestine operation with $240 billion in 10-year securities that, as it happened, were scheduled to come due in September 2001. The securities were backed by a secret CIA fund known simply as the Hammer Fund, one of a number of secret slush funds established by the US during the Cold War for a variety of reasons, some of them arguably legitimate. The Cold War against "international Communism" and the Soviet Union actually began *before* the end of World War II, but by 1991 almost fifty years of state secrecy had enabled any number of opportunists to abuse the secret funds for dubious ends, including their own personal enrichment.

Heidner theorizes that the G.H.W. Bush-led covert economic war against Russia in the 1990s was four-pronged, and included: the *actual theft* (through collusion of ex-KGB and other Soviet officials) in 1991 of *all* the gold in the Russian treasury, a coup against Gorbachev later that same year (which, incidentally, failed), a scheme to debase the ruble, and finally, a complex initiative to take control of key sectors of the Russian economy, especially the country's vast oil and gas reserves.

Heidner writes: "At its inception the program was conducted within the policy framework of the U.S. Government as defined by several Executive Orders authored by Vice President Bush and signed by President Ronald Reagan. There is good reason to believe that the plan was initially formulated by Reagan's CIA Director, William Casey.... Many of the program operatives were probably engaged through official CIA and National Security channels."[3]

Heidner reasons that the operation, however, soon crossed over into illegality, probably out of expedience, thus repeating the pattern of the October Surprise and Iran-Contra: covert operations which subverted the US Constitution and violated international law. Although Heidner does not mention the Bosnian War, it is also likely that the same individuals in the US power elite came to view the ethnic strife in the former Yugoslavia as yet another opportunity.

As noted (see Chapter Five, note 49), Bill Clinton had been compromised from the days of his Arkansas governorship and thus, was in no position as president to pursue an independent, let alone an enlightened, foreign policy. So, it should be no surprise that Clinton's policy in the Balkans amounted to neither. The Bosnian war pitted US-backed Islamic jihadists, including fighters loyal to Osama bin Laden, along with members of the KLA, a Kosovo terrorist group with known ties to the drug trade, against a Serbian nation whose only natural ally was fellow Slavic Russia.[4] It is hardly surprising that astute observers of the war identified Moscow as the West's ultimate target.

According to Heidner, the covert economic war against Russia eventually sparked at least nine independent investigations by federal agencies and foreign governments into securities fraud and money laundering. Any one of which might have exposed the operation and the conspirators. He goes on to argue that the growing threat of exposure through the decade of the 1990s eventually compelled the conspirators to take their clandestine operation to the next level.

Circa 1998, Heidner says, the group hatched plans for a false-flag terrorist attack on the World Trade Center and Pentagon to destroy

D see Parenti assessment

critical evidence, shut down the ongoing investigations, divert attention away from themselves, and generally cover their tracks. The diabolical plot may also have served other converging interests, one of them being to create a pretext for a vastly expanded use of US military force worldwide.

The neocons boldly outlined such a plan in their strategy paper, *Rebuilding America's Defenses*, which went up on the Internet in September 2000, a year before 9/11. The paper includes a passage that is chilling in retrospect: "The process of transformation, even if it brings revolutionary change, is likely to be a long one, absent some catastrophic and catalyzing event – like a new Pearl Harbor."[5]

Chilling indeed. The neocon paper is still posted, to this day.

Heidner agrees with my conclusion that the point of impact on the newly renovated west wing of the Pentagon was no coincidence (see Chapter Three), although be argues that the primary target was not the Accounting Office but the Office of Naval Intelligence (ONI). According to Heidner, the ONI had been investigating crimes associated with the plundering of Russia. What we know for sure is that a month before the attacks, the ONI inexplicably moved to its new quarters in the outer "E" ring, from a much less vulnerable location within the Pentagon. On 9/11, ONI suffered total destruction: thirty-nine out of forty ONI staffers died, including the entire chain of command.[6]

Heidner argues that specific offices at the World Trade Center were targeted, as well, especially Cantor-Fitzgerald, the leading US security broker. Cantor-Fitzgerald had offices in the North Tower (on floors 101-105) above the impact point of American Airlines 11, and lost more personnel in the attacks (661 employees) by a wide margin than any other occupant of the WTC.

Heidner believes that a little-known FBI office on the 23rd floor of the North Tower was likewise targeted, as evidenced by numerous eyewitness accounts of explosions on the 22nd floor.[7] Another security broker, Garbon Inter-Capital, had offices on the 25th floor of WTC-1, just above this zone, and may also have been a target. The early reports of near-total destruction of this portion of the North Tower, 70 floors below the AA 11 impact zone, is hard to explain by jet fuel-caused fires.

A third important security firm, Eurobrokers, was based on the 84th floor of the South Tower, immediately above where United

Flight 175 struck at 9:03 A.M. Eurobrokers also suffered heavy loss of life (i.e., 61 fatalities). All together, brokerages accounted for 41% of the total casualties at the WTC. Another target may have been the actual securities themselves. According to the Federal Register, the attacks destroyed unknown thousands of certificates stored in vaults maintained by the broker-dealers.[8]

Heidner argues that the offices of securities brokers were specifically targeted and offers the following rationale: "a critical mass of brokers from the major government security brokerages in the Twin Towers had to be eliminated to create chaos in the government securities market. A situation needed to be created wherein $240 billion dollars of covert securities could be electronically 'cleared' without anyone asking questions."[9]

Another likely target was the El Dorado Task force, an interagency money-laundering watchdog group led by the US Customs Service and the Internal Revenue Service. At the time of 9/11, the interagency task force was based in the US Customs Office in Building Six, and was responsible for coordinating federal and state money laundering investigations.[10]

Building Six ⟶

Its location in Building Six is noteworthy, because the destruction of WTC-6 remains one of the strangest mysteries from 9/11. Aerial photos of the WTC site taken after the attack show an enormous cavity in the middle of Building Six. The pictures are extraordinary, and raise obvious questions. The hole has been compared to a crater.[11] What, other than a huge explosion, could have hollowed out the core of this eight-story building? According to the official story, WTC-6 was wrecked by falling debris during the collapse of the adjacent North Tower. But subsequent inside photos of the huge cavity fail to show any of the tell-tale exterior columns or other identifiable debris from the North Tower. Indeed, judging from the available photos, the cavity was remarkably free of *any* type of debris.

After 9/11, an official FEMA photographer, Kurt Sonnenfeld, descended with several others into the wreckage of Building Six. The team located the US Customs vault in the basement and, according to Sonnenfeld, were surprised to find the vault door sprung partly open. They managed to wriggle inside, and when they did were shocked to find it was completely bare.[12] Evidently, someone had cleaned it out *before* the attacks. Sonnenfeld's electrifying report about WTC-6, posted in 2009, strongly points to foreknowledge and is powerful supporting evidence for Heidner's general thesis. Later, Sonnenfeld endured government harassment when he dared to question the official 9/11 story. He and his wife emigrated from the US, for this reason, and at last report were living in Argentina.

This brings us to the unexplained collapse of WTC-7: a 47-story skyscraper that was untouched by any airliner on 9/11 and, judging from photos and videos, suffered only minor fires on a few floors. Yet, at 5:20 P.M. on the afternoon of the attacks, the building dropped into its own footprint at free fall speed.[13] Fortunately, we have an excellent video record of the belated collapse of WTC-7 from several different angles, and this remarkable footage is compelling evidence that the building was taken down in a controlled demolition.

But why WTC-7? Again, Heidner thinks that several offices in the building were specifically targeted. These include the Securities and Exchange Commission on floors 11, 12 and 13, the Secret Service offices on floors 9 and 10, and the Internal Revenue Service offices on floors 24 and 25. All three agencies suffered the total loss of files and records for ongoing investigations which had been stored in WTC-7. Although SEC officials later refused to discuss how many ongoing cases had been impacted by the attacks, the agency claimed that it lost only two weeks' worth of computer data which had not been backed up.

But New York securities lawyers who practice before the SEC told a different story. One of them, Bill Singer, stated that a case he had pending was settled quickly because so many of the pertinent documents had been destroyed. Said Singer: "Regardless of what the regulators say, they lost a ton of files. In my opinion it was a wholesale loss of documents."[14]

It is quite possible that other federal offices were also targeted in WTC-7. The largest CIA facility outside of CIA headquarters at Langley was housed on the building's 25th floor, and the Department of Defense also had offices in WTC-7. The destruction of Building Seven thus, would have been the capstone to a covert operation of sweeping extent, which involved the targeting of government offices that were investigating financial crimes, for the purpose of destroying the documentary evidence they had accumulated, in the process killing many of the staff involved. Admittedly, such a plan would have been fiendishly clever.

FOLLOW THE MONEY

To sum up, Heidner proposes that at the very time George H.W. Bush was extolling a New World Order, Bush and those around him hatched a diabolical scheme involving a secret war chest controlled by the CIA and certain Wall Street bankers: to buy out, undermine, and ultimately wreck the Russian economy; and that while waging this covert program the policymakers overstepped a number of legal boundaries, both at home and abroad, transgressions that came back to haunt them.

While it is not yet possible to confirm Heidner's thesis definitively, it is important to understand that the premise of a secret CIA slush fund is nothing new, and has a sound basis. In his memoirs, Israeli whistleblower Ari Ben-Menashe confirms the existence of one CIA slush fund created in the 1980s during Iran-Contra.[15] Ben-Menashe, an Iraqi Jew, served as Israeli PM Yitzhak Shamir's personal envoy during this momentous period, and was intimately involved in Israel's secret arms pipeline to Iran, which continued throughout the Iran-Iraq war.

Ben-Menashe had access to highly sensitive information, and was one of the primary sources for Seymour Hersh's 1991 book about Israel's nuclear weapons program, *The Samson Option*. According to Hersh, "Ben-Menashe's account might seem almost too startling to be believed, had it not been subsequently amplified by a second Israeli, who cannot be named."[16]

Ben-Menashe's role as insider gave him a unique perspective on the US arms-for-hostage negotiations with Tehran in 1980, including President Carter's failed initiatives but also the ultimately "successful" channel secretly arranged by Ronald Reagan's then campaign chairman William Casey. During World War II, Casey headed the Secret Intelligence Branch of the OSS (the CIA's predecessor) and, as noted, later became Ronald Reagan's Director of Central Intelligence. According to Ben-Menashe, the Iranian arms deal, which has become known as the October Surprise, was worked out in secret meetings, starting in August 1980.[17]

In June 1992, Ben-Menashe told a closed session of the Senate Foreign Relations Committee that he had been present in Paris in October 1980 for the final round of the secret negotiations with the Iranians. Ben-Menashe explained that he personally witnessed George H.W. Bush, former Director of Central Intelligence, enter the conference room along with William Casey.[18]

Weeks earlier, Saddam Hussein had invaded southwestern Iran, and, according to Ben-Menashe, the Iranians, desperate for arms, would have gladly released the US embassy hostages immediately if an arms deal could be struck with the Carter administration. As we know, such a deal never materialized. The talks broke down, probably because of Carter's reluctance to trade arms for hostages.[19]

Bush and Casey, however, had no such scruples, despite Ronald Reagan's rhetoric to the contrary. Bush and Casey insisted that the hostages must remain in captivity, thus insuring Carter's defeat in the presidential election. As per the terms of the agreement, the hostages were subsequently released within minutes of Reagan's presidential inauguration on January 20, 1981. The strange timing elicited hardly a peep from the US press, which apparently was too preoccupied with Reagan's "decisive" victory over the "inept" Carter to notice.

Israel served as middleman, (or "cut out" in spy-speak), and made the actual arms deliveries on behalf of the cabal around Reagan. The deal was not "on behalf of the United States" since this channel was wholly unauthorized, arranged behind the back of President Jimmy Carter. In his memoirs, Ben-Menashe refers to the secret arrangement as the "Joint Committee," and he names David Kimche as the senior Israeli negotiator who worked closely with the CIA's Robert Gates on the implementation. The first arms deliveries to Iran commenced in March 1981.

I found surprising support for Ben-Menashe's explosive charges in Bob Gates' own 1996 memoir, *From the Shadows*. In 1981 Gates served as CIA director Casey's chief of staff, and in his memoir he brags that he was "closer to him [Casey] professionally and knew him better than anyone else at CIA or in government." Gates also writes that he "was in on virtually all of his [Casey's] meetings." This surely means that Gates was in the loop on sensitive issues.[20]

So who else would Casey have turned to, other than Gates, his go-to guy, to coordinate the most sensitive issue of them all, the clandestine arms pipeline to Iran that was being stage-managed by Israel?

Gates also corroborates Ben-Menashe on another point. He confirms the key role played by the Israeli Mossad agent, David Kimche.[21] Gates would go on to become President H.W. Bush's Director of Central Intelligence. After a profitable stint in the private sector followed by four years as president of Texas A&M University, Gates returned to "public service" in 2006, replacing the embattled Donald Rumsfeld as Secretary of Defense.

Ben-Menashe claimed that the arms pipeline to Iran continued for years with the full involvement the CIA: "There were deals going on all the time in the years 1981 to 1987, far too many to enumerate."[22]

Needless to say, the Senate Foreign Relations Committee buried Ben-Menashe's testimony.

After the Iran-Contra scandal broke in October 1986, an embarrassed Reagan admitted to a stunned American public that he had done what he said he would never do: supply arms to so called terrorists to secure the release of US hostages, in this case hostages kidnapped by Hezbollah in Lebanon. Americans eventually learned about the secret 1984-86 arms channel to Iran managed by Oliver

North and Admiral John Poindexter, Reagan's National Security Advisor. But the Reagan administration succeeded in keeping most of the story secret, including the arguably treasonous 1980 dealings with Tehran behind President Carter's back by William Casey and H.W. Bush.

According to Ben-Menashe, Israel ultimately choked off Oliver North's attempts to establish a second arms channel, which in any event never approached the scale of the already extant arms pipeline under joint Israeli-CIA management. Incredibly, the secret arms deliveries to Iran via the original channel continued even during the Iran-Contra hearings and sham investigations.[23] To this day, the average American remains clueless about this important history.

Now to the point: Ben-Menashe claims that the joint Israeli-CIA arms pipeline generated huge profits, and he was in a position to know. At the time, the Israelis were handling the money transfers. The Iranians were desperate for weapons to fend off Saddam Hussein's well equipped army, and the Israelis made them pay a whopping mark-up ranging from 50% to 400%.[24] As a result of this profiteering, cash piled up in a secret Israeli account, and a second parallel CIA account, each of which eventually totaled some $780 million.[25]

Heidner argues that H.W. Bush used the CIA slush fund to support the August 1991 coup against Gorbachev, and he might be right. Ben-Menashe writes that the CIA slush fund inexplicably ended up in the hands of media mogul Robert Maxwell,[26] whom Seymour Hersh outed as a Mossad agent in *The Samson Option*.[27]

Maxwell had close ties to H.W. Bush, after being introduced by a mutual friend, Senator John Tower, who was also Maxwell's business associate.[28] As we know, President Reagan had appointed Tower to head up the official commission (that bears his name) charged with the sham investigation of Iran-Contra. Tower knew which questions to ask and, more importantly, which ones to avoid. He could have been briefed about every aspect of the sordid affair by his aide, former Marine Colonel Robert "Bud" MacFarlane, who had played an important role in the secret arms-for-hostages negotiations orchestrated by Casey in 1980.[29]

Maxwell had large investments in the eastern bloc, and high-level connections that, amazingly, included KGB chief Vladimir Kryuchkov, the leader of the plot to oust Gorbachev. According to various accounts, Maxwell had contacts with Kryuchkov in the weeks before the coup.[30] Former Mossad agent Victor Ostrovsky claims that the two actually met on Maxwell's yacht, during this period.[31] Maxwell had a long history of money laundering and shady dealings with both the intelligence community and underworld figures, and it is entirely plausible that he served as a bag-man for Bush.[32]

There are other fishy details. Several weeks after the failed coup, Maxwell was murdered on his yacht, possibly by the Mossad. Senator Tower also died when his commuter plane crashed during a landing approach in Georgia, killing all aboard.[33] As in the case of narcotrafficker Barry Seal (see Chapter Five, note 49), people who got close to Bush had a curious way of turning up dead.

THE US GOES BACK ON ITS WORD

After the Berlin Wall came down, then-President H.W. Bush assured Gorbachev that the US would not expand NATO into eastern Europe, on the condition that Russia would not oppose the reunification of Germany. However, in retrospect it is clear that the Cold War never ended. At the G-7 summit in June 1990, Bush demanded that Russia and the eastern bloc submit to shock therapy as prescribed by the International Monetary Fund; which, of course, meant auctioning off valuable state industries for pennies on the dollar.[34]

Russia was true to its word regarding German reunification. However, President Clinton reneged on Bush's promise and expanded NATO to the Russian frontier. Clinton's Secretary of State, Madeleine Albright, went on tour promoting NATO expansion which, she argued, would stabilize central Europe politically and economically. But more thoughtful critics, such as former Senator Sam Nunn (D-GA), a long-time nuclear policy expert, warned that the consequences would be dire since Moscow would naturally view the eastward expansion of NATO as a grave threat to its national security.

Although Clinton (and the US press) made light of Moscow's fears of encirclement, the critics were correct. The expansion of NATO into Poland, Czechoslovakia, and Hungary was not in the best interests of Europe; far from it. The only beneficiaries were US arms manufacturers and their financial backers on Wall Street, who viewed the break-up of the Soviet bloc as an opportunity to enrich themselves. At the time, the relatively poor nations of eastern Europe could ill afford to purchase advanced US weaponry, a NATO requirement. Decades of communism had devastated their economies, and their top priority should have been to rebuild their infrastructure. Although the US pledged to support their entry in the European Union, which most of western Europe opposed at the time, this enticement was an illusion because the purchase of large quantities of US arms actually slowed their economic recovery.

Clinton's NATO policy set the stage for his successor G.W. Bush's arguably insane decision to shred the 1972 ABM Treaty and to deploy advanced ABM technology in Poland and the Czech Republic. Although Bush claimed that the ABM system was strictly defensive: to guard against a presumed missile threat from the Mideast, i.e., Iran, the argument was hardly convincing. As Russian leader Vladimir Putin pointed out, "missile weapons with a range of about five to eight thousand kilometers that really pose a threat to Europe do not exist in any of the so-called problem countries."[35] Retired US Lieutenant General Robert Gard admitted that the ABM deployment in Poland would defend against Iranian missiles and warheads at some unspecified time in the future.[36] Implicit in his statement was that Iran had no such missiles, at present.

Serious analysts also questioned why the US had not selected a site much closer to Iran, say, for example, in Turkey, or perhaps Kuwait, both US allies. When Putin offered the US the joint-use of a Russian radar site in Azerbaijan, very near the Iranian border, Bush responded with deafening silence.[37] A White House spokesman announced that the president had taken ill.

But what could Bush say, in any event? Putin had called his bluff, and exposed the real policy. The only logical reason for siting an ABM system in eastern Europe, on Russia's doorstep, was to "defend" against a Russian nuclear counterattack. Which of course, means that the ABM deployment was part of a broader US plan, probably set in motion during the 1990s, under Clinton, to achieve a nuclear first-strike capability.[38] Such a strategy vis a vis Russia, involving an implied threat of nuclear blackmail, goes far beyond even economic warfare. If US leaders were capable of this, then they are truly capable of anything.

Today, all of this is transparently obvious in retrospect and, I would argue, highly relevant to E.P. Heidner's 9/11 thesis.

The CIA Iran/Contra slush fund of $780 million was a substantial sum, certainly large enough to finance a coup or a large covert operation. But it is mere petty-cash compared to the $240 billion in ten-year bonds that, Heidner alleges, came into play in the covert program against Russia. Heidner's figure is so large, in fact, that initially I dismissed his thesis out of hand, that is, until I learned about another CIA slush fund on a similarly vast scale. This other secret fund came into existence at the close of World War II when US intelligence agents in the Philippines recovered a enormous treasure trove, primarily gold bullion but also substantial quantities of platinum, silver, diamonds, gemstones and priceless artistic treasures.

The story of "Yamashita's gold" or the "Black Eagle Trust," as it came to be known, is an extremely important piece of history that the US government has kept from us for more than half a century. As we will learn, the bare facts, and the back story, i.e., why it was kept secret, are nothing short of mind-boggling.

ENDNOTES

1   Kevin Fenton, *Disconnecting the Dots* (Walterville, OR: TrineDay, 2011).

2   E.P. Heidner, "Collateral Damage," June 2008. Posted at http://www.wanttoknow. info/911/Collateral-Damage-911-black_eagle_fund_trust.pdf

3   E.P. Heidner, op. cit., p. 5. The quote regarding Casey's role with the Board of Economic Warfare is from Joseph E. Persico, *Casey: The Lives and Secrets of William J. Casey From OSS to the CIA* (New York: Penguin, 1990), pp. 364-65.

4   Nafeez Mossaddeq Ahmed, *The War on Truth* (Northhampton, MA: Olive Branch Press, 2005), p. 41.

5   http://www.newamericancentury.org/RebuildingAmericasDefenses.pdf, p. 51

6   Richard Leiby, "The Last Watch," *Washington Post*, January 20, 2002.

7   "Collateral Damage," note 9.

8   "The difficulty with lost certificates was dramatically demonstrated during the September 11,2001, tragedy when thousand of certificates were destroyed in vaults maintained by broker-dealers." Federal Register / Vol. 67, No. 151 / Tuesday, August 6, 2002 / Notices.

      Posted at http://www.thefederalregister.com/d.p/2002-08-06-02-19783

9   "Collateral Damage," p.1.

10   http://www.ice.gov/cornerstone/eldorado.htm

11   http://killtown.911review.org/wtc6.html

12   http://www.voltairenet.org/9-11-FEMA-videographer-at-Ground

      In late October - early November 2001, a separate hoard of gold, silver, platinum and palladium worth hundreds of millions of dollars was recovered from a different vault, under WTC-4. Jim Dwyer, "A Nation Challenged; the Vault; below ground zero, silver and gold," *New York Times*, November 1, 2001. Posted at http://www.nytimes.com/2001/11/01/nyregion/a-nation-challenged-the-vault-below-ground-zero-silver-and-gold.html?pagewanted=print&src=pm

13   This was confirmed by NIST in its final report on the collapse of WTC-7.

14   Matthew Goldstein, "Document Chaos Isn't Sorted Out," *The Street*, September 9, 2002.

15   *Profits of War*, p. 351

16   Seymour Hersh, *The Samson Option* (New York: Random House, 1991), p. 299.

17   *Profits of War*, p. 59 and note 15, pp. 190-91. Also see Barbara Honegger, *October Surprise* (New York: Tudor Publishing, 1989); also see Gary Sick, *October Surprise* (New York: Random House, 1991); also see Joseph Trento, *Prelude to Terror* (New York: Carroll and Graf, 2005), p. 207.

18   *Profits of War*, p. 344.

19   Gary Sick, *October Surprise*, p.130-131.

20   Robert M. Gates, *From the Shadows* (New York: Simon & Schuster, 1996), p. 199 and 222.

21   Ibid., p. 395-6.

22   *Profits of War*, p. 115.

23   Israel continued to secretly supply arms to Iran throughout its eight-year war with Iraq. This should come as no surprise, since the Israelis were clearly motivated by existential fear of Saddam Hussein whom they perceived as the more immediate threat. Ayatollah Khomeini was viewed as the lesser evil. According to Ben-Menashe, the US policy of arming both sides (including support for Iraq's chemical weapons program) and playing one side off against the other caused a serious hiccup in the special relationship, because the US policy did not resonate in Israel. In this admittedly rare instance, the Israelis were on the right side of history. *Profits of War*, p. 191; 193; 238-239.

24   Ibid., p. 118.

25   Ibid., p. 351.

26   Ibid.

27   *The Samson Option*, p. 212.

28   Tower actually accompanied Maxwell to eastern Europe in the spring of 1990. Gordon Thomas and Martin Dillon, *Robert Maxwell: Israel's Superspy* (New York: Carroll & Graf, 2002), p. 194; 196.

29   Ari Ben-Menashe, see note 15, pp.190-91; Joseph Trento, see note 18, p. 207.

30   Ibid.

31   Victor Ostrovsky, *The Other Side of Deception* (New York: Harper Collins, 1994), p. 285.

32   According to Thomas and Dillon, the underworld criminals included Simeon Yukovich Mogilevich, among others. *Robert Maxwell: Israel's Superspy*, p. 189.

33   Ibid., p.197-198.

34   F. William Engdahl, *Full Spectrum Dominance* (Wiesbaden: Engdahl Press, 2009), p. 26.

35   Ibid., p. 21.

36   Ibid.,- p. 23.

37   F. William Engdahl, "G7 Play Thermonuclear Chess with Putin," *Global Research*, June 18, 2007. Posted at http://www.globalresearch.ca/index.php?context=va&aid=6020

38   Bruce Gagnon, "The Sword and the Shield: Surround Russia and China with Mobile 'Missile Defense' Systems," *Global Research*, February 5, 2010. Posted at http://www.globalresearch.ca/index.php?context=va&aid=17422

Also see Keir A. Lieber and Daryl G. Press, "The Rise of U.S. Nuclear Primacy," *Foreign Affairs*, March/April 2006. Posted at http://www.foreignaffairs.com/articles/61508/keir-a-lieber-and-daryl-g-press/the-rise-of-us-nuclear-primacy

THE COVERT HISTORY OF YAMASHITA'S GOLD

HOW WASHINGTON SECRETLY RECOVERED IT TO SET UP GIAN
COLD WAR SLUSH FUNDS AND MANIPULATE FOREIGN GOVERNMENT

GOLD
WARRIORS

STERLING & PEGG
SEAGRAVE

"The Seagraves have uncovered one of the biggest secrets of
twentieth century." — Iris Chang, author of *The Rape of Nank*

Chapter 7

Black Gold

Authors Sterling and Peggy Seagrave brought the story of the Black Eagle Trust to light in their riveting book, *Gold Warriors*, released in 2002. Their account is so shocking it would beggar belief, had it not been so meticulously researched. The authors back up their book with three CDs loaded with supplementary documentation, which, by the way, I reviewed. Multiple sources have also confirmed their conclusions. The late Chalmers Johnson was convinced.[1] And Iris Chang, author of the *Rape of Nanking*, said the Seagraves had unearthed "one of the biggest secrets of the twentieth century."[2]

Most Americans probably believe, as I once did, that World War II left Japan in ruins, much like Nazi Germany. The atomic destruction of Hiroshima and Nagasaki, plus the fire bombing of Tokyo, have no doubt contributed to this strong impression. But as horrible as those events were (and they were horrible), they were the exceptions to the rule. Most of the cities in Japan survived the war intact, as did most of the nation's industrial infrastructure. Although the US government has assiduously perpetuated the view that Japan was bankrupted by the war, the truth is exactly the reverse.

Despite losing World War II, Japan emerged much richer than before, as a result of having systematically plundered a dozen Asian countries over a period of decades. Have you ever wondered why there was no Marshall Plan in the East, as in Europe? The reason is simple: none was needed; and this also explains Japan's rapid post-war recovery.

While it is true that the Nazis also plundered outrageously, they did so within a much shorter time frame. The Nazi regime lasted less than fifteen years. By contrast, Japan's fascist march across Asia commenced with the invasion and humiliation of Imperial China in the Sino-Japanese War of 1894-95 and the simultaneous annexation of Korea, and continued through the last days of World War

II. The plundered Asian nations, with their long histories and deep distrust of officialdom, contained much more off-the-books gold *in private hands* than anyone in the West ever imagined.

Japan's plundering of East Asia was well organized and ruthlessly efficient. The Japanese army carried off everything worth taking. Acting under the supervision of royal princes appointed by Emperor Hirohito, they systemically ransacked each nation they occupied, and transferred the wealth back to Japan. After 1943, when US submarines made the sea lanes around Japan impassable, the booty was packed aboard freighters painted to look like hospital ships, and rerouted to the Philippines, where Japanese engineers had secretly begun excavating a network of underground storage sites. The Japanese selected the Philippines because they believed Japan would retain the islands in a post-war peace settlement. Many of the vaults were carved out deep under cathedrals and hospitals, and on former US military bases: on sites the Japanese rightly judged would be excluded from US bombing.

When the work was done, the Japanese insured secrecy by entombing the slave laborers who had worked to construct the sites. Tens of thousands of men were buried alive, including US prisoners of war. When the last underground treasure crypts had been completed and packed with gold, over one hundred and seventy Japanese engineers were lured to a "farewell party" inside Tunnel-8 and likewise sealed along with the treasure, even as they drank toasts to Hirohito's health.

Of course, things did not turn out as the princes had hoped. Japan lost control over its colonies, including the Philippines, under the terms of the US-imposed unconditional surrender. Moreover, a team under the command of General Douglas MacArthur soon heard rumors about hidden gold, which were promptly confirmed. The team extracted the locations of a dozen sites by torturing the personal chauffeur of General Yamashita, Japan's most brilliant military strategist during the war: the man who had conquered Singapore. In the waning days of the conflict, Yamashita had been assigned to organize the defense of the Philippines.

The US intelligence community was involved, from the outset. MacArthur's team included Ed Lansdale, an OSS officer who later became one of the CIA's most celebrated Cold Warriors. It is strangely fitting that Lansdale launched his inglorious CIA career as a torturer. The team also included a Filipino-American, Severino Garcia Santa Romana, who would also play a key role.

MacArthur sent Lansdale back to Washington to report the gold discovery to former OSS chief General Magruder and to General Hoyt Vandenberg who then headed the interim Central Intelligence Group. Lansdale next briefed President Harry Truman, who promptly sent him back to the Philippines accompanied by Robert B. Anderson, one of Secretary of War Henry Stimson's top advisers. According to the Seagraves, Anderson and MacArthur toured several underground caverns north of Manila, the first to be opened, where they strolled down row after row of gold bars piled to the ceiling.[3]

Even as the US military was presiding over the initial gold recoveries, Truman made a decision that would prove fateful. It was a decision that he may also have come to regret, given Truman's belated second-thoughts about the CIA. In 1945, the president decided to keep the plunder secret, off the books. Rather than return the treasure to its rightful owners, the US would retain the gold and make it serve US geopolitical objectives.

A small group around Stimson administered the creation of the so called Black Eagle Trust, named after the gold bullion stamp of the Nazi eagle and swastika. The name is curious, and may itself have been a calculated piece of deception, another false flag, because although recovered Nazi war loot was also folded into the trust, the Japanese hoard made up by far the largest portion. US secrecy in the disposition of the plundered gold also accounts for the oddities of US foreign policy vis a vis Japan since World War II.

It explains, for instance, why Truman's special envoy to Japan, John Foster Dulles, crafted a postwar treaty in 1951 that made it legally impossible for US POWs and other victims of Japanese war crimes to sue Japan for restitution or reparations, unlike the victims of the Nazis. The black gold (in this case a term with a rather explicit meaning, not a metaphorical reference to petroleum) also explains why the US exonerated Hirohito and rehabilitated the royal family. And it explains why MacArthur, the de facto ruler of postwar Japan from 1945-51, reinstalled the same corrupt elite to power who had been responsible for the war, in the first place.

MacArthur, by the way, also specifically exempted from any war-crime trials the leading Japanese "scientists" who had practiced vivisection and other unspeakable horrors on living prisoners, because of their valuable biological/chemical-warfare expertise. Unit 731's obscene experimentation was hushed up, and the few survivors of *this* Holocaust, almost all Chinese and Korean, never got to tell *their* stories, which would have absolutely discredited the official history.[4]

In addition to the booty stashed in the Philippines, much treasure had already made its way to the Japanese homeland, where it was very effective in keeping the extreme right wing party in power, over many years. This explains why, as Chalmers Johnson pointed out, Japanese-style democracy has over the years remained so corrupt, inept, and weak.[5] The purported justification for all of this, the consuming war on communism, was just another part of the same tapestry of lies.

Even as MacArthur was exonerating the actual war criminals, he ordered the execution of an innocent man, General Yamashita, who according to the Seagraves was actually a moderate and had not engaged in war crimes. Nor had he been responsible for the live burials of the slave laborers. Yamashita had to die, quite simply, because he knew too much. Months before the start of the Nuremberg trials, the general was hauled before a kangaroo court, convicted of war crimes based on false testimony, and summarily hanged to get him out of the way. The black gold also explains why most US government documents about Japan's predatory looting remain classified, even to this today.[6]

In addition to Anderson, the small group that administered the gold trust included Truman's closest adviser, Clark Clifford, and also John L. McCloy, an ally of the Rockefellers. Later, McCloy headed the World Bank, served as chairman of Chase Manhattan, and was even appointed to the Warren Commission. Anderson became Secretary of the Navy, probably to facilitate the secret transshipment of vast quantities of gold out of the Philippines aboard US naval vessels.

During this period Anderson traveled to banks all over the world setting up black gold accounts. The key role he played probably also explains why Anderson was named as Treasury Secretary during Eisenhower's second term. Late in life, Anderson was convicted of money laundering and died in disgrace.[7] Clark Clifford's reputation was also ruined due to his involvement in the BCCI scandal, which the *Wall Street Journal* called the "world's largest bank fraud."[8]

The group around Stimson included Robert Lovett, formerly an executive at Brown Brother's Harriman where, no doubt, he rubbed elbows with fellow Yale Bonesman Prescott Bush, father and grandfather of two presidents. During World War II, Lovett oversaw the massive expansion of US military forces, and played such a vital role that after the war Truman at first refused to accept his resignation. Lovett went back to Wall Street, but he returned to Washington to become George Marshall's Under Secretary of State in 1947. When Marshall became Secretary of Defense in 1950, Lovett joined him there as Deputy Secretary, then became Truman's last Secretary of Defense when Marshall stepped down in 1951. Described as one of the most capable officials who ever served in Washington, Lovett's specialty was international currency transactions.

According to the Seagraves, Lansdale worked with Severino Garcia Santa Romana supervising the early gold recoveries in the Philippines, which continued through 1947. Lansdale also inventoried the loot and provided for security. A number of the early gold accounts were placed in Santa Romana's name to conceal the CIA as the actual owner. Although the Santa Romana personal accounts are thought to have contained more than $50 billion in gold (at the then-current value), this was only a fraction of the total hoard.

Twenty years after the initial searches ended, the treasure hunt resumed in the late 1960s under the sponsorship of Philippine President Ferdinand Marcos, who had learned about the underground vaults. Like most Americans, I had always assumed that Marcos acquired his obscene wealth by skimming US and international aid to his impoverished nation. Although such skimming did occur,[9] the fabulous Marcos fortune was primarily based on a second series of gold recoveries, which continued into the 1980s. Marcos also pressured Santa Romana to cede the power of attorney for his Manila bank accounts, and when Santy passed away in 1974, Marcos seized some of these accounts, greatly enriching himself. At about the same time, Ed Lansdale also managed to transfer Santy's remaining gold accounts into his name, thus insuring CIA control.

Marcos succeeded in opening a number of underground sites thanks to the competent assistance of an American mining engineer and metallurgist, Robert Curtis, whom Marcos recruited in 1974. Though Curtis nearly fell prey to treachery at the hands of Marcos, the engineer survived and eventually became one of the leading experts on the Japanese gold.

After World War II, the Philippines had served as a staging area for US military and CIA operations throughout Southeast Asia,[10] and this continued under Marcos, who proved a valuable ally during the Vietnam War. For example, Marcos assisted the CIA by providing false end-user certificates which enabled the CIA to launder arms shipments for various covert operations, and thereby, to evade US law.[11]

But Marcos eventually fell out of favor with Washington. The man's unbridled greed was his own worst enemy; and in 1986, as pro-democracy protests were spreading throughout the country, Reagan's CIA chief William Casey intervened to terminate the regime. Ferdinand and his wife Imelda were flown to Hawaii and placed under house arrest. By this point, Marcos was also in failing health. The CIA meanwhile expedited the removal of vast quantities of gold from vaults in the presidential palace. Billions in gold certificates were also confiscated from Imelda Marcos' person.

When Imelda protested, the US announced that the certificates were fakes, a standard ploy to prettify theft on a grand scale.[12] While it is not entirely clear why the US moved when it did against Marcos, it is likely that Casey and H.W. Bush deemed the seizure of Marcos' gold stockpiles as vital to shore up a number of US banks, which were in deep trouble because of reckless lending in the Third World, during the late 1970s and early '80s.[13]

In 1987, a team of US generals, including ex-CIA superstar John Singlaub and Reagan's National Security Advisor, Robert Schweitzer, organized another attempt to open up new sites in the Philippines and recover more gold, both for personal profit and to set up a new slush fund for covert action.[14] The team sought to recruit Curtis, just as Marcos had done.

However, the earlier betrayal had made Curtis wary; and although he was persuaded initially to participate, he withdrew soon after from what he judged to be a poorly led venture. Although the Singlaub initiative came to nothing, it nonetheless showed the continuing interest of the US intelligence community in the Japanese plunder, *an estimated third of which had not been recovered.*

How much gold did the Japanese stash in the Philippines? No one knows for sure, but the Seagraves provide some tantalizing hints. One of the larger sites was a series of three natural caverns located near the San Fernando army camp. The largest of these, Tunnel-8, was said to be the size of a football field, while the other two were gymnasium-sized; and all had been packed with bars of gold bullion.[15]

Among the Seagraves' documents that I reviewed is the transcript of a 1987 conversation with engineer Robert Curtis, who in the course of discussing the Singlaub fiasco proffered an educated guess about the size of the stash. According to Curtis, 172 underground sites contained about $500 billion in gold, at $35/ounce.[16] Assuming his figure is accurate, the Japanese treasure would have totaled more than 400,000 tonnes (metric tons: 2,000 kilograms, about 2,250 pounds) of gold, worth some $3.9 trillion at the 2000 market price of $279/ounce. With gold presently valued at roughly $1,650/ounce, you do the math.

These figures are roughly consistent with an accounting authorized by Marcos himself, which certified that, as of 1987, a little more than two-thirds of the original hoard had been recovered, totaling some 280,000 metric tons.[17] Contrast the Japanese total with the Nazi plunder from World War II, estimated at only about 11,000 tonnes, and the US Treasury gold (reputed to be) inside Ft Knox, which, at the time of the last known audit, many years ago, contained only about 8,000 tonnes.[18]

I should add, however, that when I checked with the Seagraves they cautioned against placing too much weight on these estimates, which involve a considerable amount of guesswork. In an email, Sterling Seagrave pointed out that there were actually 175 sites, not 172, and that Curtis's estimate did not include these three sites, his favorites, which he never recovered.[19] Seagrave also mentioned that Marcos re-smelted and eventually rehid a great many ingots to prevent the US from confiscating them.

All of which suggests that the above estimates could actually be on the low side. In any event, the official world total of 130,000 metric tons of gold is obviously much too low.[20] Although the figure is supposed to include all existing gold in the form of coinage, bullion and jewelry, the true amount, or at least the best estimation, is no doubt among the world's most closely kept secrets. For our purposes, it is enough to show that the best estimates of the gold recovered in the

Philippines, even when shared out and siphoned off, would be far more than enough to collateralize the Hammer Fund as described in an April 2000 deposition by Erle Cocke, one of the fund's managers. In the next chapter, we will examine this important document.

The Seagraves argue in their book that the Black Eagle Trust was used to buy elections in Italy, Greece and Japan, for the purpose of preventing the rise of left-wing political parties in those countries. The events in Italy and Greece they describe correspond with the covert operations involving Operation Gladio, NATO's stay-be-hind-army project, organized by Frank Wisner, the CIA master of dirty tricks who suffered a mental breakdown in the late 1950s.[21] As we are about to learn, the Hammer Fund, a part of the larger Black Eagle Trust, was similarly used during the Cold War to shore up South African Apartheid, and to impede and reverse democratic movements elsewhere in Africa.

The authors believe that the trust also came into play in 1971-72 during Nixon and Kissinger's backdoor negotiations with China over the thorny issue of Taiwan. At the time, longstanding US support for Chiang Kai-shek and his Nationalist Chinese base on Taiwan was the principal obstacle to a US rapprochement with the Peoples' Republic of China (PRC). The dangerous alternative to a settlement was the implicit threat of a communist invasion of the island, which Mao Tse-tung insisted must eventually be reunited with the mainland.

As we know, the US made concessions as a quid pro quo for Mao's promise to forego an invasion, and to be helpful in winding down the Vietnam War. In return, Nixon agreed to remove US forces from Taiwan, and to cease US open hostility to the PRC at the United Nations.[22] It was a major victory for Mao and a decisive defeat for the remnant power of Chiang Kai-shek. The PRC was ultimately given China's permanent seat, with concomitant veto power, on the UN Security Council.

The Seagraves examined bank documents showing that during this period Nixon secretly transferred large amounts of gold bullion to the People's Republic, which suggests that Nixon and Kissinger paved the way for their celebrated renewal of formal US-China relations in 1973 with a sweetener: they returned some of the loot previously carried off by the Japanese imperialists.[23]

From these few examples, it will be evident just how useful a secret fund of black gold might be in geopolitics, whether for good or ill.

19-MAR-96 THU 21:45 ATLANTIC METALS CORP   +632+8150672   P.01

CROWN COMMODITY HOLDING INT'L

151 BGY. SAN JOSE, CALAMBA, LAGUNA
PHILIPPINES

SPECIAL POWER TO VERIFY

ALFREDO R. RAMOS
CROWN COMMODITY HOLDING INT'L.
151 BRGY. SAN JOSE
CALAMBA, LAGUNA
PHILIPPINES

© 2000

MARCH 14, 1998

I, ALFREDO R. RAMOS, WITH PHILIPPINE PASSPORT NO. AA-409998
OWNER, HOLDER, AND SELLER, ACTING WITH FULL CORPORATE AND
PERSONAL LEGAL RESPONSIBILITY, HEREBY APPOINT MOSCHA CIRIC,
GERMAN CITIZEN, PASSPORT NUMBER 5067803618, OWNER OF
MARKETING SERVICES LOCATED AT HARDTRLAND STR 200, 41169
MONCHENGLADBACH, GERMANY AS MY TRUE AND LEGAL ATTORNEY IN
FACT TO PERFORM CERTAIN ACTS ON MY BEHALF TO WIT:

TO   : UNION BANQUES SUISSES (UBS)
               BAHNHOFSTRASE 45
               8021 ZURICH, SWITZERLAND

ATTN   : HON. CHAIRMAN/PRESIDENT
               BANK BULLION OFFICER MR. MARTIN WULF/MR. ALEX
               WULF

SUBJECT   : AUTHORITY TO VERIFY AND PERFORM ALL DEEDS AND
               ACTS NECESSARY FOR THE TRANSACTION FROM:

ACCOUNT NAME   : MAJ. GEN. EDWARD LANDSDALE
CODE NO.   : 429-3284-5
CODE CLIENT   : A112934
ABA ACCOUNT NO.   : G72570367-D-UBS
METAL ACCOUNT NO. : 725-70367-D
MASTER ACCOUNT NO. : 7257
VAULT NO.   : 88 RWRP

THIS SPECIAL POWER TO VERIFY IS VALID TO CHECK AND TAKE ALL
NECESSARY INFORMATION IN MY NAME FROM THE PRESENT BANK AND
BANK OFFICER.

Bank document showing vast Swiss Union Bank gold bullion account in the
name of CIA agent Ed Lansdale.

TED,
The fingerprints, palmprints and footprints (originals) are with the MDM. Pineda. *Ernie*

ACCOUNT HOLDER : **VICTORIANO A. BAYABAN**

NAME OF BANK : **CITIBANK, NEW YORK**
FORMERLY KNOWN AS : **FIRST NATIONAL CITY BANK NEW YORK**

METAL ACCOUNT NO. : **430-20-2011-797637**

REFERENCE CODES : **JAP-2281908** AND **YAB-2281908**

REFERENCE NAME : **BERGET: HARBOUR KING**

VOLUME : **116,000 M.T. AU**

JUNE 14, 1995

Dear Ted,
Above is the bank coordinates of a huge gold account of CITIBANK, N.Y. Please check if the account holder is the real person because I'm in direct contact with the holder of the Power of Attorney. I have seen all the documents pertaining to the Holder but there is no OBC or warehouse receipt (all costs). Thanks,
Ernie Hidalgo

RECEIVED FROM 010 244 6301   6.14.1995 18:03   P. 9

Citibank document showing gold bullion account in the amount of 116,000 metric tones of gold bullion in the name of Victoriano A. Bayaban, one of many aliases used by CIA asset Severino Garcia Santa Romana.

ENDNOTES

1   Chalmers Johnson, "The Looting of Asia," *London Review of Books*, September 203. Posted at http://www.lrb.co.uk/v25/n22/chalmers-johnson/the-looting-of-asia

2   From the cover. Sterling and Peggy Seagrave, *Gold Warriors* (New York: Verso, 2005 edition).

3   *Gold Warriors*, p. 95-96.

4   Hal Gold, *Unit 731 Testimony* (North Clarendon, VT: Tuttle Publishing, 2004)

5   Chalmers Johnson, "The 1955 System and the American Connection: A Bibliographic Introduction," *Japan Policy Research Institute Working Paper No. 11*, July 1995.

6   Nonetheless, the Seagraves' diligent research paid off. An official US Army report came into their hands indicating that General MacArthur and his staff were fully aware that wholesale looting had occurred during Japan's imperial march across Asia. The official report acknowledges that "one of the spectacular tasks of the [US] occupation dealt with collecting and putting under guard the great hoards of gold, silver, precious stones, foreign postage stamps, engraving plates, and all currency not legal in Japan..." "Reports of General MacArthur, MacArthur in Japan: The Occupation: Military Phase," Volume 1 Supplement, Prepared by his General Staff, Library of Congress Catalogue Card Number 66-60006, facsimile reprint, 1994. The Seagraves archived the key parts of the above report. See page 10 of the SCAP document (a pdf file) on the second of three archival CDs, available from from the Seagraves at http://www.bowstring.net/

7   Frank J. Prial, "Ex-Treasury Chief Gets 1-Month Term in Bank Fraud Case," *New York Times*, June 26, 1987.

8   *Gold Warriors*, p. 98.

9   David Chaikin, "Tracking the Proceeds of Organized Crime -- The Marcos Case," Paper presented at the Transnational Crime Conference convened by the Australian Institute of Criminology in association with the Australian Federal Police and Australian Customs Service and held in Canberra, March 9-10, 2000.

10   Although US entanglements in SE Asia lie beyond the scope of this book, the importance of this history cannot be overstated. The gist is that the US intelligence community found it expedient to cooperate with narcotraffickers in SE Asia after World War II, just as in Italy during the war. But whereas the objective in Europe was the defeat of the Nazis, the goal in China was to encircle China. In 1950, when Mao Tse-tung drove Chiang Kai-shek's defeated KMT army across the border into Burma, a decision was made to keep Chiang's remnant forces, which numbered about 10,000 men, on life support. The CIA began supplying the KMT via two front companies, Civil Air Transport (which later became Air America) and Paul Helliwell's Sea Supply Corporation, based in Bangkok. The KMT also funded itself by developing and controlling the region's one reliable crop: opium. Thus was born the same type of marriage of convenience that we later witnessed in Vietnam, and more recently in Afghanistan. The CIA aircraft would fly in military supplies to the KMT, then, return to Thailand or Taiwan loaded with opium. Jonathan Kwitny, *The Crimes of Patriots* (New York: Norton, 1987), pp. 43-52. Also see Alfred McCoy, *The Politics of Heroin* (Toronto: Lawrence Hill, rev. edition, 2003).

11   Sterling Seagrave, *The Marcos Dynasty* (New York: Fawcett, 1988), p. 371 and 375.

12   According to the Seagraves, a former US Attorney General, Norbert Schlei, was imprisoned when he attempted to redeem a bona fide gold certificate. *Gold Warriors*, p. 130-137.

13   David Guyatt, "Project Hammer," *Nexus*, Vol 9, No. 2, February - March, 2002.

14   Former CIA agent Ray Cline was one of the key sources for the Seagraves' account. *Gold Warriors*, p. 204-215; also see p. 227-228.

15   *Gold Warriors*, p. 81.

16   See page 33 of the Foringer document (a pdf file) on the first of three archival CDs, available from the Seagraves at http://www.bowstring.net/

17   *Gold Warriors*, p. 358, note #245.

18   *Gold Warriors*, p. 96 and 197.

19   email from Sterling Seagrave, August 7, 2011.

20   *Gold Warriors*, p. 9.

21   Multiple sources confirm that Wisner implemented the stay-behind-army project, though Soviet expert George Kennan was the architect. The CIA gave it a vanilla name: Office of Policy Coordination (OPC). Burton Hersh, *The Old Boys* (New York: Charles Scribner's, 1992), pp. 226-227 and 274-277; also see Tim Weiner, *Legacy of Ashes* (New York: Anchor Books, 2007), p. 37.

22   Seymour Hersh, *The Price of Power* (New York: Summit Books, 1983), p. 367-368. Also see Henry Kissinger, Years of Upheaval (Boston: Little, Brown & Co, 1982), p. 46-47.

23   *Gold Warriors*, p. 192-193.

Chapter 8

The Cocke Deposition

T he existence of a vast slush fund created by the CIA after World War II was confirmed in April 2000 by a banker, Erle Cocke, who had been personally involved in the fund's management. Cocke's testimony was recorded in New York District Court just ten days before he passed away from pancreatic cancer, and thus, also carries the weight of a deathbed confession.[1]

The 68-page deposition was first posted on the Internet by David Guyatt, a London-based investigator, but unfortunately, has received scant attention. For easy access, I have included excerpts in the appendix of *Black 9/11* so that the reader can follow this discussion and make up his/her own mind.

Guyatt himself had a 28-year career in investment banking. His research into the Black Eagle Trust, aka the Hammer Fund, and what he calls "the parallel economy" has been featured in *Nexus* magazine.[2]

E.P. Heidner describes the deposition as "a critical starting point for understanding the [Hammer] fund."[3] By any standard, it is an extraordinary document. In my case, a careful reading precipitated one of those humbling experiences: I rudely awakened to the fact that the world is a much bigger (and darker) place than I had ever dared to imagine.

The document is the transcript of an interview in which an attorney plies Cocke with questions about the so called Hammer Fund. Three individuals named as litigants on the first page had brought suit in a New York court, contending that they had been swindled out of their commissions for a particular transaction. The three were probably brokers or traders. Erle Cocke and another attorney were hired to arbitrate on their behalf and hopefully to reach a settlement. Cocke states that he made several trips to New York and a lot of phone calls trying to mediate, but got the run-around and was ultimately unsuccessful (Cocke Deposition (CD), pages 43-44).

For our purposes, however, we are less concerned with the specifics of the suit than with the story of the Hammer Fund itself.

On page 17, Cocke confirms its existence and begins to explain what it was all about. He says the fund originated in the 1940s and 1950s as a hush-hush project to "repatriate monies" back to the US "from all types of activities, both legitimately and illegitimately." Cocke acknowledges that he does not know who created the Hammer Fund, but says it had to be "somebody at a pretty high level." Then, he adds (CD, page 18): "obviously [it] got way out of proportion as time went on..." He explicitly confirms the involvement of the US intelligence community, including the CIA and FBI, as well as the Departments of Defense and Treasury. Curiously, he also mentions the Federal Reserve.

Cocke identifies the primary depository for the fund as the New York offices of Citibank, which became Citigroup after a 1998 merger (CD, pages 19-20). Cocke states: "They [i.e., Citibank] were going to be the trustees. They were going to be running the program. They were going to be the disbursing agency. They were the cheese." Incidentally, this is the same Citibank, as noted (see Chapter Five), that was implicated during the 1990s in a $100 million money laundering scandal involving the former Mexican president Salinas, and which, in 2001, under the "leadership" of former Treasury Secretary Robert Rubin, acquired the second largest bank in Mexico, Banamex.

The Hammer Fund apparently constituted a block of at least 30 accounts (CD, p. 37) at Citibank's New York branch, with parallel accounts in Citibank's Athens, Greece office. At one point in the interview the attorney asks (p. 19): "It sounds like it would involve many different commercial or financial banking institutions, over the years." To which Cocke replies: "No question about it. Everybody got into the act that could." Evidently, much of the international banking community was involved through Citibank's numerous correspondent accounts.

Cocke also names Citibank's John Reed, a former bank vice president and CEO at the time of the deposition, as the coordinator and primary trust officer for the Hammer Fund (CD, p. 20 & 26). Later, in an implicit reference to the compartmentalization of duties that is standard in covert actions, he observes (CD, p. 26), "I can see the President of the United States with no trouble. [but] I cannot see

Reed." John Reed retired from Citigroup in May 2000 after a 35-year career.

So, who was this man who could "see the President of the United States with no trouble," but was unable to arrange a meeting with a fellow banker and primary trust officer of the enormous secret fund he had helped to manage?

Erle Cocke was somebody, the scion of a well known Georgia banking family. Both his great grandfather and grandfather had founded banks in Georgia, and his dad rose to become president of Fulton National Bank. His father Erle Sr., was also at one time the president of the American Bankers Association and Chairman of the Federal Deposit Insurance Corporation.[4]

Erle Jr. served in three wars with distinction: World War II, Korea, and Viet Nam. He entered World War II as an artillery officer and eventually became a division staff officer. He was captured by the Germans on three different occasions, and each time he escaped. On the third occasion he survived the execution of his entire unit by a Waffen SS firing squad by playing dead. Hours later, a local villager found him and tended his wounds until he could be rescued.

In short, Cocke was a genuine war hero. His division commander, Maj. Gen. Anthony McAuliffe, later stated that he had "displayed courage of the highest degree, enthusiasm, and excellent judgement." By war's end, Cocke had earned the silver star, a purple heart with three clusters, the Bronze Star, the French Croix de Guerre, and numerous other citations.[5] He left the service after the war, but was later recalled for the Korean conflict, during which he served as liaison between Secretary of Defense Marshall and General Douglas MacArthur, who commanded the UN expeditionary forces.

Cocke was recalled again for Vietnam, and served as an aide to General William "Light-at-the-End-of-the-Tunnel" Westmoreland. He also rose to the rank of Brigadier General in the Georgia National Guard, and eventually became the national commander of the American Legion.

Earlier, Cocke also had an eleven-year civilian career at Delta Airlines, where he was a special assistant to the airline president and vice-president. He also served as a US delegate to the United Nations (with the rank of ambassador), and did a four-year stint at the World Bank from 1961-64. From 1962 to the time of his deposition in 2000, he was CEO of Cocke and Phillips, a consulting firm with offices on "K" Street, in downtown Washington.

In his deposition Cocke makes an astounding claim (CD, p. 9) about the World Bank: "After the UN, I was the first full time US representative at the World Bank ... At that time *I owned 28 percent of the stock* [my emphasis] and, of course, I had all kinds of people at the Treasury tell me what to do. Don't get me wrong, I made all the decisions."

Until you remember Cocke's family pedigree, his claim that he owned 28 percent of the World Bank might seem like outrageous braggadocio, or even senility. But perhaps not for the son of the former president of the American Bankers Association. Cocke mentions (CD, p. 12) that "He [i.e., his dad, Erle Sr.] was the commercial banker, and I was the international banker. So we had ways that we came together. My banking experience has been mostly at the other side of the table. Not the banking side of the table, but the person coming to the bank to do business with."

Cocke's expertise was as an arbitrator and in this capacity he made himself available for various banking duties. He apparently had a talent for closing deals, and perhaps for this reason served at the beck and call of every president from Truman to Clinton, although Cocke admits in his deposition that some of these duties were minor.

MISSION TO NORTH KOREA

Cocke's skills as a mediator extended to diplomacy. In 1987, CIA Director William Casey recruited him for a highly sensitive mission to North Korea. It seems that the North Koreans had just been approached by Pakistan with an offer to assist them in developing nuclear weapons. The North was already supplying Pakistan with nuclear-capable missiles, and a deal could be struck to have the missile sales offset a portion of the cost of a nuclear program. North Korea's leaders were reluctant to accept the Pakistani offer, however, because they knew their nation could not afford the immense expense of a nuclear weapons effort.

At the time, the North Korean economy was in terrible shape. Things were so bad that the country was facing widespread famine. The North Koreans decided that if they could reach a political accommodation with their only true enemy, the United States, they might forego the expensive need to invest in a nuclear deterrent. This is how the diplomatic opening with the US came about.

Although Cocke was suffering from prostate problems, at the time, he agreed to make the secret trip to Pyongyang with William Zylka, another Casey associate. The two Americans spent several weeks in North Korea, and were no doubt shocked when the North Koreans informed them that the US had secretly supplied some of the hardware for Pakistan's nuclear bomb program.

The discussions went more smoothly than expected. According to Cocke, the North Koreans offered to begin to negotiate a pledge not to develop nuclear weapons in exchange for a $1 billion-dollar loan from the US to purchase food and avert a country-wide famine. In sum, the prospects for a non-proliferation treaty with the North were excellent.

Unfortunately, by the time Cocke and Zylka returned to the US the nation was focused on the breaking Iran Contra-gate scandal, and Casey was dying from brain cancer. Moreover, because Casey had failed to inform the Reagan White House about the backdoor channel with Pyongyang, the good news fell on deaf ears. Nor did the subsequent Bush presidency show any interest. Cocke reportedly said, "I could not get anyone in the new Bush administration to pay attention. They did not want to hear about Casey." Which is how both the Reagan and Bush administrations fumbled a rare opportunity to keep the nuclear genie in the bottle in NE Asia.[6]

THE NUGAN-HAND BANK

Cocke's career also had a dark side. In his deposition (CD, p. 15) he acknowledges his long-time involvement with the US intelligence community:

> Attorney: Were you engaged in assisting, for example, international companies with their banking operations?
>
> Cocke: Oh yes, they always call on you for all kinds of odd chores.
>
> Attorney: Would this be true also of some of the government intelligence agencies?
>
> Cocke: Oh, yes. One thing is if they trusted you, they practically came in and said, what do I do? I mean, you didn't argue with them. You sort of proceeded with the program and gave them

a few choices....But [they] practically always followed what we did. I was administrator, arbitrator. I was a moderator, bringing people together.[7]

US Treasury documents show that during 1979-1980 Cocke's Washington offices doubled as the US branch of the notorious Australian Nugan-Hand Bank, which laundered money in the 1970s for various CIA covert operations. Cocke and the nominal bank president Admiral Earl P. Yates, who was also based in the Washington office, were probably not themselves involved in the money-laundering, but had been brought in due their military backgrounds, to lend Nugan-Hand the appearance of respectability. Cocke was a shrewd choice for the Washington office because he had connections within the Carter administration and was willing to tap them. Like Carter, Cocke was a Georgia boy, and he later acknowledged that he had arranged White House meetings for bank cofounder Frank Nugan.[8]

Nugan-Hand was a bank that did no banking. Most of its employees were salesmen rather than clerks or experienced investment counselors. The bank employees hustled to keep new deposits coming in the front door faster than cash was leaking out the back to cover bank cofounders Frank Nugan and Mike Hand's high salaries and lavish expenses. Alfred McCoy, author of *The Politics of Heroin,* describes Nugan-Hand as "a carnival shell game, courting depositors for cash and moving money from branch to branch to conceal one fundamental fact: the bank simply had no assets behind it."[9]

Nugan-Hand specialized in complex currency transactions for clients who wished to hide money and evade government taxes. The bank became a laundry for a wide array of shadowy Asian business interests, including known narcotraffickers. Indeed, it catered to this clientele. While Nugan was milking clients in the main office in Sydney, Hand, a former green beret and CIA operative, spent much of his time on the road establishing new branch offices that laundered drug money, engaged in arms trading, and provided cover for CIA operations.

A third partner, Maurice Bernard Houghton, assisted Hand in the off-shore side of the "business." Houghton was a soldier of fortune who for years had run a seedy restaurant in Sydney, the *Bourbon and Beefsteak*, that was a hangout for CIA officers, American GIs on leave from the Vietnam war, gangsters, and corrupt Australian politicians. Hand and Houghton had long-standing relationships with senior CIA spooks Theodore "Ted" Shackley and Thomas Clines; and Houghton was also connected with Australian intelligence.

Nugan-Hand Bank collapsed in 1980, just days after Frank Nugan was found dead from a gunshot wound. Although his death was officially ruled a suicide, knowledgeable individuals, including Mike Hand, believed that Nugan had been murdered. Six months later, Hand himself dropped out of sight, apparently having fled Australia to escape legal prosecution.[10] His subsequent whereabouts have never been revealed.

During the 1970s, the Nugan-Hand Bank assisted the CIA by expediting international arms deals, including one scheme involving Libya. The bank may have served as a financial laundry for the sale of military hardware forbidden to Libya under US law.[11]

The linkage to the drug trade is well established. A number of Nugan-Hand's clients were known narcotraffickers, some of them convicted felons.[12] Just to give some insight, in 1977, the bank opened two new offices in Thailand, one in Bangkok, another in Chiang Mai, an unlikely outpost in the northern part of the country. The town has only one export. Just as Napa is famous for fine wine, and Germany has a reputation for sausages and beer, Chiang Mai is known for heroin. For many years, ever since Mao Tse-tung drove Chiang Kai-shek's Kuomintang army out of China, the town of Chiang Mai had functioned as a drug outlet for the legendary Golden Triangle, including Burma's Shan province, which lies to the north.[13]

Some of the evidence linking Nugan-Hand to the drug trade was made conspicuous by its omission. In March 1983, when an Australian Task Force on Drug Trafficking released its final report on the failed Nugan-Hand Bank, it was immediately evident that government censors had deleted portions of the report, including all nine pages of Chapter 34. The title of the missing chapter was: "Nugan Hand in Thailand." The stated reason for the official redactions: "....release of material is contrary to public interest," either because of "likely interference with ongoing or future inquiries..." or because "disclosure is likely to identify informants or other confidential sources of information."[14]

THE CIA'S OTHER MONEY-LAUNDERING BANKS

Nugan-Hand was not the first phony bank to serve as a conduit for CIA black money. It was simply a larger version of predecessors Castle Bank and Mercantile Bank, both formed by infamous CIA operative Paul Helliwell.[15] Castle and Mercantile banks were shell companies that shared common offices and directors. Each owned large blocks of stock in the other, and each deposited substantial funds with the other. As in the case of Nugan-Hand, both were chartered in the Cayman Islands, and as with Nugan-Hand, both ultimately collapsed because they ran afoul of the law.

It is no coincidence that Nugan-Hand expanded its global money-laundering operations in 1976-77, just as Castle and Mercantile were going under.[16] Similarly, when Nugan-Hand suddenly collapsed in 1980 its intelligence functions shifted to the notorious Bank of Credit and Commerce International (BCCI), which was then expanding. Founded by Agha Hasan Abedi, a Pakistani national, BCCI was the first global Third World Bank, and was officially committed to providing financial assistance to developing countries. This and Abedi's charismatic personality drew considerable international support for BCCI, even as the bank robbed depositors of their life savings, assisted dictators in the looting of their own countries, and regularly did business with terrorists, drug lords, and CIA operatives.[17]

In the 1970s, subsequent to Watergate, when President Jimmy Carter and Congress were pressuring the CIA to reform itself, the Saudis emerged to take up the slack in the spy world; and BCCI became one of the primary vehicles. According to investigative journalist Joseph Trento, the idea for an expanded Saudi intelligence role did not originate with the royal family, but was the brainchild of the much respected Washington attorney Clark Clifford, who had longtime CIA connections.[18] The CIA-Saudi relationship blossomed after Clifford approached Saudi intelligence chief Sheikh Kamal Adham with a request that he set up an informal intelligence network outside the US. Adham was the brother-in-law of the late King Faisal, and one of the driving forces behind BCCI.

Adham was also close to H.W. Bush, who maintained an account at BCCI's Paris branch. Bush also served as director (and, later, chairman) of First International, a bank used by BCCI to finance its intelligence operations.[19] According to Norman Bailey, a former senior member of President Reagan's National Security Council, Reagan's CIA chief William Casey and other Reagan administration officials frequently asked Adham to fund covert CIA operations in Afghanistan and elsewhere, as a convenient way to bypass Congress.[20] Casey is also known to have met regularly with BCCI founder Abedi, both in Washington and Islamabad.[21]

From the late 1970s until it was forced to close, BCCI served as a laundry for a wide variety of black operations, even nuclear proliferation. According to Trento, during the 1980s, hundreds of millions in US foreign aid money meant for the Afghani Mujahedeen resistance was diverted by Pakistani intelligence (ISI) through BCCI and ultimately funded Pakistan's clandestine nuclear weapons program. This happened with the full knowledge and support of the Saudis, who were also secretly funding the program.

It is quite likely that H.W. Bush also knew about the diversions and approved them. Trento argues that Bush's overarching Mideast strategy was to establish parity between Saudi Arabia and Israel, which, of course, meant that Pakistan would become the nuclear proxy for the Saudis. In June 1994, Muhammad Khilewi, the deputy chief of the Saudi mission to the UN, defected to the US with thousands of classified documents showing that Saudi Arabia had financed the Pakistani Bomb program. Some of the documents showed that the two nations even forged a secret pact, whereby Pakistan would deploy its nukes in defense of Saudi Arabia should the kingdom ever come under nuclear attack.[22] But Khilewi was forced into hiding when the US government denied him asylum, a likely indication of high level US complicity in the secret Pakistani bomb program. BCCI, however, came to an ignominious end in July 1991 when a British magistrate finally ordered the closure of the bank.

I have covered Erle Cocke's fascinating career in detail to establish his credibility and to place his 2000 deposition in the proper context. Cocke clearly had the necessary background, connections and abilities to help manage a secret trust.

COVERT USES

The Hammer Fund was a long-term project, and over time its uses evolved. According to Cocke (CD, p. 27), in the 1970s and 1980s portions of the fund were used to channel arms into Mozambique and Angola, probably for counter-insurgency campaigns in support of South African Apartheid. As Cocke also notes, later the fund supported US-backed mayhem in Sudan (CD, p. 27). One of the plaintiffs mentioned on page one, Roelf Ignatius Johannes Van Rooyen, had been a member of the South African military, or security police. In a separate deposition (see the Appendix) van Rooyen describes the Hammer Fund as an *"extremely large very delicate operation* in cooperation with the authorities of various countries" that were involved with his company Oceantec. Just *how large* is indicated by the following exchange (CD, p. 36), in which the interviewer presents Cocke with a document identified as exhibit one:

> Attorney: All right, with respect to that exhibit, and the question I asked earlier about the size of some of those Hammer transactions, do you see a number on the bottom of the page?
>
> Cocke: Yes.
>
> Attorney: First of all, can you tell us what that number means?
>
> Cocke: That on this date they thought this was the value.
>
> After a brief interruption, the attorney continues: Okay. What was the number as of whatever date that is?
>
> Cocke. This number, and I am going to read it properly, $223,104, 000,008.03", in other words, $223 billion.

While this is a vast sum, according to David Guyatt the $223 billion was not the size of the Hammer Fund itself but merely the profits it had generated over a certain time period.[23] The date is also given (CD, p. 49): November-December 1991.

In short, the Hammer Fund was a secret cache of wealth so vast as to be almost beyond human comprehension. Over time, the covert trafficking in arms became secondary as the fund developed into a collateral trading program. The financial managers began to realize the fund's incredible potential for generating still more wealth, which they accomplished by using the asset base as collateral for sales of large numbers of leveraged derivatives or banking instruments that were then marketed at a discount. In other transactions, certain types of derivatives were also treated like collateral (CD, p. 31).

Evidently, the Hammer Fund underwent a significant expansion over the twelve year period from 1988 to 2000. Cocke confirms (p. 55) that the fund generated very large profits: "we moved from one hundred million to a billion type of movement, and now we are doubling, about a trillion..."

Curiously, this time frame closely follows the CIA's ouster of Philippine dictator Ferdinand Marcos and its seizure of untold billions of gold then in Marcos' possession. It also coincides with the wholesale looting of Russia during the 1990s, and with AIG's expansion into financial services and its subsequent period of uninterrupted growth.

Cocke states that the Hammer Fund expanded not only due to profits, but also because new assets were added (CD, p. 51), a likely reference to the CIA's seizure of the Marcos gold:

> Attorney: I have been advised that a chunk of the Hammer Project funds that were used to trade, to invest and reinvest, came from a large block of assets that CIA put in the bank.
>
> Cocke: *And they pulled that several times from several sources. Nobody is going to confirm it.* [my emphasis]
>
> Attorney: Are those sources reliable?
>
> Cocke: Certainly they are educated guesses.

OPERATING OFF LEDGER

That gold-backed securities would have special appeal to private investors is obvious. But the fund held another attraction, as indicated by the following lengthy exchange (CD, p. 48-49):

> Attorney: Internally, inside the bank, would there be a department or division where they kept records on these kinds of transactions, Exhibit 1?
>
> Cocke: They are bound to. Every big bank is [so] inundated with inspections that they are ready to show the records, any time. Just move on, get it off my desk.
>
> Attorney: But the records....relating to these type of accounts, these collateral trading accounts, [such as] Hammer? Would they be separate?
>
> Cocke: Ledger, off ledger account.
>
> Attorney: What is that?
>
> Cocke: An off ledger account means that if we took out a big sum of money from the bank it wouldn't change the basic banking bal-

ance for that day. And therefor off ledger. When it is off ledger it doesn't affect the bank....

Attorney: Now, are those off ledger accounts inspected?

Cocke: They are reset is about the same way to say it. You get your balance sheet, this is running a small bank, now. You get your balance sheet at the end of the day, and then you come back and take the second balance sheet, which is off there, and then you find [that] the boss slipped a little paper his two figures, and you can go home. The responsibility is...

Attorney: The bank examiners come in, do they examine those off ledger accounts?

Cocke: yes.

Attorney: Excuse me, straighten me out, would these kind of accounts be handled by the private banking department of the bank?

Cocke: Generally, you have a ledger account, off ledger account. Now, they may give some other fancy name for putting it on the door of the building; but, yes, every big bank has got an off ledger balance. And they pull it every day. This is not something you do monthly, you do it at the close of every business day.

Attorney: You believe that's where...

Cocke: *That's where you hide money.*

Attorney: *Would that be where the Hammer operation would go?*

Cocke: *I am sure it is.* [my emphasis]

In other words, by operating two sets of books, one for public scrutiny and another in private, Citibank managers could easily hide transactions of any size. As long as they designed the various transactions and obligations to cancel out at the end of each banking day, so that the off ledger balance would remain unchanged, the total amount of business conducted that day would be off the record, hence, invisible, even if the trading was in the trillions.[24]

David Guyatt argues that because the Hammer Fund was based in US dollars the trading was very lucrative for the US government. He thinks the US Treasury, by prior arrangement, received a percentage of the take. This would explain the complicity of various federal agencies, including the Treasury Department, and perhaps even a private bank like the Federal Reserve. It might also explain, in part, the CIA's continuing involvement, assuming, of course, that the Agency exists for the purpose of serving investment bankers, a role that I will discuss in more detail in the next chapter.

What a system! Whatever part of its principal (described by Cocke as "hardly touched") originated in the Black Eagle Trust, one can readily appreciate why the Hammer Fund would attract private investors looking to both hide and multiply wealth. Using the off-ledger account, fund managers could create limitless amounts of money and securities which, though heavily leveraged, were still gold-backed, and hence more secure than the US dollar and more desirable from a trading standpoint. A manager could safely play the world market, extending credit, making loans, buying and selling, in the process moving assets around (by 2000 in milliseconds) via electronic transfers through a network of correspondent banks, while neatly avoiding foreign taxation and regulatory oversight.

One could hide a billion dollars or a hundred billion with equal ease, and with very little risk. And because these transactions were secret and off-ledger one could also divert the profits as desired, to serve whatever purpose. Assets could easily be concealed through the use of anonymous offshore accounts, shell companies, phony loans, and endless "creative" accounting schemes. Not only was the Hammer Fund an ideal means for investment bankers to make piles of money at low risk, it was also a made-to-order source of black funding for covert intelligence operations, including state sponsored terrorism.

Now, let us explore how the marriage of bankers and the US intelligence community was institutionalized.

ENDNOTES

1   The deposition is posted in its entirety at http://www.bibliotecapleyades.net/socio-politica/projecthammer/contents.htm

2   For example, see David Guyatt, "Project Hammer: Covert Finance and the Parallel Economy," *Nexus* magazine, Vol. 9, Number 1, December 2001 - January 2002.

3   "Collateral Damage," footnote #6.

4   "Project Hammer: Covert Finance and the Parallel Economy."

5   According to former Wall Street Journal reporter and author Jonathan Kwitny, the description of Cocke's military honors runs to eight lines of small print in *Who's Who in America*. Jonathan Kwitny, *The Crimes of Patriots* (New York: Norton & Co., 1987), p. 200. Also see Joseph P. Trento, *Prelude to Terror* (New York: Carroll & Graf, 2005), p. 288 and 382.

6   *Prelude to Terror*, p. 288-289.

7   Cocke deposition, p. 15.

8   *The Crimes of Patriots*, p. 201.

9   Alfred McCoy, *The Politics of Heroin* (Chicago: Lawrence Hill, 2nd edition, 1991), p. 461-472.

10   *The Crimes of Patriots*, p. 333-336.

11   Ibid., p. 312-313.

12   Jonathan Kwitny deserves much credit for researching the drug angle. See chapter 16 of his book. *The Crimes of Patriots*, p. 229-242.

13   Ibid, p. 206-7.

14   Ibid.

15   For a more detailed discussion see Alan A. Block and Constance A. Weaver, *All is Clouded by Desire* (London: Praeger Publishers, 2004), p. 37-47.

16   *The Crimes of Patriots*, p.162-163.

17   Peter Truell and Larry Gurwin, *False Profits* (New York: Houghton Mifflin, 1992).

18   Trento's source was Robert Crowley, former CIA associate director. *Prelude to Terror*, p. 98 and 101.

19   *Prelude to Terror*, p.105 and 139.

20   *False Profits*, p. 153.

21   Ibid., p.133.

22   *Prelude to Terror*, p.102-103; 317; 325-326.

23   "Project Hammer: Covert Finance and the Parallel Economy"

24   Ibid.

Chapter 9

Rise of the National Security State

One of the most successful frauds ever perpetrated upon the American people is the notion that the CIA exists to provide intelligence to the president. In fact, the CIA's intimate links to Wall Street suggest that the CIA was created to serve the perceived interests of investment bankers. The well documented links to Wall Street can be traced to the founding of the agency.

According to former CIA director Richard Helms, when Allen Dulles was tasked in 1946 to "draft proposals for the shape and organization of what was to become the Central Intelligence Agency," he recruited an advisory group of six men made up almost exclusively of Wall Street investment bankers and lawyers. Dulles himself was an attorney at the prominent Wall Street law firm, Sullivan and Cromwell. Two years later, Dulles became the chairman of a three-man committee which reviewed the young agency's performance. The other two members of the committee were also New York lawyers.[1] For nearly a year, the committee met in the offices of J.H. Whitney, a Wall Street investment firm.[2]

According to Peter Dale Scott, over the next twenty years, all seven deputy directors of the agency were drawn from the Wall Street financial aristocracy; and six were listed in the New York social register.[3] So we see that from the beginning the CIA was an exclusive Wall Street club. Allen Dulles himself became the first civilian Director of Central Intelligence in early 1953.

The prevalent myth that the CIA exists to provide intelligence information to the president was the promotional vehicle used to persuade President Harry Truman to sign the 1947 National Security Act, the legislation which created the CIA.[4] But the rationale about serving the president was never more than a partial and very imperfect truth.[5]

Col. L. Fletcher Prouty, an early critic of the agency, has referred to this oft-repeated notion as "the CIA's most important cover story."[6] In his important book *The Secret Team*, Prouty argues that the cover story was actually a front for the CIA's main interest, what he calls "fun and games," in other words, clandestine operations.[7]

Prouty was in a position to know the facts. For nine years, from 1955 - 1964, he served as the focal point for contacts between the CIA and the Pentagon on matters pertaining to "special operations," officialese for covert activities. In this capacity Prouty worked directly with CIA Director Dulles and his brother John Foster, who was then Secretary of State, and also with several different Secretaries of Defense and chairmen of the Joint Chiefs, and many other government officials. Col. Prouty's work with the CIA took him to CIA offices and hot spots in more than sixty countries, where he observed various covert operations then in progress.

For some reason, perhaps through an oversight, Prouty was never required to sign a security oath, and so, was unencumbered, completely free to write a detailed expose of the agency, released in 1972. In his book Prouty does not mince words. He describes Allen Dulles' concept of intelligence as only 10% intelligence, and 90% clandestine operations.[8] In another passage, he fleshes out his meaning: "the CIA is at the center of a vast mechanism that specializes in covert operations...or as Allen Dulles used to call it, 'peacetime operations.' In this sense, the CIA is the willing tool of a higher level Secret Team, or High Cabal, that usually includes representatives of the CIA and other instrumentalities of the government, certain cells of the business and professional world, and, almost always, foreign participation."[9]

If this sounds conspiratorial it is because Allen Dulles and his allies on Wall Street managed to get around the law and thwart the will of Congress. The National Security Act, which created the CIA, included no provision for intelligence gathering or covert operations because, as Prouty points out, the intent of Congress was for the CIA to function as a central clearinghouse for intelligence collected by *other* government departments and pre-existing intelligence agencies. This is why Congress placed the CIA under the direct authority of the newly created National Security Council.

But Allen Dulles and those around him wanted to take the new agency into the shady world of clandestine operations to serve the interests of the US financial and corporate elite, interests that in their distorted world view were synonymous with the interests of the United States of America. Dulles and his allies achieved their goal by exploiting a loophole in the legislation, a catch-all provision stating that the CIA would "perform such other functions and duties related to intelligence affecting the national security as the National Security Council (NSC) may from time to time direct."

As worded, the passage grants the CIA no authority on its own to stage operational activities, but only as instructed by the National Security Council. Moreover, the passage "from time to time" indicates that Congress never intended that such operations would become a full time program. Prouty argues that the CIA and the Secret Team immediately "tested this clause in the act and began to practice their own interpretation of its meaning."[10] Unfortunately, the National Security Council failed to live up to the role that Congress intended, that of providing leadership and direction.

In part, this happened because NSC members had other full-time duties and were not able to allocate sufficient time and energy to direct the CIA and keep it honest. Before long, the NSC had delegated its primary responsibilities to subcommittees, which the CIA easily captured by packing them with its supporters through patient maneuvering and unrelenting pressure. Soon, the NSC became a rubber stamp for a full-time program of endless black operations.

The CIA also insinuated its supporters and agents throughout the other branches of government: into the FAA, the Departments of State and Defense, even within the White House. From that point on, in the words of Prouty, the agency created "its own inertial drift....without the knowledge of most higher level authorities." Through the use of organizational strategies like compartmentalization and plausible deniability, and by limiting the flow of information to "a need to know basis," the CIA succeeded in keeping its covert operations, even large ones, secret from the very government officials charged with oversight.

Prouty relates one instance where he briefed General Lyman L. Lemnitzer, then chairman of the Joint Chiefs of Staff, on the subject of the largest covert operation that the CIA had ever mounted, up to that point. Whereupon, Lemnitzer, in shock, said to the other Chiefs, "I just can't believe it. I never knew that."[11]

Allen Dulles was up to such tricks even *before* becoming director. In his voluminous history of the CIA, *Legacy of Ashes,* journalist Tim Weiner describes how in 1951 Allen Dulles, then deputy director of plans (i.e. covert operations), and Frank Wisner routinely stonewalled their boss, CIA Director Bedell Smith, about ongoing covert projects. At the time, Wisner headed up the bland-sounding Office of Policy Coordination, newly instituted to counter the USSR threat in Europe.[12] That meant staging covert operations throughout western Europe (i.e., Operation Gladio).

Smith fumed at being kept in the dark, and was also aghast that the CIA budget being proposed by Dulles had mushroomed eleven-fold since 1948, with most of the increase allocated for covert operations–––three times the budget for espionage and analysis. Smith correctly worried that "this posed a distinct danger to CIA as an intelligence agency," because "the operational tail will wag the intelligence dog."[13]

Smith was an Army General, and clashed sharply with the lawyer Dulles, who made a habit of evading direct orders. Weiner cites the CIA's Tom Polger, who observed the two men trying to work together. Said Polger: "Bedell clearly doesn't like Dulles, and it's easy to see why. An Army officer gets an order and carries it out. A lawyer finds a way to weasel..."[14] Weiner recounts how Dulles lied to Congress to conceal an unbroken string of failed covert operations during the Korean war.[15]

General Bedell Smith never succeeded in bending Dulles and Wisner to his authority. As we know, Dwight D. Eisenhower won the 1952 election on a platform of confronting Communism and rolling back the iron curtain. Ike's closest foreign policy advisor was none other than John Foster Dulles, Allen's brother. So, when the time came for Ike to pick his new CIA chief, it was no surprise that he tapped Allen Dulles for the job, over Bedell Smith's strong objections.

With the appointment of Dulles as CIA Director, the US financial elite finally achieved through peaceful means the perversion of democracy it had sought to achieve through a violent coup in 1934, when a cabal of Wall Street bankers and industrialists attempted to overthrow the presidency of Franklin Delano Roosevelt. During the 1930s, a number of prominent individuals on Wall Street, including

Prescott Bush, father of George H.W. Bush, viewed FDR as a traitor to his class and wanted to replace him with a fascist puppet government.

In 1934, the plotters enlisted a genuine war hero to their cause: two-time Congressional Medal of Honor winner General Smedley Butler. Although Butler initially appeared to go along with the conspiracy, much to his credit, the general remained loyal to the Constitution and ultimately alerted Congress to the plot.[16]

The attempted coup against FDR failed, but the bankers' moment finally arrived after World War II with the onset of the Cold War. The Red Menace was made-to-order for Wall Street. The international threat of communism, real or imagined, was the perfect rationale for a national security apparatus with the power to undermine and ultimately trump our democracy. Along with this went the systematic manipulation of public opinion through mass propaganda and spin.

In 1947, the "War Department" was re-christened the "Defense Department." That same year, the English writer George Orwell sat down to finish his dystopian masterpiece *1984* in which he prophetically describes a fictional world-turned-upside-down: which has since become all too real. Words and expressions that Orwell coined, like "Big Brother", "Newspeak", "Ignorance is Strength", "Freedom is Slavery", "War is Peace", even the term "Orwellian," have long since become integral to our language.

Truman lived to regret his role in creating a monster. One month to the day after the murder of JFK in Dallas, the elder statesman posted a letter in the *Washington Post,* in which he addressed the nation. In the letter Truman explained that he had set up the CIA to provide raw intelligence to the office of the president, but that in practice things had turned out very differently. Truman wrote that

> I think it has become necessary to take another look at the purpose and operations of our Central Intelligence Agency.....For some time I have been disturbed by the way CIA has been diverted from its original assignment. It has become an operational and at times a policy-making arm of the Government. This has led to trouble and may have compounded our difficulties in several explosive areas.
>
> *I never had any thought that when I set up the CIA that it would be injected into peacetime cloak and dagger operations.*

Some of the complications and embarrassment I think we have experienced are in part attributable to the fact that this quiet intelligence arm of the President has been so removed from its intended role that it is being interpreted as a symbol of sinister and mysterious foreign intrigue...there are now some searching questions that need to be answered.

I, therefore, would like to see the CIA be restored to its original assignment as the intelligence arm of the President....and that its operational duties be terminated or properly used elsewhere. We have grown up as a nation, respected for our free institutions and for our ability to maintain a free and open society. There is something about the way the CIA has been functioning that is casting a shadow over our historic position and I feel that we need to correct it.[17] [my emphasis]

Truman's line about the CIA "casting a shadow over our historic position" may have been a thinly-veiled reference to the assassination of President John F. Kennedy in Dallas, *exactly one month before*, an assassination which new research suggests was a rogue CIA operation conducted with the cooperation of Chicago mobsters.[18] It is quite possible that by December 1963 Truman had privately reached the same conclusion.

But he may also have been referring to the CIA's many inglorious foreign policy disasters in the Mideast, Latin America, and Southeast Asia, about which the aging Truman surely must have been painfully aware. The most obvious example, of course, was the Bay of Pigs fiasco in 1961 that led to the 1962 Cuban missile crisis which brought the world to the brink of nuclear Armageddon. Another was the CIA's 1953 plot to overthrow the popular and democratically elected leader of Iran, Mohammad Mossadegh, and replace him with the dictatorial Shah, the fallout from which continues to bedevil geopolitics, many years later.

No example of US treachery has ever done more harm to American prestige, world wide, than the CIA's destruction of the fledgling Iranian democracy. At the time, Iran was friendly to the West and a US ally. During World War II, Iran had played a key role in US efforts to resupply the Soviet Union and prevent a Nazi victory on the eastern front. Yet, the US repaid Tehran with betrayal. And there are many other examples.[19]

It appears that Truman's successor, Dwight D. Eisenhower, despite his eminent role as Cold Warrior, may in due course have learned to distrust the CIA. During Eisenhower's two terms the CIA often kept him in the dark, when they were not actively manipulating him. There is some evidence that the CIA may even have gone so far as to wreck Ike's scheduled 1960 peace summit with Nikita Khrushchev by secretly arranging for the Soviets to shoot down an American U-2 surveillance plane piloted by Gary Powers.[20]

The incident embarrassed Eisenhower, causing renewed hostility between Washington and Moscow at the very moment when a thaw in the Cold War seemed within reach. Like the murder of JFK, three years later, the U-2 incident is suspicious and may have been a calculated move by CIA hardliners. This dark possibility may even have motivated Eisenhower to warn the American people in 1961 about the growing threat to democratic institutions posed by "the military-industrial complex."[21]

But while most Americans have at least heard of Ike's famous warning, delivered in his final address to the nation, by contrast, Truman's remarkable letter has been forgotten. No doubt, Truman ruffled some powerful feathers, because, later that day, his letter was mysteriously yanked from subsequent editions of the *Post*.

As we now know, by the early 1960s the CIA had enlisted many frontline journalists for undercover work. Estimates of how many range from 50 to 400, or more.[22] But the exact number is less important than the confirmed fact that selected journalists at every major US magazine and newspaper, including the *Post*, were on the CIA payroll, in sufficient numbers to leak disinformation into the media and deceive the American people on a range of issues. The willing CIA operatives were only too happy to plant phony "news" or, as in the case of Truman's letter, to make troublesome stories disappear. One or two phone calls from Langley may have done the trick.

There was no follow up in the press regarding the Truman letter, not in subsequent weeks, months, or years. None of Truman's biographers mention it, probably because they did not even know about it.[23] This includes David McCullough, author of the 1992 bestseller, *Truman*, which won the Pulitzer Prize and has been called "the most thorough account of Truman's life yet to appear."[24] Thorough, perhaps, but not thorough enough. I searched McCullough's account in vain for any mention of the 1963 letter. Soon after it appeared in print, Truman's letter vanished down an Orwellian memory hole and nearly disappeared from human consciousness.

It is noteworthy that the original edition of Prouty's pathbreaking CIA expose, *The Secret Team*, suffered a similar fate. In 1975, on hearing from a professor acquaintance that forty copies of the book had inexplicably vanished from the shelves of a university library, Prouty visited the Library of Congress in Washington to see if his book was still in the stacks where he had seen it on a previous visit. Not only was it missing, his book was no longer even listed in the library card catalogue. Someone had expunged every trace of its existence. Until the occasion of its re-publication in 2011, *The Secret Team* remained, in Prouty's words, "an official non-book."

Shades of Orwell.

ENDNOTES

1   Richard Helms with William Hood, *A Look Over My Shoulder: A Life in the Central Intelligence Agency* (New York: Random House, 2003), p. 82-83; 99.

The two other members of the committee were William H. Jackson and Mathias F. Correa. The committee had been authorized by Secretary of Defense James V. Forrestal, an old colleague of Allen Dulles. Burton Hersh, *The Old Boys* (New York: Charles Scribner's Sons, 1992), p. 233.

The Dulles-led committee produced a report dated January 1, 1949, that was submitted to President Truman upon his re-election. According to Fletcher Prouty "No report on the broad subject of intelligence has ever been more important than this one was." Prouty continues: "The report....clearly and precisely outlined what Allen Dulles was going to do; and to his credit, he did just that, and more. During that busy summer of election year, 1948, Allen Dulles was officially the speechwriter for the Republican candidate, Governor Thomas E. Dewey of New York. All through the campaign it had been generally accepted that Dewey would defeat President Truman. Allen Dulles, his brother, John Foster Dulles, and the others of that Dewey team fully expected to move into Washington on the crest of a wave with the inauguration of their candidate. In this context the Dulles-Jackson-Correa report takes on a special meaning. Although this select committee had been established by President Truman, they had timed their work for delivery to the President during his———they expected———"Lame Duck" period. Then they planned to use it as their own plan of action in the new Dewey administration. In one of the greatest political upsets of all time, Truman beat Dewey, and the Republicans were forced to wait another four years. Thus it happened that this crucial report was reluctantly delivered into Truman's more than hostile hands on January 1, 1949." According to Prouty, only 10-12 copies of the 193-page report were published, and later, efforts were made to collect and destroy the copies not under CIA control. L. Fletcher Prouty, *The Secret Team* (Delaware: Skyhorse Publishing, 2011), p.174 and 213.

2   Burton Hersh, *The Old Boys* (New York: Charles Scribner's Sons, 1992), p. 185; 233.

3   Peter Dale Scott, Drugs, *Oil and War* (Lanham, MD: Rowman & Littlefield, 2003), p.187; 200-201.

∆ - A disappearance so complete that the Ballontine pb edition vanished overnight (literally) from bookstores in Cambridge, Mass & emptied itself from warehouses in Australia

4   Other provisions of the same act created the National Security Council and reorganized the US military force structure.

5   The notion is also refuted by the facts surrounding the Gulf of Tonkin incident. See Ray McGovern's excellent analysis, in which he shows that the CIA deceived then President Johnson. Assuming the CIA's mission was to provide intel to the chief, why did they lie to LBJ? The only reasonable explanation is that the CIA was serving the perceived interests of Wall Street. At the time, Wall Street wanted LBJ to expand the Viet Nam war. Why? Simple. Because warfare is vastly more profitable than peace. Wall Street achieved the desired objective by means of CIA manipulation. The rest is history. http://www.consortiumnews.com/2008/011108a.html

6   *The Secret Team*, p.xxx.

7   Ibid.

8   Ibid., p 79.

9   Ibid.

10   Ibid., p. 116.

11   Ibid., p.xx.

12   *The Old Boys*, p. 226.

13   Tim Weiner, *Legacy of Ashes* (New York: Anchor Books, 2008), p. 60.

14   Ibid., p. 59.

15   Ibid., p. 65.

16   Smedley D. Butler, *War is a Racket* (Port Townsend, WA: Feral House, 1935).

17   Washington Post, December 22, 1963. The complete text of the letter may be viewed at http://www.maebrussell.com/Prouty/Harry%20Truman's%20CIA%20 article.html

It is notable that Clark Clifford, one of the bankers involved in the drafting of the 1947 National Security Act, echoed the same concerns as Truman when he testified in 1975 before the Senate Select Committee investigating CIA abuses. The committee was chaired by Senator Frank Church (D-Idaho). Clifford's testimony is important because Clifford had been one of Truman's most trusted aide's and, no doubt, was instrumental in persuading Truman to sign the bill, in the first place. The full text of Clifford's statement is posted at http://www.aarclibrary.org/publib/church/reports/vol7/pdf/ChurchV7_8_Clifford.pdf

18   James W. Douglas, *JFK and the Unspeakable* (Maryknoll, NY: Orbis Books, 2008).

19   The CIA-assisted murder of Congo's Prime Minister Patrice Lamumba in 1960 produced a long reign of terror under the US-backed butcher Mobutu, and fueled decades of bloody cvil war in the mineral-rich heart of Africa. Stephen R. Weissman, "Congo-Kinshasa: New Evidence Shows U.S. Role in Congo's Decision to Send Patrice Lamumba to His Death, *All-Africa.com*, August 1, 2010. Posted at http://allafrica.com/stories/201008010004.html

Another "success" was the CIA plan to overthrow the legitimate ruler of Cambodia, Prince Sihanouk, a non-communist whose only crime was that he tried to remain neutral in a US war zone. Sihanouk's ouster and the decision by Nixon and Kissinger to carpet bomb Cambodia helped bring Pol Pot to power and led to the subsequent mayhem of the killing fields. There is also the case of Indonesia, where the US-assisted slaughter of a half-million communists in 1965 led to many years of crony-capitalism under the US-backed Suharto, during which time the forests of Indonesia were devastated and the people impoverished. For dozens of similar examples see William Blum, *Killing Hope: US Military and CIA Interventions Since World War II* (Monroe, ME: Common Courage Press, 1995).

20   *The Secret Team*, p. 445-456; also see Travis Kelly, "Mayday, 1960," Counterpunch,

November 27, 2009. Posted at http://www.counterpunch.org/kelly11272009.html

21   The key part of Ike's speech may be viewed on line. http://www.youtube.com/watc h?v=8y06NSBBRtY&eurl=http%3A%2F%2Fwww%2Eorangemane%2Ecom%2FBB %2Fshowthread%2Ephp%3Ft%3D81836&feature=player_embedded

22   Hugh Wilford, *The Mighty Wurlitzer* (Cambridge: Harvard University Press, 2008), p. 227; also see Carl Bernstein, "The CIA and the Media," *Rolling Stone*, October 20, 1977, archived at http://www.informationclearinghouse.info/article28610.htm

23   This is according to scholar Martin Schotz, who has been researching Truman's let- ter since 1966. W. Martin Schotz, *History Will Not Absolve Us: Orwellian Control, Public Denial, and the Murder of John F. Kennedy* (Brookline, MA: Kurtz, Ulmer and DeLucia Press, 1996), appendix VIII, p. 237.

24   The quote is by Alan Brinkley, whose review appeared in the *New York Times Book Review*.

Chapter 10

BoNY and the Fed

Official White House documents declassified in the 1990s show that, starting in 1982, Ronald Reagan signed at least three national security directives that declared economic warfare on the Soviet Union. According to oil expert James R. Norman, "the most pivotal" of these, "NSDD-66, launched a huge effort which marshaled the CIA, the Pentagon, Treasury, and other governmental agencies to devise ways to increase economic pressure on the Soviets."[1] NSDD-66 gave rise to a series of internal papers, one of which was a "massive secret study on international oil pricing" which the Treasury Department completed in early 1983.

The study determined that oil was the USSR's principle cash-producing export, and that a sustained drop in world oil prices would, therefor, have a devastating impact on the Soviet economy. The Reagan White House moved quickly to exploit this perceived weakness, in part, by engineering a world oil glut. OPEC nations, especially the Saudis, were encouraged to increase production at the wellhead. The US also took steps to block a Soviet natural gas pipeline to Europe then under construction. The US succeeded in delaying its completion by two years, which deprived Moscow of an estimated $20 billion in revenue. Meanwhile, a new factor also came into play: the emergence of speculative "short" sellers on the New York Mercantile Exchange.

In his 2008 book, *The Oil Card*, Norman writes that the identity of the "short" sellers "was never clear, since the ultimate buyers and sellers of NYMEX contracts were known only to the brokers handling their trades. [And] even then, the identity of futures buyers could be disclosed as no more than a nominee in the Cayman Islands."[2] And because the futures margin requirement per thousand-barrel-contract was only 5%, relatively small amounts of cash, persistently applied, had a "snowballing effect."

The speculative shorting of oil futures ultimately decoupled prices from supply-and-demand fundamentals, and helped cause a world collapse in the price of oil that continued for years. The resulting chronic shortfall in oil revenues dealt the Soviet Union a mortal blow, according to a Russian academic, Yegor Gaidar, who had served as Russian prime minister from 1991-1994.[3] In his book, *The Soviet Collapse,* Gaidar states that the Soviet government ran out of funds in November 1991, at which time the Soviet Union effectively ceased to exist.[4]

That same month, Gosbank director Victor Geraschenko announced that the gold vault in the country's Central Bank was empty. Incredibly, some 2-3,000 metric tonnes of gold, worth an estimated $22-33 billion, had simply vanished.[5] Geraschenko's statement, reported by *Izvestia,* was confirmed the same day by Aleksandre Orlov, a member of the Supreme Soviet. The Russian gold was never recovered; nor has its disappearance ever been explained. The failed coup against Gorbachev had occurred just three months earlier, i.e., in August 1991; and Gorbachev resigned on Christmas day, 1991.

Also, during 1991-92, vast quantities of rubles were illegally laundered out of Russia, in what came to be known as the "great ruble scam." 400 billion rubles were embezzled from the Central Bank alone, a crime that many Russians believe was a cyber-attack.[6] The Central Bank did not finally staunch the looting until encryption software was introduced in December 1992.

At the time, the ruble was not traded on world currency markets. Its value was artificially set by Soviet decree. As reported by the *New York Times,* the ruble was then worth 57 cents, which means that the 400 billion rubles looted from the Central Bank was worth about $228 billion in US dollars.[7] Notice, this approximates the $223 billion figure mentioned in the Cocke deposition. Moreover, the date of the transaction discussed in the deposition (CD, p. 49), i.e., November-December 1991, also appears to line up with events in Russia.

Is this merely coincidence? Or, was the $223 billion a secret slush fund derived from the Hammer Fund, or perhaps part of an even larger collateralized slush fund of $240 billion in ten-year bonds created for the purpose of debasing the ruble, as E.P. Heidner charges in "Collateral Damage"?[8] We may never know. In September 2006, Andrei Kozlov, a Russian official who had been investi-

gating the 1991-92 looting of Russia's Central Bank, was murdered
in Moscow along with his driver.[9] The two men were gunned down
by unknown assailants as they exited a soccer match. Kozlov had
been a leading bank reformer, and at the time of his death served
as first deputy chairman of Russia's Central Bank. Authorities described the deaths as "a contract killing."

"A POCKET WITH HOLES"

During the critical period of 1991-92, Russian officials issued
public statements that the nation was under outside attack. In
1991, Premier Valentin Pavlov went so far as warn of an "imperial-
ist plot." Although Pavlov was ridiculed in the West, at least one
western journalist, Claire Sterling, concluded after a two-year investigation that the premier's suspicions were "not far off." In 1993,
Sterling wrote that *propagandist*

> "the flow of rubles out of Soviet Russia was heavy enough to sug-
> gest a conspiracy, and a lot of it was moving through western
> banks. It was moving through Russian banks also, however. Ev-
> erybody with any rubles to speak of was racing to exchange them
> illicitly for hard currency, starting with those who had the most:
> communists on the way out, politicians on the way in, and the
> Russian mafia."[10]

During 1991-92, shady western "businessmen" were "running fabulous joint ventures in Moscow," but they "were only part of the story":

> "While they were in it for money, others were in it to manipulate
> the politics of a dying Soviet state. In the end, the case that shook
> Russia turned out to be an enormous and almost indecipherable
> conspiracy in which elements of the KGB, in collusion with the
> international underworld, set out deliberately to destabilize the
> Soviet Union's currency, almost certainly with the tacit consent if
> not active participation of the western intelligence community."[11]

As pressure on the ruble mounted, its value dropped. Before it
hit bottom the ruble was trading for fifty to one, or less.[12]

By 1992-1993, vast quantities of rubles were also being smuggled
back into Russia to purchase timber, rare metals and especially oil,
at fire-sale prices. The commodities were then shipped out and

By past performance, Sterling reports only what she's told to report.

peddled on the world market for a fortune. The asset stripping was too easy. The old Soviet state was gone. Russia stood defenseless, without custom controls, laws or procedures for confiscating contraband and prosecuting corruption. A Brookings scholar, Raymond Baker, has called this rip-off of Russia's natural resources "the greatest theft of resources that has ever occurred from any country in a short period of time."[13]

Asset stripping was Russia's baptism by fire into the world of "free" markets. And it happened thanks to men like Marc Rich, named by *Business Week* as the most powerful commodity trader in Russia in the early 1990s.[14] Rich has another dubious distinction. At the time he was pardoned in 2001 by President Bill Clinton on his last morning in the Oval Office, Rich had been a fugitive from the US since 1985, and faced a combined 325-year prison sentence for fifty-one charges of racketeering, mail and wire fraud, tax evasion on $100 million of unreported income, not to mention trading with the enemy, i.e., Iran during the hostage crisis.[15] The FBI had even offered a $750,000 reward for his capture. Yet, Clinton set Rich free with the stroke of a pen. Why? Was the pardon Marc Rich's reward for helping to bring Russia to her knees?

To be sure, the hemorrhaging of gold, rubles, and assets out of Russia would not have been possible without co-conspirators inside the country, i.e., corrupt Party and KGB officials, willing Russian businessmen, oligarchs, not to mention the Russian mafia. All of whom were eager to squeeze whatever profits they could from the dying Soviet system and move it out of the country. Indeed, after the failed coup, this became an urgent priority for certain high-ranking KGB officials, who became pariahs overnight. Between 1991-1997, the flight of capital swelled to a flood, prompting one western observer to describe Russia as "a pocket with holes in it."[16]

ELECTRONIC MONEY LAUNDERING VIA BoNY

Western banks extended a helping hand, especially the Bank of New York (BoNY), which in 1999 became embroiled in a major international money laundering investigation. The full story would easily fill this entire volume, so I will limit the discussion to a summary.

It seems that in 1995-1996, BoNY executives, working under the authority of senior vice-president Natasha Kagalovsky, set up a com-

& Rich colluded with Iranian Mossad assets to seize the hostages in the first place.

puterized wire transfer system to enable the speedy washing of funds out of Russia.[17] Records later confirmed that Russian gangsters and even the Cali drug cartel made use of the system.[18] Some of the laundered money may also have included loans to Russia from the International Monetary Fund, which points to the likely involvement of corrupt Russian officials.[19] Curiously, Ms. Kagalovsky's husband had been an economic adviser to Russian President Boris Yeltsin, and was also an associate of Russian oligarch Mikhail Khodorkovsky.[20]

As many as 160,000 separate money transfers were spun through the system over a period of several years: an average of 170 transfers each business day.[21] Some of the individual transfers were very large, in the range of $200 million, and they totaled at least $10 billion, though a lawsuit filed in 2007 by the Russian government put the total much higher, at $22 billion.[22] Much of the cash ended up in off-shore accounts in the Cayman Islands, Liechtenstein and other safe havens.

A story in the *New York Times* hinted at the background role played by the US intelligence community.[23] The article named Israeli banker Bruce Rappaport, one of BoNY's principal shareholders, whose Inter-Maritime Bank in Geneva had directed BoNY's initial expansion into Russia. Rappaport, a long-time US intelligence asset, had been William Casey's golfing buddy, one of a select group of cronies who made regular use of Casey's private elevator when visiting their pal at CIA headquarters.[24] A source at the CIA confirmed that Rappaport and Casey even shared a private phone line.[25]

In the mid-1980s, at the time of Iran-Contra, Rappaport had served as Oliver North's personal banker. Three different sources have confirmed that a $10 million contribution to North's Contra War effort from the sultan of Brunei had been deposited in one of Rappaport's Swiss accounts.[26] Also during the 1980s, Rappaport and several other traders including Marc Rich reportedly made a fortune supplying oil to South Africa, in defiance of the world economic embargo against Apartheid.[27]

Curiously, the Cocke deposition includes what may be a reference to Rappaport's Swiss American Bank. When Cocke was asked by the interviewing attorney (CD, p. 53) if he knew the origin of the name "Hammer," his response was: "I do not. And certainly [I] don't know where the name Rosebud comes from. Rosebud seems to be the secondary code name to Hammer. But nobody can tell me who is Rosebud, and who is not Rosebud, and I asked a half dozen people..."

In their pathbreaking study of global banking, money laundering and international organized crime, *All is Clouded by Desire,* Alan Block and Constance Weaver mention that Rosebud Investments was a shell company set up in 1985 by the Irish Republican Army (IRA) for the purpose of laundering drug money through a branch of Rappaport's Swiss American Bank, based in Antigua. While the name could be a coincidence, Rappaport's shady dealings have done nothing to allay suspicions; on the contrary.

In 1987, when US authorities rolled up the IRA ring and attempted to recover $7 million in laundered funds under the RICO act, Rappaport's bank refused to cooperate and ultimately handed over the cash to the Antiguan government, which, needless to say, was also firmly under Rappaport's personal control. According to Block and Weaver, in the early 1980s Rappaport and Marvin L. Warner, a business associate, "practically took over the small Caribbean Island." In subsequent years, Antigua earned a reputation for Russian money laundering.[28] Rappaport even served in an official capacity as the Antiguan ambassador to Russia.[29]

In 1990, Rappaport made the news again when it was revealed that Israeli mercenaries had been running arms through Antigua to the Medellin drug cartel. The mercenaries had used a "melon farm" owned by Rappaport as a base for training paramilitary forces for the Columbian cartel.[30] Incredibly, the property had been purchased with funds provided by an agency of the US government: the US Overseas Private Investment Corporation. The loan totaled more than a million dollars, courtesy of the US taxpayer.[31]

In 1985, Rappaport bought out Marvin Warner after an Ohio court convicted his partner of fraud and conspiracy, sentencing him to thirty-two years in prison. In 1997, another business associate, Abbas Kassimali Gokal, who had served on the board of Rappaport's Inter-Maritime Bank from 1978-1982, was sentenced to 13 years for his involvement in the notorious money laundering BCCI.[32] But Rappaport proved more capable than his unsavory associates at staying one step ahead of the law.

As the BoNY money laundering investigation deepened, bank officials brought in the Wall Street firm Sullivan and Cromwell to represent them, the very firm where CIA chief Allen Dulles had worked, once upon a time.[33] Some things never seem to change.

The investigation into the BoNY money laundering scam was delayed by the 9/11 attacks, but it eventually resumed. In 2007, two BoNY executives who had pled guilty to conspiracy were finally sentenced to six months' house arrest and a five-year probation period. The two were also ordered to pay a $20,000 fine and $685,000 in compensation: a hand slap.[34] The Bank of New York reportedly paid $38 million in penalties and compensation, and agreed to "sweeping internal reforms to ensure compliance with its antifraud and money laundering obligations."

Natasha Kagalovsky, who had supervised what may have been the largest money laundry in history, was never charged with a crime.[35] After reportedly cutting a deal with BoNY, she testified on behalf of the bank, and was allowed to exercise millions in stock options.[36] Did BoNY's defense attorneys purchase Kagalovsky's testimony (and her silence) in order to limit the scope of the federal probe?

While many questions remain unanswered, it is absolutely clear that BoNY failed to reform itself. On February 14, 2012 New York Attorney General Eric Schneiderman filed suit against BoNY Mellon (in 2007 BoNY merged with Mellon Financial Shares) for defrauding thousands of clients out of some $2 billion in a foreign currency exchange manipulation scheme. According to Schneiderman, BoNY had hatched the scheme in 2001, which of course means that securities fraud was ongoing even during the earlier money laundering investigation and settlement![37] Even as they were agreeing to reform bank practices, BoNY managers were busily fleecing customers! Speaking of chutzpah. In retrospect, there was scarcely a time from the mid-1990s up to the present when BoNY was not engaging in criminal activity. Now we will explore why this matters.

BoNY and the 9/11 Attacks

As we know, the attacks on the World Trade Center on 9/11 proved devastating to the New York financial district. The loss of life was concentrated in the financial industry, which accounted for at least 74% of the civilian casualties. The collapse of WTC-7 sent "I" beams crashing into the Verizon building at 140 West Street, causing telecommunications outages across lower Manhattan.

Due to the attacks, the New York Stock Exchange and the Nasdaq Stock Market never opened. The government securities market was especially hard hit because it opens earlier. Trading of government securities starts at 8 A.M., and the borrowing and lending starts at 7 A.M. On a typical day, most of the trading occurs before 9 A.M. and, as a result, at the time of the 9/11 attacks nearly $600 billion in transactions had already been executed.[38]

The Bank of New York had offices in the financial district (at One Wall Street and at 101 Barclay Street) and was compelled to evacuate some 8,300 employees. BoNY immediately shifted to its back-up systems and contingency sites, all of which were located outside the City of New York. Although the press reported otherwise, none of BoNY's backup facilities were affected by the attacks.

The initial backlog was heavy and was due mainly to the widespread phone outages. However, according to Thomas P. (Todd) Gibbons, BoNY's executive vice president in charge of risk management, BoNY was able to continue processing transactions through its backup facility located in Utica, New York. The initial disruptions lasted for only 2-3 days and by Friday September 14th, the bank had returned to normal processing.[39] BoNY actually issued a press release to this effect. Over the weekend of September 15-16, BoNY staff succeeded in clearing the backlog. On Monday the 17th, the New York stock exchange reopened, after a four-day closure, the longest stoppage since the Great Depression.

BoNY is one of the largest funds transfer banks in the world, and at the time of 9/11 was responsible for clearing about 50% of government securities traded in the United States. Chase Manhattan was the other important clearing bank (though in November 2001 it merged with J.P. Morgan to form J.P. Morgan-Chase).

At the time of the attacks, the Federal Reserve Bank of New York also shifted to backup contingency procedures and, thereafter, it functioned smoothly throughout the crisis. The Fed facilitated the markets' return to normalcy by relaxing the rules on trading, and by waiving overdraft fees and penalties. The Fed also made monies and securities available to Wall Street to mitigate the liquidity problems that continued for many weeks.

The biggest problem was the persistence of failed transactions, known as "fails," which happen when sellers are unable to deliver securities on time. The volume of fails jumped from $1.7 billion a day during the typical week of September 5, 2001, to $190 billion a day during the week ending September 19th; and it remained high for several weeks. [See chart below] Fails continued to be a problem through the end of the year, but the worst was over by mid-October.

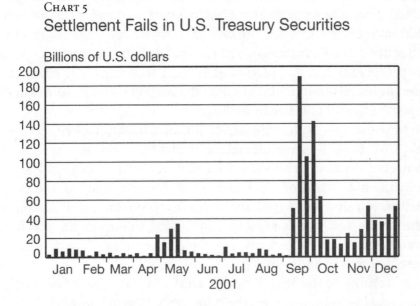

CHART 5
Settlement Fails in U.S. Treasury Securities

Billions of U.S. dollars

Jan Feb Mar Apr May Jun Jul Aug Sep Oct Nov Dec
2001

Source: Federal Reserve Bank of New York.

Note: The chart plots daily average settlement fails to deliver of U.S. Treasury securities as reported by the primary dealers for the weeks ending January 3 through December 26, 2001.

According to a 2002 study prepared by Federal Reserve officials, the rate of failed transactions "rose initially because of the destruction of trade records and communications facilities. They remained high because the method typically used to avert or remedy a fail, i.e., borrowing a security through a special collateral repurchase agreement (RP), proved as costly as failing to borrow the security."[40]

RPs (or repos) are short-term borrowing instruments, and are commonly used by some market participants, especially dealers and owners of hedge funds, who often commit themselves to making purchases in excess of their balances, or commit to selling more securities than they own at a given moment in time.

Fails multiplied, in large part, because one failed transaction caused others, setting in motion a type of chain reaction known on Wall Street as a "daisy chain." If a seller, for example, had not yet received the securities in settlement of a previous purchase, he might not be able to meet an obligation to deliver those same securities in a timely manner, for a subsequent unrelated transaction. In simple language, the system backed up.

The problems persisted even after the Fed relaxed the rules because the interest rate on repos fell to near zero. Lenders, as a result, had no incentive to lend. The system of repo borrowing stalled. On October 4, the Fed attempted to resolve the issue by announcing an unprecedented "snap" auction of 10-year securities. The snap auction pumped about $6 billion into the markets, and in subsequent days the rate of fails began to drop.[41]

Anyhow, this is the official version of what transpired, according to Federal Reserve officials. E.P. Heidner was not convinced, however, because in his view the Fed never satisfactorily explained why the fails problem was largely concentrated at BoNY, the same institution that had laundered at least $10 billion out of Russia in the 1990s, and which, as noted, continued to engage in securities fraud after 9/11, indeed, even as the earlier money laundering investigation was underway.

According to the *Wall Street Journal*, at times, the fails at BoNY exceeded $100 billion.[42] Yet the other large clearing house, J.P. Morgan, reported no such problems. Nor did Deutschebank, which was located just across the street from WTC-2 and suffered much more extensive damage.

It is also curious, as BoNY executive Todd Gibbons later acknowledged, that the press chronically misrepresented the situation at BoNY.[43] Several articles in the *Wall Street Journal*, for instance, wrongly stated or implied that the location of BoNY's Wall Street offices near the WTC rubble pile in lower Manhattan was somehow responsible for its continuing fails problem.[44] Not so. And the *Financial Times* and *New York Times* made similar errors.[45] But were these errors simply honest mistakes?

Heidner argues in "Collateral Damage" that 9/11 was the mother of all money laundering scams. He proposes that the reported $100 billion in fails at BoNY was but the "tip of a three-day operation," during which the Fed conspired with BoNY to launder the $240 billion in covert securities that the cabal around H.W. Bush had collateralized in 1991, and which were coming due at the time of the attacks.[46] Heidner thinks the Fed surreptitiously pumped hundreds of billions of dollars into the system, and may even have held down the interest rate on repos to provide the necessary cover for this subterfuge.

The truth is that BoNY and the Fed could have gotten away with almost anything in the confusion that prevailed after the 9/11 attacks. Unfortunately, we will probably never learn the truth, unless we succeed in generating sufficient political support to compel a genuine audit of the Fed and the Bank of New York.[47]

The machinations of Wall Street tend to be opaque to outsiders. Except for one last thing...

PRE-9/11 CURRENCY SPIKE

Although the Fed has acknowledged pumping more than $100 billion into the system in the weeks following 9/11,[48] to this day the American people have never been told about the sharp spike in the US currency supply that occurred in the weeks *before* the attacks. I learned about this from William Bergman, a former financial market analyst at the Federal Reserve Bank of Chicago, where he worked for fourteen years. Bergman contacted me in February 2011 after reading one of my articles online. He believes the whole truth about 9/11 remains to be told.[49]

In December 2003, soon after accepting a new money laundering assignment at the Chicago Fed, Bergman learned about a supervisory letter that the Federal Reserve Board of Governors had issued to staff on August 2, 2001. The letter was concerned with suspicious activity reporting, and although it did not explicitly mention terrorism or terrorist financing, it nonetheless got Bergman's attention because these were known to be important elements of self-policing initiatives to curb money laundering activities.

Bergman had studied the financial data for June - August 2001, and he had some related concerns about the unusual growth in the money supply during this period. Indeed, the expansion in the currency component of the M1 aggregate (which includes demand deposits in checking accounts and the total currency in circulation) was unprecedented. The expansion of currency in circulation in the US between June and August, 2001, which Bergman estimated at $5 billion, was the largest such increase since the Fed began record-keeping in 1947.[50]

The increase in August alone was the third highest for any month ever recorded, trailing only the millennial Y2K bug concerns in December 1999 and a spike in January 1991, the month preceding

Operation Desert Storm; and which is explainable in terms of war fever, and possibly the liquifying of assets and other financial maneuvering associated with the BCCI scandal.

The currency expansion in July-August 2001 largely consisted of $100 bills, and could be evidence of foreknowledge of the September 11 attacks. Bergman reasoned that someone had withdrawn large amounts of cash beforehand, perhaps to protect himself, assuming he had reason to believe that the US government would seize his assets *after* the attacks. There were historical precedents. For example, the US government froze Iranian assets at the time of the 1979-81 hostage crisis, and a similar seizure occurred following the 1998 al-Qaeda attacks of the African embassies. Bergman speculated that something similar might have occurred in the weeks before 9/11, though he acknowledges that the August increase could also have been due in part to the Argentinian banking crisis that was ongoing at that time.[51]

Bergman contacted the Fed's board of governors about these concerns *after* first consulting with his supervisor, who instructed him to follow up. However, about a week later Bergman was summarily terminated from his position, and his credentials were canceled. He was told that he had committed a serious breach of protocol. But rather than replacing him, the Fed eliminated the position to which Bergman had been assigned, and his department was absorbed into another department. In March 2004, Bergman accepted a severance package and left the bank.

The Government Accountability Project, a whistleblowers' organization, summarized Bergman's case in a January 2006 letter sent on his behalf to Fed chairman Alan Greenspan. A copy apparently also went to Mr. Harvey Witherspoon, the Fed's Inspector General. In the letter GAP urged Greenspan to respond to the questions Bergman had raised, noting that "The Fed's failure, to date, to publicly address the growth in currency in mid-2001 is conspicuous. If a benign explanation exists, or if for whatever reason the currency growth is irrelevant, the Fed should say so publicly, and explain why this is the case. A failure to do so raises....troubling questions."

OK. Here is one troubling question: Why did the Federal Reserve Board of Governors issue a supervisory letter to its bankers on August 2, 2001, just weeks before 9/11, emphasizing the importance of monitoring "suspicious" activity?

Here is another: Why did the Fed terminate a 14-year employee simply for doing his job?

This much, at least, ought to be clear: Someone with foreknowledge of the 9/11 attacks withdrew very large amounts of cash beforehand, from US bank accounts. The total was at least $5 billion, a vast sum compared to the paltry half-million that, according to the 9/11 Commission, financed al-Qaeda's plot against America.[52] As professor R.T. Naylor suggests in his fine book *Satanic Purses*, the movement of large amounts of money in association with a terrorist event is an indicator of state terrorism.[53]

This would tend to rule out al-Qaeda as the moving force behind 9/11, and brings us back to the event itself.

As we are about to learn, several different new lines of evidence challenge the official view that 9/11 was organized and carried out by a loose-knit cadre of Islamic terrorists operating from a cave in Afghanistan.

ENDNOTES

1   James R. Norman, *The Oil Card* (Walterville, OR: Trineday, 2008), p.18-19.

2   *The Oil Card*, p. 3.

3   Other important factors included the Soviet occupation of Afghanistan, and the Chernobyl disaster, both of which drained the Soviet economy.

4   Yegor Gaidar, *The Soviet Collapse: Grain and Oil*, American Enterprise Institute for Public Policy Research, April 2007.

5   Claire Sterling, *Thieves' World* (New York: Simon & Schuster, 1994), p. 175; also see note 20, p. 277.

6   This is according to Regnum, a Russian news agency. Posted at http://www.regnum.ru/english/749825.html

7   "Exchange Rate Cut for Ruble," *New York Times*, November 4, 1991. Posted at http://www.nytimes.com/1991/11/04/world/exchange-rate-cut-for-ruble.html

8   "Collateral Damage," p. 26.

9   C.J. Chivers and Andrew E. Kramer, "Russian Bank Reformer Dies after Shooting," *New York Times*, September 14, 2006. Posted at http://www.nytimes.com/2006/09/15/world/europe/15russia.html?_r=1&oref=slogin&pagewanted=print

    Also see http://www.regnum.ru/english/749825.html

10 *Thieves' World*, p. 185.

11 *Thieves' World*, p.176.

12 "Exchange Rate Cut for Ruble"

13 Raymond W. Baker, "Biggest Loophole in the Free-Market System," *The Washington Quarterly*, Autumn 1999, p. 39.

14 "Investigative report: The Rich Boys," *Business Week*, July 18, 2005.

15 *Thieves' World*, p. 204.

16 The observer was Britain's foreign secretary, Douglas Hurd, who made the remark at a meeting of the G-7 in 1993. *Thieves' World*, p. 208.

17 For a good summary see Nick Kochan, *The Washing Machine* (Mason, Ohio: Thomson/South-Western, 2005), p. 21-36.

18 Jean Martinson and Dan Atkinson, "Russian mob 'used US bank' to launder cash," *Guardian* (UK), August 20, 1999.

19 David Ignatius, "Who Robbed Russia? Did Al Gore know about the massive lootings?", *Washington Post*, August 25, 1999; also see Raymond Bonner, "Russian Gangsters Exploit Capitalism to Increase Profits," *New York Times*, July 25, 1999.

20 Timothy O'Brien, "The Money Movers: A special report; Tracking How Pair Went from Russia to Riches," *New York Times*, October 19, 1999; also see Tom Bawden, "Bank of New York accused by Russians of money laundering," *Sunday Times* (London), May 18, 2007.

21 *All is Clouded by Desire*, p.146.

22 Tom Bawden, "Bank of New York accused by Russians of money laundering," *Sunday Times* (London), May 18, 2007.

23 Timothy O'Brien with Raymond Bonner, "Russian Money-Laundering Finds a Familiar Swiss Banker in the Middle," *New York Times*, August 22, 1999.

24 *The Road to 9/11*, p.95.

25 *All is Clouded by Desire*, p.33.

26 *Profits of War*, p.181; also see *All is Clouded by Desire*, p. 89-90; also see Robert Parry, "US Ties to Russian Money Scam," *Online Journal*, August 9, 2011.

27 *All is Clouded by Desire*, p. 72.

28 *All is Clouded by Desire*, p. 51.

29 "Russian Money-Laundering Finds a Familiar Swiss Banker in the Middle"

30 Andrew and Leslie Cockburn, *Dangerous Liaison: The Inside Story of the US-Israeli Covert Relationship* (New York: Harper Perennial, 1992), p. 270.

31 Robert Coram, Caribbean Time Bomb: The United States' Complicity in the Corruption of Antigua (New York: William Morrow, 1993), p. 186-87.

32 *All is Clouded by Desire*, p. 86.

33 *All is Clouded by Desire*, p. 203.

34 "Bank of New York accused by Russians of money laundering"

35 Timothy O'Brien, "Bank Settles US Inquiry Into Money Laundering," *New York Times*, November 9, 2005.

36 The letter of agreement continues to be posted on the Internet: http://www.moscowtelegraph.com/klap_let_kag.htm

Also see http://moscowtelegraph.com/mt110601.htm

37 Gupta Rajsingh, "10 years Bank of New York Mellon manipulation in foreign currency exchange," Newsmakertoday.com, February 16, 2012; also see "Oregon Seeks to Lead Lawsuit against Bank of New York Mellon," *Bloomberg.com*, February 14, 2012.

38 Jeffrey M. Lacker, "Payment System Disruptions and the Federal Reserve Following September 11, 2001," Federal Reserve Bank of Richmond, Richmond, Virginia, November 17, 2003, p. 3-4.

39 "Emerging Stronger from 9/11/01: An Interview with Todd Gibbons," *The Risk Management Journal*, December 1, 2001.

40 "When the Back Office Moved to the Front Burner: Settlement Fails in the Trea-

sury Market after 9/11," Michael J. Fleming and Kenneth D. Garbade, *FRBNY Economic Policy Review*, November 2002, p 35.

41 Jonathan Fuerbringer, "US Acts on Shortage of Treasuries," *New York Times*, October 5, 2001.

42 Paul Beckett and Jathon Sapsford, "Rebuilding Wall Street: How Wall Street's Nerve System caused Pain," *Wall Street Journal*, September 21, 2001

43 "Emerging Stronger from 9/11/01: An Interview with Todd Gibbons"

44 "Rebuilding Wall Street: How Wall Street's Nerve System caused Pain." Also see Greg Ip and Gregory Zuckerman, "Treasury Sale Averts a Crisis in 'Repo' Market --- Unscheduled Auction of $6 Billion in Notes is a Department First," *Wall Street Journal*, October 5, 2001.

45 Saul Hansell with Riva D. Atlas, "Wall Street Lifeline Shakes Off Dust, and Critics," *New York Times*, October 6, 2001. The September 21 article in the *Financial Times* is cited in James J. McAndrews and Simon M. Potter, "Liquidity Effects of the Events of September 11, 2001, *FRBNY Economic Policy Review*, November 2002, n. 22, p.76.

46 "Collateral Damage," p. 30-38.

47 But why stop there? An honest audit of the CIA would doubtless reveal numerous unfunded black operations, that is, covert activities unsupported by any Congressionally appropriated money. It is no wonder the CIA refused to disclose the relevant documents about its pre-9/11 budget and operations to the 2002 Joint Inquiry, the first official 9/11 investigation. Check the final appendix. "Congressional Reports: Joint Inquiry into Intelligence Community Activities before and after the Terrorist Attacks of September 11, 2001," posted at http://www.gpoaccess.gov/serialset/creports/911.html

48 "Payment System Disruptions and the Federal Reserve Following September 11, 2001," p. 2.

49 According to William Bergman the Fed publishes monetary statistics, i.e., raw data, which contained this information. But the data never made it to the public. Certainly the press never reported it. Email from William Bergman, October 11, 2011.

50 Email from William Bergman, October 11, 2011.

51 For a good summary see Jim Hogue, "More evidence of pre-9/11 Insider Trading: Follow the Money. God Forbid," *Global Research*, February 10, 2008. Posted at http://www.globalresearch.ca/index.php?context=va&aid=8046

52 *The 9/11 Commission Report* (New York: W.W. Norton & Co, 2004), p.172.

53 The Russia demolition project continued after 9/11. When Mikhail Khodorkovsky was indicted in 2003 for tax evasion and fraud, the powerful Russian oligarch was, at that moment, on the verge of selling off a 40% stake in Russia's second-largest oil company, Yukos, to Exxon-Mobile and Chevron-Texaco. The talks with the western oil giants had begun soon after an unpublicized meeting between Khodorkovsky and Vice President Dick Cheney. Tanvir Ahmad Khan, "Russia's Return to Center Stage," *Dawn*, February 26, 2007.

The timing of the arrest was curious for another reason. It came just a few weeks before a decisive vote in the Russian Duma, where, according to various sources, Khodorkovsky had used his wealth to purchase a majority. Had Russian authorities not acted when they did, the vote might have enabled Khodorkovsky to legislate a pathway to political power. It was a deal-breaker---Khodorkovsky had agreed to stay out of politics in return for state patronage---and on this basis William Engdahl concluded that Khodorkovsky made himself the willing vehicle for "a Washington-backed putsch against Putin." F. William Engdahl, *Full Spectrum*

Dominance (Wiesbaden: Engdahl Press, 2009), p. 58-59.

Subsequent reports tend to bear this out. The *Washington Post* revealed that Khodorkovsky was also a consultant to the Carlyle Group, a privately held US investment company that is heavily invested in arms manufacturing. Khodorkovsky's status as consultant would have given him direct access to G.W. Bush, a senior member of the Carlyle board. Greg Schneider, "Arrested Russian Businessman is Carlyle Group Adviser," *Washington Post*, November 10, 2003.

The *Washington Times* reported another relevant tidbit. On his arrest, all of Khodorkovsky's shares in Yukos, including his voting rights, passed to banker Jacob Rothschild, according to a "previously unknown arrangement" that was to take effect if Khodorkovsky was unable, for any reason, to administer his share of the company. Khodorkovsky's controlling stake in Yukos was worth an estimated $13.5 billion. "Arrested oil tycoon passed shares to banker," *Washington Times*, November 2, 2003.

This shows that powerful western bankers were backing Khodorkovsky, no doubt, for the purpose of gaining control over a key sector of the Russian economy. As we know, Khodorkovsky's arrest touched off a flurry of angry editorials in the western press. Outraged critics chaffed that Russia was slipping backward under Putin into authoritarian rule. Western editors were only too happy to feature spirited op/eds by Khodorkovsky himself which, no doubt, he penned from prison. The oligarch's defense of liberty was less than convincing, but he nonetheless remained a cause celebre in the US and a symbol of dashed freedom. In order to sustain this mythic image of the persecuted champion, Khodorkovsky's defenders had to overlook certain unpleasantries: for starters, that he had acquired Yukos via a rigged auction; and that his bank Menatep preyed upon ordinary Russians by selling phony bank shares, which, needless to say, was illegal. David Hoffman, *The Oligarchs* (New York: Public Affairs, 2003 edition), p. 297-315; p. 211.

Khodorkovsky's defenders likewise failed to mention how he reneged on a partnership with Amoco, after the western oil company had invested $300 million to develop a promising Siberian oil field. Catherine Belton, "Khodorkovsky's High Stakes Gamble," *Moscow Times*, May 16, 2005.

For this piece of work Khodorkovsky might have been indicted in the West, but in the wild west of Russia it was business as usual. Like many others who found a way to feed on the carcass of communism, Khodorkovsky was less interested in producing something of value than making windfall profits from far more lucrative speculative schemes———including predation. When the ruble tumbled, in 1998, and bank Menatep along with it, three western banks attempted to recover their $266 million investment by cashing in their collateral, i.e., their secured shares in Yukos. But Khodorkovsky refused to sell, offering oil in lieu of cash (probably because he was strapped). When the western banks declined, the oligarch threatened to dilute their stake with an avalanche of new shares, forcing the banks to dump their stock at a huge loss. Paul Klebnikov, "The Oligarch Who Came in From the Cold," *Forbes*, March 18, 2002.

While legal in Russia, the predatory practice might have landed Khodorkovsky in a western jail cell. In their hypocrisy, western commentators failed to acknowledge what should have been obvious: that Russia, like any nation, has a right, indeed, a responsibility, to protect vital sectors of its economy in its own interest. Yukos certainly fit that profile. Here in the US no one bats an eye when our government does the very same thing. It is taken for granted that national security will always trump the free market. There were no cries of dashed liberty, for instance, when Washington recently blocked the attempted purchase of Unocal by Chinese capitalists. "China's CNOOC drops bid for Unocal," *Associated Press*, August 2, 2005.

It was obvious to everyone that China's objective was to gain control of Molycorp, a Unocal subsidiary and owner of the most important rare earth mine in North America, located in the Mojave desert.

The attempted purchase was a thinly-veiled bid by China to expand what was already a Chinese near-monopoly of the world supply of rare earth elements, a commodity that has become crucial for high-tech, hence, vital for national security. No surprise that the US government intervened on its own behalf, just as the Russian state did in the case of Yukos. Although Heidner writes that George Soros and Jacob Rothschild gained control over Yukos and the other Russian oil giant, Gazprom, Putin reportedly reassumed control over Yukos, in December 2004, by nationalizing the company. "Putin defends Yukos oil asset purchase," *CBCnews*, December 23, 2004

Similarly, in June 2005 the Russian government announced plans to acquire a controlling interest in Gazprom. "Kremlin agrees price for Gazprom," *BBC News*, June 16, 2005.

Chapter 11

Remote-Control 9/11

I n May 2010, an avionics technician named Wayne Anderson went public with testimony about a specific type of black technology long rumored to exist, but never previously confirmed. In the interview, Anderson told Rob Balsamo, co-founder of Pilots for 9/11 Truth, that in late 1996 or early 1997 he personally witnessed an avionics engineer use black software to remotely control the autopilot of a Boeing 757, in the process "locking out" the flight crew.[1] If such a test occurred, it means that this type of remote-control technology is not science fiction but reality, and already existed at the time of the 9/11 attacks. For years, critics have pointed to discrepancies in the official 9/11 conspiracy narrative, discrepancies suggesting some type of remote-control operation. But hard evidence, let alone proof, has remained elusive.

In the interview, Anderson names the engineer, David Prentice, who Anderson says was a coworker at Dalfort Aviation Services based in Dallas, Texas. At the time, the Boeing 757 was supported on jacks in a hanger at Love Field where it was undergoing maintenance. Anderson says he served as a gofer during the test, and that throughout, Prentice maintained walkie-talkie communication with him and with two other avionics technicians, who were in the 757 cockpit.

The first part of the test was a routine procedure known as a "return to service" check, a standard set of protocols done after an overhaul to insure that a plane's autopilot is working properly. While the technicians put the 757 through its paces in a ground-simulated test flight, the engineer monitored everything from the avionics lab, located at some distance from the aircraft on a second floor between the hanger bays. Once the techs had run through all of the usual protocols, Prentice launched the black software program on his laptop and keyed in a command, which was transmitted by radio signal to the 757's flight management computer via the aircraft's mode "S" transponder.

The more common mode "C" and mode "A" transponders transmit a plane's altitude and air speed to air traffic controllers. A mode "S" transponder does the same. However, in addition, it also includes a data-link capability that allows for two-way sending and receiving of "data packets." The mode "S" is standard equipment on Boeing 757s.

Prentice then took over control of the aircraft and locked out the technicians in the cockpit, who apparently were stunned. Prentice had not briefed them beforehand about what was going to happen during this additional test, which was not a part of the usual return to service check. Anderson, meanwhile, was listening to the chatter, and he says the crew became increasingly distraught when they realized they were no longer in command of the aircraft, a perfectly understandable reaction. Like pilots, avionics technicians take their control of an aircraft for granted.

The engineer, now fully in command of the 757, next used the aircraft's "S" transponder to upload a different flight plan into the aircraft's flight management computer. The new flight plan instructed the autopilot to "fly" a new course. During this time, the technicians in the cockpit were still out of the loop. All they could do was watch helplessly as the autopilot proceeded to fly the 757 on the newly designated course. Anderson says that Prentice tried to calm them down over the walkie-talkies and even had them pull various circuit breakers to see if they could regain control. But they were unable to do so.

In a subsequent debriefing with the team, Prentice explained what he had done. But he never revealed where he obtained the mysterious software that had allowed him to control the aircraft's flight management computer via remote access. The engineering manager, Prentice's boss, ordered the technicians to hand over all of the documentation for the remote control test, and also made it abundantly clear there would be no further discussion about it. According to Anderson, the manager issued the order after quietly muttering "something about this being a career basher."

Wayne Anderson believes the test utilized "high level commands," not just "control data," and that it also necessarily involved more than the black software on the laptop. The test required a hidden "back door," some kind of firmware, probably engineered into the aircraft when Boeing designed the 757 series.

After the test, Prentice instructed two technicians to thoroughly search the aircraft. But they never found any suspicious equipment or wiring. Anderson was not surprised by this, since the techs did not have authorization from the 757's owner to disassemble any equipment, only to look. In a subsequent email, Anderson explained: "What they were searching for in the aircraft would be a clandestine electrical panel that would provide a parallel source of power. The power switching electronics existed at the time to make this functional under computer control. Also, the hardware would be very small and easy to hide or camouflage. One would have to know very specifically what to look for."[2]

Anderson added that the existence of this type of back door was illegal: a blatant violation of FAA regulations that require all the components in a commercial airliner to be fully documented in the official wiring diagrams. Even so, at the time he assumed that the test only involved proprietary manufacturer's trade secrets, not "black ops stuff," as he put it. [3] After 9/11, his views evolved.

Wayne Anderson's testimony offers powerful support for a scenario posted on the Internet soon after the 9/11 attacks by the late Joe Vialls, a British aeronautical engineer who was one of the first to reject the official story about 9/11. In October 2001, Vialls charged that 9/11 was an inside job staged with black technology. Although Vialls' website has long since disappeared from cyberspace, his original paper fortunately was archived and can still be viewed. He called it "Operation Home Run."[4]

JOE VIALLS' HOME RUN

Vialls claimed that plans for an avionics back door originated as far back as the mid-1970s, when two American multinationals and the US military jointly launched a top-secret research program in response to a sharp increase in the number of terrorist hijackings during that period. According to Vialls, the research program succeeded in taking remote-control technology to a higher level.

The program's goal was laudatory: to cut the hijackers out of the control loop while empowering ground controllers to return a hijacked plane to a chosen airport, where police could then deal with the terrorists. To be truly effective, however, the new fail-safe technology "had to be completely integrated with all onboard systems." This could only be achieved by incorporating it into a new aircraft design.

According to Vialls, this is exactly what happened. A high-level decision was made, and Boeing quietly added a back door to the computer designs for its 757 and 767 commercial jetliners, which were then on the drawing boards. The Boeing 757 and 767 first went into production in the early 1980s.

The security problems inherent with this type of design ought to be self-evident, because the same technology engineered to foil hijackers might just as easily be used to commit acts of terrorism, such as flying planes into tall buildings. It all depends on who is at the controls. Assuming Vialls was correct, and Boeing did develop such a system, one has to wonder why it was never unveiled. It stands to reason that such a system would be an effective deterrent only if potential hijackers understood that they faced certain capture and prosecution.

Vialls also made another startling claim. He contended that Lufthansa airlines discovered the hidden back door soon after taking delivery of a fleet of Boeing jetliners in the 1990s. Lufthansa officials then ordered the Honeywell flight management systems to be stripped out of the Boeings, at considerable trouble and expense. The Honeywell equipment, deemed unacceptable due to the obvious security concerns, was replaced with a German-made counterpart. Although Vialls' claims have never been confirmed, insofar as I know, they have never been refuted either. Today, they need to be carefully revisited in light of Wayne Anderson's tale.

Andreas von Buelow, a former German government minister of research and technology, took Joe Vialls' Home Run scenario seriously enough that he discussed it in his controversial 2003 book, *The CIA and September 11*.[5] Von Buelow also made a stunning charge of his own. He claimed that the 9/11 attack was not the work of Islamic extremists, but was an inside job orchestrated by the CIA.

Von Buelow's provocative book probably helps to account for the dramatic shift in German public opinion about 9/11. A recent poll indicated that 89% of Germans do not believe the official version of events on 9/11.[6] Nor has von Buelow ever retracted his views. On the contrary, in subsequent radio interviews he continued to insist that 9/11 was an "inside job," and that the "hijacked" planes were most likely guided by some type of remote-control technology.[7]

Von Buelow thinks 9/11 was a covert operation carried out by a sub-group within the US intelligence community, probably numbering fewer than fifty persons. He also joined with 9/11 truth activists in calling for a new (and this time, honest) 9/11 investigation. Von Buelow reportedly served on a German intelligence committee as late as the 1990s, and in that capacity had access to classified information. Von Buelow may have been privy to the details concerning Lufthansa's experience with Boeing and perhaps other classified information about 9/11 as well.

9/11 TRUTH AS A PROCESS OF ELIMINATION

The 9/11 Commission Report describes Hani Hanjour, the alleged hijacker pilot of American Airlines Flight 77, as "the [terrorist] operation's most experienced pilot."[8] But an FBI brief released in early 2009,[9] plainly shows that Hanjour had neither the training nor the skills to fly a commercial jetliner. In 2009, after conducting my own extensive review of all the pertinent documents in the case, I estimated the likelihood that Hanjour piloted AA 77 into the Pentagon at "approximately zero."[10] Hanjour was a perpetual novice who, just three weeks before 9/11, flunked a flight test in a one-engine Cessna, one of the easiest planes to fly. One week later, Hanjour also flunked a simple test for a Virginia driver's license.

It seems clear that Hanjour would have been lost in the cockpit of a commercial airliner. Evidently, a number of professional pilots agree with this assessment. One of them, Philip Marshall, who is licensed to fly both 757s and 767s among other commercial planes, offered his professional opinion in his 2008 book *False Flag 911* that the basic flight training the four alleged hijack pilots are known to have had "in no way can explain the expert level of airmanship required for the 9/11 hit." Recounting his own career as a pilot, Marshall stated, "It took me 20 years, dozens of ground school courses, and 15,000 hours between my first lesson and taking command of my first commercial airliner."

Moreover, without advanced training and many additional hours of in-flight experience needed "to understand the momentum of a 767 [or a 757], they [the hijackers] would have been all over the sky and completely out of control."[11] As we know, such was not the case on 9/11. The 9/11 radar data show that three out of the four allegedly hijacked planes maintained tight trajectories en route to their targets. They were not "all over the sky." Anything but.

In this context, another account of 9/11 deserves mention, even though it adheres to the standard jihadists-flew-the-planes scenario. Robert Schopmeyer, owner of a software company in Los Altos, California, is the author of a unique book, *Prior Knowledge of 9/11*, in which he recounts his own stranger-than-fiction tale.[12] Schopmeyer says that seven months before the World Trade Center attacks, he was reading a magazine article about al-Qaeda while passing time on a transcontinental flight from San Francisco to Newark, when he realized that Osama bin Laden's 1998 Fatwa calling for the murder of Americans was, in his words, "nothing less than a declaration of war against the United States."[13]

Using only his native intuition, simple logic and an engineer's capacity for deduction, Schopmeyer concluded that an Islamic attack against the US was in the offing, and would probably target the World Trade Center in New York. His analysis turned out to be correct, down to the smallest details. Schopmeyer anticipated that hijacked airliners would be used as weapons, and even predicted the date of the attack to within about a week. He actually traveled to Boston's Logan Airport on September 8, 2001 in an attempt to spot terrorists surveying airport security points.

For years after the attacks, Schopmeyer endured his own personal purgatory of guilt for not having tried harder to prevent them. I realize that all of this sounds incredible, but several long telephone conversations with Schopmeyer after reading his book convinced me that he is for real.[14] His 9/11 research deserves a lot more attention than it has yet received.

At first, Schopmeyer believed the official story. However, his own personal 9/11 investigation left him "increasingly perplexed regarding the intelligence agencies' excuses for not anticipating and preventing ... 9/11."[15] A turning point occurred at the 9/11 Commission hearings of April 13-14, 2004, which he attended. Schopmeyer told me that he became enraged listening to CIA Director George Tenet spin obvious lies to the Commission.

In Schopmeyer's words, the CIA chief's testimony was "so abysmally absurd that it was impossible to understand why the mainstream media gave Tenet a pass."[16] The lying was so transparent that, according to Schopmeyer, just about everyone in the audience was aware of it, including the families of the victims sitting in the front two rows who were shaking their heads, visibly agitated by Tenet's dissembling. At the hearing, Schopmeyer handed copies of his own account (in an FBI interview) to several of the Commissioners. One of them, Bob Kerrey was so impressed that he came over and inquired in all seriousness why Schopmeyer was not working on the counter-terrorism unit at the CIA.

In subsequent days, Schopmeyer continued his own personal investigation. In July 2004, for example, he conducted a two-hour interview with Coleen Rowley and her boss in Minneapolis. Rowley, you may recall, was the whistleblower FBI agent who revealed, in an open letter to Bureau director Robert Mueller in May 2002, how the bizarre obstructionism of various intelligence officials delayed FBI agents in the Minneapolis field office from obtaining a search warrant for Zacarias Moussaoui's laptop computer, already in custody after his arrest for overstaying his visa. Moussaoui was a hypothetical "twentieth hijacker," and his laptop held information which might have prevented the attacks, if FBI agents had been granted access. Moussaoui was convicted of various terrorism-related charges in 2006 and sentenced to life in prison.

Today, Schopmeyer can cite chapter and verse from many of the official 9/11 reports, large portions of which he has apparently committed to memory. These include the 2002 *Joint Inquiry Report* prepared by the Joint House/Senate Intelligence Committee, *The 9/11 Commission Report* released in 2004, both versions of the *Department of Justice Inspector General Report* (i.e., the November 2004 redacted version and the May 2006 unredacted version), the 2006 account of FBI agent Ali Soufan, and the 2007 *Report by the CIA's Inspector General.*

One of these documents I had not even heard about. Although several of the official reports were heavily redacted to keep the public in the dark, Schopmeyer defeated the censors in several instances by aggregating and crosschecking all of the reports, which enabled him to fill in key names and connect the dots.

Schopmeyer has gone further down this particular line of research than anyone else I am aware of, including Lawrence Wright, author of the bestselling *The Looming Tower*. Whereas Wright leaves numerous loose ends, Schopmeyer offers a consistent account of what probably happened, including a rational explanation for the CIA disconnects and how, time and again, the Agency withheld key evidence that would have enabled the FBI to roll up the terrorists and prevent the attacks.

In Schopmeyer's view, these were not just missteps, but a deliberate and criminal pattern of obstruction of the honest field agents who were trying to do their job and protect the nation. Ultimately, Schopmeyer succeeded in exposing most of the chain of command at the CIA that was responsible. From the top down, the chain goes from George Tenet to Cofer Black to Richard Blee to Tom Wilshire, the foot soldier who, in May 2001, was ordered to monitor the FBI investigation, and to intervene as necessary to keep the FBI guessing.[17]

Elsewhere, I have argued that the order by Pentagon higher-ups to destroy vast amounts of intelligence data became "necessary" after a legitimate counter-terrorism operation known as Able Danger threatened to expose the plot-within-a-plot.[18] By February 2000, Lt Col. Anthony Shaffer and his fellow staffers at Able Danger, based at Ft. Belvoir, Virginia, had learned the identity of Mohamed Atta and the other hijackers by means of data-mining: sweeping the Internet with powerful search engines. When higher-ups learned of their success, they ordered the Able Danger staffers to shut down their operation and to destroy 2.5 terabytes of intelligence data.

I suspect that similar steps may have been deemed necessary where other individuals stood in the way, and therefore had to be replaced or removed to enable the plot-within-a-plot to proceed. Michael Scheuer's case is a possible example. In 1996, Scheuer set up the CIA's bin Laden desk, Alec Station (named after Scheuer's son), and directed it until Director Tenet removed him in June 1999. Scheuer's replacement was Richard Blee, whose role in the pre-9/11 period has remained obscure.

Several 9/11 Commission files refer to Blee, but never by name, either by an alias or with a nondescript label like "an intelligence officer." The US media has done likewise, referring to Blee only by a number of aliases. In his book *Ghost Wars*, Steve Coll refers to Blee as "Rich," and in his memoirs George Tenet refers to him as "Rich B." Wikipedia identifies Blee only as "Richard" or "Rich" or "Richie."[19]

Why the obscurity? Possibly to conceal Blee's role as the critical link in the chain of command between Blee's superiors Cofer Black and George Tenet on the one hand, and his immediate subordinate, Tom Wilshire, on the other. Schopmeyer thinks Wilshire was the willing foot soldier carrying out orders from above to obstruct the FBI's domestic surveillance, so that 9/11 would go off as planned. Blee's identity would have to be shielded to conceal his true role and protect his superiors.

After 9/11, Blee was reassigned to Kabul, Afghanistan, where he became CIA station chief. In that capacity, he appears to have presided over the escape of Osama bin Laden from Tora Bora.[20]

But I digress. Returning to the issue of remote control, Schopmeyer thinks the CIA was complicit in the attacks, but he also believes that the hijackings really happened and that the terrorists actually flew the planes into the buildings. Although I disagree, his conclusions are otherwise so credible that his argument deserves mention.

Schopmeyer is a pilot himself, and he argues that the hijacker pilots' lack of experience gave them a surprising advantage. He thinks they achieved the near impossible, not despite their lack of training but, strangely, because of it. How so? Quite simply, because Hani Hanjour, Mohamed Atta, and Marwan al Shehhi did *not* stop to consider the level of difficulty of what they were attempting to do. They succeeded *precisely because* they did not stop to think. They simply shoved the stick forward with a single-minded determination, and flew into history.

I do not buy this scenario, because the available evidence shows that the alleged terrorist pilots did not have nerves of steel, quite the contrary. Hani Hanjour, for example, the most experienced of the four terrorist pilots according to the 9/11 Commission was a rather timid and incompetent fellow. Hanjour's personal issues were not limited to his inability to learn English: the man could not even remember the PIN number for his own bank account.

I simply cannot picture him having the resolve to hold the stick firm to the very end. I see his hand wavering. At the speed of AA 77, the slightest waver would have plunged the craft nose-down into the Pentagon lawn, long before striking the building.

WERE THE HIJACKERS HIJACKED?

My own beliefs have evolved by degrees. I have come around to the view that the Islamic plot to hijack planes was probably real, and that it may even have originated with Osama bin Laden and his cohorts. But the evidence also points to the likely involvement of private corporate interests, with the complicity of various members of the G.W. Bush administration and elements of the US military and intelligence establishments, possibly freelancers. I also wonder about Israeli involvement.

Indeed, I suspect it was the Israelis who initially penetrated bin Laden's operation in Afghanistan. The sum total of evidence points to a plot within a plot. Evildoers guided the jihadist plan, semi-controlling it, augmenting it in various ways, and ultimately making it serve a very different purpose, for which the only adjective is "diabolical." In short, the spooks hijacked the hijackers, and they succeeded because of cutting-edge technology, which was the handmaiden of the operation. Reality can be stranger than fiction, a lot stranger.

According to Sir Arthur Conan Doyle's legendary detective Sherlock Holmes, "When you have eliminated the impossible, whatever remains must be the truth." Holmes' logic applies to the unsolved crimes of September 11, and has a special relevance to the question of who was flying the planes.

If Hani Hanjour was not at the helm of AA 77, there are only two other possibilities, each involving a different type of remote-control technology. Either perpetrators remotely accessed and controlled the flight control systems of the "hijacked" planes using the type of black technology described by Wayne Anderson, or they somehow managed to replace all of the "hijacked" planes with look-alike drones wired for remote control in the more conventional manner.

Over the years, a number of 9/11 researchers have entertained one or another version of the plane-swap hypothesis, which in my opinion deserves consideration because a plane-swap was included in a Cold War-era plan that almost became operational. Operation Northwoods was a covert false-flag terrorist scheme hatched by the Joint Chiefs of Staff in 1962 as a pretext for a US invasion of Cuba. The previously secret memoranda documenting the proposals were declassified upon release in 1997 by the J.F.K. Assassination Records Review Board.

One of Northwoods' mock attacks (the plan also proposed real attacks on Americans) involved the mid-flight swap of an identical drone for a chartered civilian aircraft, which would then be safely diverted. The identical drone would continue on the chartered plane's designated flight path, carefully selected to overfly Cuba, where it would transmit false MAYDAY signals indicating attack by Cuban MIG's. The drone would then be exploded over the Caribbean by radio signal.

First revealed in 2001 by former National Security Agency employee James Bamford,[21] the plan was never implemented. President John F. Kennedy rejected it out of hand and fired the Chairman of the Joint Chiefs, General Lyman Lemnitzer (who had already antagonized the president in other ways). The record plainly shows that US military strategists are capable of such schemes. Yet, insofar as I am aware, no one has produced a scintilla of evidence that a plane swap occurred on September 11, 2001.

This is no surprise because the plane-swap scenario suffers from insurmountable difficulties. Northwoods assumed an unquestioning compliance by the unharmed crew and passengers of the diverted flight, who were to be sworn to secrecy, while a new list of dummy aliases was substituted for the actual passenger list. Taking that level of compliance for granted was unlikely in 1962, and certainly unimaginable in 21st century America.

Other nagging questions also bedevil the plane-swap scenario. If commercial aircraft were swapped for drones on 9/11, what became of the passengers and crew? And what happened to the swapped planes? These are salient questions. It seems obvious that the planned scenario of Operation Northwoods does not translate well to September 11, 2001.

True, not all of the difficulties would apply in the case of a different variant of the plane-swap hypothesis. Journalist Christopher Bollyn thinks the Israeli Mossad somehow staged a plane swap *before* flights AA 11 and UAL 175 took off from Boston's Logan International Airport. Bollyn has been investigating IAI (Israeli Aerospace Industries, formerly known as Israeli Aircraft Industries), which controls several aircraft leasing and maintenance companies in the United States, one of which, ATASCO, began operating in the early 1970s.[22] Bollyn says [23]that within hours after he contacted Shalon Yoran, the former Israeli chairman of ATASCO, three undercover policemen arrived at his house, tasered him, and broke his elbow in front of his wife and children.

IAI reportedly specializes in converting Boeing aircraft into tankers, and has done this for a variety of customers since the early 1980s. According to the *Jerusalem Post*, IAI completed its first conversion of a Boeing 767 passenger jet into a cargo plane in 2000.[24] For these reasons, it is theoretically possible that Israeli agents helped arrange a plane swap just prior to 9/11. To date, however, neither Bollyn nor anyone has presented any evidence that this actually happened, and his scenario must be viewed as purely speculative.

In recent years, Bollyn's online articles have explored the suspicious role on 9/11 of an Israeli-owned security firm, International Consultants on Targeted Security International (ICTS), which was founded in 1982 by former members of El Al (Israeli Airlines) and the Shin Bet (currently known as Shabak), the Israeli equivalent of the FBI. A subsidiary of ICTS, Huntleigh USA, reportedly shared security duties at Logan International on September 11, 2001. Curiously, ICTS also handled security at Charles de Gaulle Airport near Paris in December 2001, when the mentally disturbed "shoe bomber" Richard Reid successfully boarded a US-bound jetliner.

Nor is this all. The Israeli company also had the security contract for London's bus system at the time of the infamous July 7, 2005 terrorist bombings in London.[25] According to an Associated Press report, then-Israeli Finance Minister (and once-and-future Prime Minister) Benjamin Netanyahu that morning canceled plans to attend an economic conference in a hotel located above the subway stop where one of the blasts occurred, *after* receiving a last-minute warning from the British police.[26] In a bizarre twist, the AP subsequently retracted the story following an emphatic denial from the Israeli embassy.

Meanwhile, Stratfor, a private security firm, reported that the press got it exactly backwards. Stratfor claimed it was actually Israeli government officials who warned Scotland Yard, not vice versa. According to Stratfor, the Israeli warning came several days *earlier*, but the British chose not to act.[27]

An ICTS subsidiary was also responsible for security at Amsterdam's Schiphol Airport on Christmas day 2009, when the so called "underwear bomber," a Nigerian named Umar Farouk Abdulmutallab, successfully boarded Northwest Airlines Flight 253, bound for Detroit.[28] Abdulmutallab was arrested after he attempted to detonate plastic explosives hidden in his underwear, which fortunately failed to go off. This means that ICTS personnel were at the scene of four of the most notorious terrorist attacks of recent years, and on each occasion failed to prevent the attack.[29] Was this merely a set of coincidences?

But whatever role Isrealis may have had in the events of 9/11, the complexities of a plane-swap operation make this an unrealistic alternative to the elegant simplicity of remote control. In March 2007, after posting an article on the Internet in which I speculated about the use of remote-control technology on 9/11, I heard from a veteran pilot with more than forty-five years flying experience. "If there truly is a back door," he wrote, "then it would be a simple matter to have remotely done 9/11." According to this veteran pilot, a single transmitter in a window of each World Trade tower and at the Pentagon would have provided all of the necessary guidance for a "routine autopilot coupled approach."[30]

Although generally unknown by the public, the computerized flight management system in commercial airliners is so advanced that pilots seldom touch the controls. A modern autopilot, officially termed the "flight director," is more than capable of flying a modern passenger jet from takeoff to landing. Moreover, as good as the system already was, in the mid-to-late 1990s the airline industry achieved a quantum jump in navigation performance with the rapid development of Global Positioning System (GPS) technology, a critical path that my colleague Aidan Monaghan covers very thoroughly in this book's Foreword and Afterword.

Despite strenuous efforts, however, I have not been able to independently confirm that the remote control test reported by Wayne Anderson actually took place. In August 2010, I located the engineer David Prentice, who was then employed in Houston at Continental Airlines. I reached Prentice at work and spoke with him over the telephone. He remembered Wayne Anderson from his days at Dalfort Aviation; this in itself was a partial confirmation. However, Prentice denied staging a remote control test at Love Field.[31] I was left with the frustration that so often attends 9/11 research, a field wherein promising leads so often play out in fuzzyland, or sputter in the face of denial.

Wayne Anderson was not in the least surprised by David Prentice's response, however, and he may have the right perspective. After all, Prentice still works in the airline industry. Were he to acknowledge his central part in staging an unauthorized test of what surely must have been a highly classified type of software (assuming Anderson's story is accurate), it is a safe bet that disclosure might wreck Prentice's career. The likely loss of both job and retirement benefits would be reason enough to deny everything. And who knows? An affirmation could have even more serious consequences. The national security apparatus does not look kindly upon impertinent leaks of black technologies that officially do not exist. Individuals have been made to disappear for less.

There is a simple way to determine if Wayne Anderson is telling the truth. If Boeing did hardwire a back door into its commercial airliners, records of this must exist, records that a genuine 9/11 investigation could subpoena. And if it turns out that the records have gone missing, or, if by some act of God a raging fire should sweep through the Boeing offices where the records are stored, well, there would still be the physical evidence, i.e, the firmware.

Ten years after 9/11, roughly a thousand Boeing 757s and more than eight hundred 767s remained in active service. Not even the most inventive covert agent is going to find a way to vanish every last one of them.

(ENDNOTES)

1   http://pilotsfor911truth.org/forum/index.php?showtopic=20048.

2   Ibid.

3   Email from Wayne Anderson, March 30, 2011.

4   http://www.sweetliberty.org/issues/war/homerun.htm.

5   von Buelow, Andreas, *Die CIA und der 11. September. Internationaler Terror und die Rolle der Geheimdienste.* (München: Piper Verlag GmbH, 2003)

6   http://911blogger.com/news/2011-01-21/poll-germany-895-doubt-official-version-911.

7   An audio file of one of these interviews is available at http://www.prisonplanet.tv/audio/200406vonbuelow.htm.

8   The source cited by the Commission is a CIA-prepared report based on the CIA interrogation of Kalid Sheikh Mohammed (aka KSM), who, as former President George Bush recently acknowledged, was waterboarded 183 times. Might this explain the comment about Hani Hanjour's flight experience? As Jesse Ventura recently told Larry King, "Give me Dick Cheney, a waterboard, and one hour, and I'll have Cheney confessing to the murder of Sharon Tate." *The 9/11 Commission Report*, p. 530.

9   http://911myths.com/images/2/2a/PENTTBOM_About_Hanjour.pdf.

10   http://www.globalresearch.ca/index.php?context=va&aid=14290.

11   Philip Marshall, *False Flag 911* (Amazon.com: BookSurge Publishing, 2008), p. 33.

12   Robert Schopmeyer, *Prior Knowledge of 9/11* (Palo Alto: Palo Alto Publishing, 4th ed. 2010)

13   Email from Robert Schopmeyer, April 14, 2011.

14   Conversations with Robert Schopmeyer, September 22, 2010, December 20, 2010, and April 5, 2011.

15   See note 13

16   See note 13

17   The complex means by which CIA personnel blocked FBI investigaters' discovery of two watchlisted al-Qaeda terrorists (who became 9/11 hijackers) known by the CIA to be residing openly in the San Diego area are discussed in detail by Kevin Fenton, *Disconnecting the Dots* (Walterville, OR: TrineDay, 2011)

18   Mark H. Gaffney, *The 9/11 Mystery Plane* (Walterville, OR: TrineDay, 2008), pp. 117-19.

19   http://en.wikipedia.org/wiki/Bin_Laden_Issue_Station.

20   Kevin Fenton, "Identity Of CIA Officer Responsible For Pre-9/11 Failures, Tora Bora Escape, Rendition To Torture Revealed," *9/11 Blogger*, September 11, 2009, posted at http://911blogger.com/news/2009-09-11/identity-cia-officer-responsible-pre-911-failures-tora-bora-escape-rendition-torture-revealed.

21   James Bamford, *Body of Secrets* (New York: Anchor Books, 2001), pp. 85-87.

22   *Washington Post*, September 11, 1978.

23   http://www.bollyn.com/solving-9-11-the-book#article_11260

24   *Jerusalem Post*, April 4, 2000.

25   Patrick Martin, "Why is the American press silent on the Israeli role in NW Flight 253?," *World Socialist Web Site*, January 16, 2010, posted at http://www.wsws.org/articles/2010/jan2010/f253-j16.shtml.

26   Amy Teibel, "Netanyahu Changed Plans Due to Warning," Associated Press, July 7, 2005, posted at http://web.archive.org/web/20050709002013/http://news.yahoo.com/s/ap/20050707/ap_on_re_mi_ea/israel_britain_explosions_1.

27   The chronology of the July 7, 2005 London bombings is posted at http://www.historycommons.org/timeline.jsp?complete_911_timeline_alleged_al_qaeda_linked_attacks=complete_911_timeline_2005_7_7_london_bombings&timeline=complete_911_timeline

28   Yossi Melman, "Israeli firm blasted for letting would-be plane bomber slip through," *Ha'aretz*, January 10, 2010, posted at http://www.haaretz.com/print-edition/news/israeli-firm-blasted-for-letting-would-be-plane-bomber-slip-through-1.261107.

29   Patrick Martin, see note 21.

30   Email from "old geezer pilot." February 25, 2007.

31   Conversation with David Prentice. June 21, 2010.

Hani Hanjour

Chapter 12

Key Evidence Suppressed

In August 2004 when the 9/11 Commission completed its official investigation of the September 11, 2001 attacks, the Commission transferred custody of its voluminous records to the National Archives and Records Administration,[1] where the records remained under lock and key for four and a half years. In January 2009, NARA released a considerable fraction (about 35% of the total) for public viewing. Each day, more of the released files are scanned and posted on the Internet, making them readily accessible.

Although most of the newly released documents are of little interest, a select few contain important new information. Several files show that the FBI and 9/11 Commission suppressed crucial evidence about Hani Hanjour, the alleged hijack pilot of American Airlines Flight 77. By undermining the official explanation that Hani Hanjour crashed AA 77 into the Pentagon at high speed after executing an extremely difficult top-gun maneuver, this evidence indirectly supports the case for remotely controlled aircraft. But to understand how all of this plays out, it is best to approach the story in bite-sized pieces.

As we know, the 9/11 Commission did not begin its work until late 2003, more than two years after the attacks. By this time, a number of journalists had already done independent research and published articles about various aspects of 9/11. Some of this work was of excellent quality. The *Washington Post*, for example, interviewed aviation experts who said that AA 77 had been flown "with extraordinary skill, making it highly likely that a trained pilot was at the helm."[2] Experts told CNN the same story: the hijackers, including Hani Hanjour, must have been extremely knowledgeable and capable aviators. "They knew what they were doing," said one pilot who had been with a major carrier for more than thirty years.[3]

Air Traffic Controllers agreed. Danielle O'Brien, who was working in the radar room at Dulles Airport on 9/11 and who handled the routine, on-time departure of American Flight 77, later tracked the blip as it sped toward the Pentagon. "The speed," she told *ABC News*, "the maneuverability, the way that he turned, we all thought in the radar room, all of us experienced air traffic controllers, that that was a military plane."[4]

CBS interviewed experts who said that the hijacker pilot of AA 77 executed a difficult high-speed descending turn, during which the aircraft dropped 7,000 feet in two and a half minutes. "The steep turn was so smooth, the sources said, it's clear there was no fight for control going on. And the complex maneuver suggests the hijackers had better flying skills than many investigators first believed."[5] In a related story, the *Washington Post* quoted an expert who described the steep, accurate descent into the Pentagon as the work of "a great talent ... virtually a textbook turn and landing."[6]

Yet, strangely, when journalists investigated Hani Hanjour himself, they found a trail of clues indicating he was a novice pilot, wholly incapable of executing any top-gun maneuver, let alone in a Boeing 757. By early 2003, this independent research was a matter of public record, which created a serious problem for the 9/11 Commission.

By all accounts, 29-year-old Hani Hanjour was a diminutive fellow. He stood five-feet-five and was slight of build. As a young man in his hometown of Taif, Saudi Arabia, Hanjour cultivated no great dreams of flying airplanes. The man was satisfied with a more modest ambition: he wanted to become a flight attendant. That is, until his older brother Abulrahman encouraged him to aim higher.

Even so, Hani's aptitude for learning appears to have been rather limited. Although he resided in the US for about thirty-eight months during the ten-year period leading up to September 11, 2001, Hanjour never learned to speak or write English.

While it is true that Hani Hanjour trained at various flight schools in the US, the evidence shows he was a perpetual novice. Hanjour dropped out of his first school, the Sierra Academy of Aeronautics, located in Oakland, California, after attending only a few classes. Next, he enrolled at Cockpit Resource Management (CRM), a flight school in Scottsdale, Arizona. But his performance as a student was less than satisfactory. Paul V. Blair, the school's controller, told the

New York Times that Hanjour was a "a lackadaisical student who often cut class."[7]

Duncan K.M. Hastie, owner of the school, described Hanjour as "a weak student" who was "wasting our resources."[8] After several weeks, Hanjour withdrew from the program, but then returned in 1997 for another short period of instruction. This on-and-off pattern of behavior was typical of the man. Hastie says that over the next three years Hanjour called him at least twice a year, and each time wanted to return for more training.

By this time, however, it was obvious to Hastie that his erstwhile student had no business in a cockpit. Hastie refused to let Hanjour come back. "I would recognize his voice," Hastie said. "He was always talking about wanting more training. Yes, he wanted to be an airline pilot. That was his stated goal. That's why I didn't allow him to come back. I thought 'You're never going to make it.'"[9]

Rejected by CRM, Hanjour enrolled at nearby Sawyer Aviation, also located in the Phoenix area. Wes Fults, a former instructor at Sawyer, later described it as the school of last resort: "It was a commonly held truth that, if you failed anywhere else, go to Sawyer." Fults remembers training Hanjour, whom he describes as "a neophyte." He says Hani "got overwhelmed with the instruments" in the school's flight simulator. "He had only the barest understanding of what the instruments were there to do," said Fults. Hanjour "used the simulator three or four times, then disappeared like a fog."[10]

I must emphasize to the reader: I am not making this up. The record is clear on this point. Other accounts cited here, by *Newsday*, the *New York Times* and the FOX network, all agree that Hani Hanjour was a novice pilot.

In 1998, Hanjour enrolled at another flight school in the area, Arizona Aviation. There, his initial trainer was a Japanese flight instructor who later submitted a detailed statement to the FBI about his impressions of Hanjour. We do not know the instructor's name, which is redacted from the document, but he claimed that he instructed Hani Hanjour "for about four months," from May to September 1998.

The instructor's comments are telling: "I knew him only professionally; he was generally quiet, and his English was poor.... He was not well educated nor was he very intelligent.... As a person I found Hanjour fairly easy to get along with. He smiled often and was easy going. I did not think that he was the type of person to become an airline pilot. He was a follower and not a leader, had few opinions of his own and had, in my view, almost no initiative. Consequently I very seriously doubt that he had any organizational or leadership role in the events of September 11th.... As a pilot Hani Hanjour was very poor. His knowledge of the academic side of training was weak, his flying skills were marginal, but most significantly his judgment was very poor."[11]

The Japanese instructor goes on to explain that on one occasion Hanjour failed to remember even the most rudimentary protocol: he was about to take off on a training flight with a near-empty fuel tank, and would have if the instructor had not caught the error and reminded him to be more careful. Strangely, when the instructor "questioned him about the lack of fuel," Hanjour "seemed mildly amused rather than appalled by his possibly life-threatening mistake."

The instructor concludes his testimonial as follows: "In retrospect, Hani Hanjour was not someone cut out to be a pilot. He had no motivation, a poor understanding of the basic principles of aviation, and poor judgment, combined with poor technical skills. His personality was weak and I have no doubt that he could have been easily persuaded to do almost anything."[12]

The Japanese instructor's description appears to fit the profile of a patsy – not a determined suicide bomber with the flying skills of a seasoned test pilot.

EVADING THE LANGUAGE REQUIREMENT/OBSCURING THE RECORD

In the United States, fluency in English is required to qualify for a pilot's license, for which reason Hanjour's atrocious English should have barred him from ever obtaining a license. But it appears that Hanjour exploited a loophole in the Federal Aviation Administration system, which for years has outsourced the pilot certification process. According to a June 2002 story in the *Dallas Morning News*, Hanjour was certified in April 1999 as an "Airplane Multi-Engine Land/Commercial Pilot" by Daryl Strong, one of the FAA's 20,000 designated pilot examiners.[13]

Although an FAA official later defended the agency's policy of using private contractors, some critics, including Heather Awsumb, took issue with it. Awsumb is a spokesperson for the Professional Airways Systems Specialists Union, which represents more than 11,000 FAA and Defense Department employees. She pointed out that the FAA does not have anywhere near enough staff to oversee its 20,000 designated inspectors, all of whom have a financial interest in certifying as many pilots as possible.

It seems that Hanjour evaded the language requirement by finding an examiner willing to ignore the rule. Said Awsumb, "They receive between $200 and $300 for each flight check. If they get a reputation for being too tough, they won't get any business." According to Awsumb, the present system allows "safety to be sold to the lowest bidder."[14]

I must also emphasize that Hani Hanjour's commercial license did *not* qualify him to fly commercial airliners, only *to begin training* to fly them. When he subsequently enrolled at Jet Tech International, another flight school in the Phoenix area, Hanjour's horrible English prompted school officials to question the authenticity of his FAA-approved pilot's license. Peggy Chevrette, operation manager at Jet Tech, later told *FOX News*: "I couldn't believe that he had a license of any kind with the skills that he had."[15] She explained that Hanjour's English was so bad it took him five hours to complete an exam that normally should have taken about two.

But it wasn't just his poor English that failed to impress. In his evaluation, the Jet Tech flight instructor Rodney McAlear wrote, "Student made numerous errors during his performance and displayed a lack of understanding of some basic concepts. The same was true during review of systems knowledge ... Hani is very intelligent, but to move beyond the comprehension level (or rote level in some cases) Hani needs more experience ... I doubt his ability to pass an FAA [Boeing 737] oral [exam] at this time or in the near future." The 737 instructor also concluded his evaluation of Hanjour with a significant comment: "He will need much more experience flying smaller A/C [aircraft] before he is ready to master large jets."[16]

Thus, although McAlear differed from the Japanese flight instructor in his estimate of Hanjour's intelligence, he nonetheless reached the same conclusions about Hanjour's poor flying skills.

The 9/11 Commission Report fails to discuss or even mention these negative written evaluations, even while presenting Hanjo-

ur's substandard performance in a Boeing 737 simulator as sufficient evidence that Hanjour could fly a Boeing 757, an even larger
plane. The wording of the final report succeeds in giving this dubious impression, while obscuring the facts: an amazing achievement
of propaganda.[17]

Early in 2001, Peggy Chevrette, the operation manager at Jet Tech,
contacted the FAA repeatedly to convey her concerns about Hanjour. According to Chevrette, a federal inspector eventually showed
up at the school and examined Hanjour's credentials, but found
them to be in order and took no further action. Apparently he even
suggested that Jet Tech provide Hanjour with an interpreter. This
surprised Chevrette, because it was a violation of FAA rules.

"The thing that really concerned me," she later told *FOX News*,
"was that [the inspector] had a conversation in the hallway with
Hani and realized what his skills were at that point and his ability to
speak English."[18] Evidently, the inspector also sat in on a class with
Hanjour.

FOX News was unable to reach the inspector for comment, but
FAA spokesperson Laura Brown defended the FAA employee.
"There was nothing about the pilot's actions" she said, "to signal
criminal intent or that would have caused us to alert law enforcement."[19] This is true enough. The Jet Tech staff also never suspected
that Hani Hanjour was a terrorist.

But that is not the point. According to Marilyn Ladner, vice-president of Pan Am International, which owned Jet Tech: "It was more
of a very typical instructional concern that *'you really shouldn't be
in the air'*" [my emphasis].[20] Although Pan Am dissolved its Jet Tech
operation shortly after 9/11, a former employee who knew Hanjour
expressed amazement "that he could have flown into the Pentagon.
He could not fly at all."[21]

The "Scouting" Flights

We know that in the months before the September 11, 2001 attacks, Hani Hanjour rented planes at several small airports
on the outskirts of New York City and Washington DC. *The 9/11
Commission Report* mentions these local flights and suggests that
Hanjour was scouting the terrain: familiarizing himself with possible targets.[22]

But the record here also shows the same pattern described above. For example, on May 29, 2001 Hanjour rented a plane at a small airport in Teterboro, New Jersey and flew the "Hudson Tour," accompanied by a flight instructor. However, the next day, when Hanjour returned for a repeat flight, the same instructor "would not allow it because of Hanjour's poor piloting skills."[23] *The 9/11 Commission Report* actually cites this incident, but in a context that diminishes its significance.[24]

This pattern played out again on August 16 and 17, 2001, when Hanjour attempted to rent a plane at Freeway Airport, in Bowie, Maryland, about twenty miles from Washington. According to a report in *Newsday*, although Hanjour presented his FAA license, the Freeway manager insisted that instructors first accompany him on a test flight to evaluate his piloting skills. During three such flights over two days in a single-engine Cessna 172, instructors Sheri Baxter and Ben Conner observed what others had before them.

Hanjour had trouble controlling and landing the aircraft. Afterward, Baxter interviewed Hanjour extensively about his flight training and experience, and she also reviewed his flight log, which documented six hundred hours of flight time. On the basis of that record, she and Conner declined to approve a current license rating until Hanjour returned for more training. On their recommendation, Freeway's chief instructor Marcel Bernard refused to rent Hanjour a plane.[25] This was less than a month before 9/11.

When I reached Bernard by phone, he confirmed the details of the *Newsday* account.[26] So did Ben Conner when I spoke with him.[27]

The 9/11 Commission Report acknowledges Hanjour's poor English and substandard flying skills. The report even mentions that flight instructors had urged Hanjour to give up trying to become a pilot.[28] As stated previously, however, an endnote describes him as "the operation's most experienced pilot," suggesting that the Commission may have had a mixed opinion about Hanjour.[29] In the end the official investigation evidently interpreted Hanjour's FAA license as sufficient proof he had "persevered" in overcoming his aviation handicaps.[30]

But why did the Commission ignore the multiple open-sourced accounts cited above, all mutually corroborative, indicating that Hanjour would have been lost in the cockpit of a Boeing 757 and that he was barely qualified to fly a single-engine Cessna? It is astonishing that *The 9/11 Commission Report* fails to mention the negative written evaluations by the Japanese instructor and the instructor at Jet Tech.

The omission of the latter is particularly troubling, because a glance at the timeline shows that Hanjour's five to six weeks of training at Jet Tech occurred in February and March 2001, that is, *after* he had already earned his FAA license. Perseverance obviously was not enough. The instructor's negative evaluation was based on Hanjour's skill set at the time.

Nor does the final report mention Hanjour's failed test flight at Freeway Airport. These are telling omissions. The Commission clearly screened out testimony that conflicted with the official narrative of what happened on that terrible day.

THE OTHER FLIGHT INSTRUCTOR

The NARA files released since 2009 raise further issues. It turns out that just three days after Hani Hanjour failed a flight evaluation in a Cessna 172 at Freeway Airport, he showed up at Congressional Air Charters, located down the road at Montgomery County Airpark in Gaithersburg, Maryland, also in the Washington suburbs. Once again, Hanjour attempted to rent a plane, and again he was asked to go up with an instructor for a flight evaluation to confirm his flight skills. The plane was the same: a Cessna 172.

Yet, on this occasion Hanjour passed with flying colors and this other instructor later gave testimony to the commission that turned out to be crucial. Their *Report* mentions the instructor's name only once, in a brief note buried at the back in small print, as is typical of its treatment of crucial data:

> Hanjour successfully conducted a challenging certification flight supervised by an instructor at Congressional Air Charter of Gaithersburg, Maryland, landing at a small airport with a difficult approach. The instructor thought Hanjour may have had training from a military pilot because he used a terrain recognition system for navigation. Eddie Shalev interview. (Apr. 9, 2004)[31]

The note gives a name, "Eddie Shalev," but no other information about him. Indeed, his identity remained a mystery until January 2009, when NARA released the 9/11 files.[32] But David Ray Griffin had already identified the key questions in his 2008 book *The New Pearl Harbor Revisited*: "How could an instructor in Gaithersburg have had such a radically different view of Hanjour's abilities from that of all of the other flight instructors who worked with him? Who was this instructor? How could this report be verified?"[33]

These are important questions because two individuals' assessments of Hani Hanjour's flight skills, separated by only three days, are so radically different that both cannot be correct. Contradictory reports raise the question of who is telling the truth.

THE FBI FILE

Fortunately, one of the newly released documents, an FBI file on Hani Hanjour, sheds additional light on the case.[34] The file includes a timeline, and it evidently was compiled to document the government's case against Hanjour. I learned about it from Miles Kara, who served as a staffer on the 9/11 Commission, and who insisted to me in an email that the file verifies Hani Hanjour's expertise as a pilot.

At a glance it appears to do that. On closer examination however, the file is much less impressive, and I have to wonder if Kara actually studied it. As we will see, the document not only falls short of confirming Hanjour's flight skills, it shows signs of having been "enhanced" to obscure the record.

Crucially, the FBI file includes not one scintilla of evidence that Hani Hanjour ever trained in a Boeing 757. Although, as we know, Hanjour did some sessions in a *Boeing 737 simulator*, the press accounts, and more importantly his own instructors' written evaluations, offer a clear and unambiguous assessment of his actual skills.

It is also important to realize that even if Hanjour *had* mastered the controls of a Boeing 737 on the simulator, this would *not* have qualified him to fly a Boeing 757, which is a significantly larger and less maneuverable aircraft. These are the views of commercial pilots who fly these planes every day.[35]

Philip Marshall, one such pilot who is licensed to fly Boeing 727s, 737s, 747s, 757s and 767s, in his book *False Flag 911*, states categorically that none of the alleged 9/11 hijacker pilots could have flown 757s and 767s into buildings at high speed without advanced training and practice flights in that same aircraft over a period of months. As Marshall put it: "Hitting a 90-foot target [i.e., the Pentagon] with a 757 at 500 mph is extremely difficult—absolutely impossible for first-time fliers of a heavy airliner. It's like seeing Tiger Woods hit a 300-yard one-iron, and someone telling you he never practiced the shot."[36]

Marshall speculates that the hijackers may have received advanced flight lessons from Arabic-speaking instructors at a secret desert base somewhere in Arizona or Nevada, possibly arranged by complicit Saudi diplomats or by members of the Saudi royal family.[37] However, Hanjour's inability to pass a test flight evaluation in a one-engine Cessna at Freeway airport, just weeks before 9/11 effectively rules out Marshall's theory of advanced instruction.

Close inspection of the FBI file shows that someone padded the record, evidently to put the best face on Hanjour's flight training. This was done in a curious way. Instead of simply informing us that Hanjour took courses "x," "y" and "z" at such-and-such a flight school between certain dates, the FBI file gives *an itemized record of every single day* that Hanjour showed up for training at the various schools

This creates the appearance of more extensive instruction than actually occurred. Even so, the enhancement becomes transparent upon examination. The day-by-day detail also obscures Hanjour's tendency to jump around from school to school and his inability to finish anything he started, which would appear clearly in a more standard, summary account.

The FBI file also conspicuously fails to mention the Jet Tech instructor's written evaluation of Hani Hanjour's flying skills. The omission is serious, and qualifies as suppression of evidence, because we know the FBI had the document in its possession. The document was first made public at the trial of Zacarias Moussaoui in 2004, when it was submitted as evidence. This means, of course, that the 9/11 Commission also had the document and suppressed it.

The FBI file also grossly mischaracterizes what happened at Freeway Airport. The file mentions Hanjour's visits, but wrongly indicates that Hanjour received flight instruction. When I specifically asked Marcel Bernard about this, he categorically denied it and emphasized that Hanjour's test flights included no lessons and were strictly for the purpose of evaluation.[38]

The FBI should have known this because Bernard and his two flight instructors notified the FBI after 9/11 about Hanjour's visit, and they were subsequently interviewed by FBI agents. The file, however, makes no mention of these interviews. The file also conspicuously fails to mention that Hanjour flunked his test flight evaluation. Whether through incompetence or deception, the FBI failed to state the facts correctly.

The FBI file does, however, offer some fresh insights into Hani Hanjour the man. On August 2, 2001, according to the timeline, Hanjour showed up at the Virginia Division of Motor Vehicles in Arlington, where he flunked a standard written test for a Virginia driver's license. This is significant, and it ought to make us wonder how Hanjour ever managed to acquire his previous driver's licenses—a 1991 Arizona license and a Florida license issued in 1996—let alone master the controls of a Boeing 757.

There is another interesting item. The record indicates that on September 5, 2001, *just six days before 9/11*, Hanjour showed up at the First Union National Bank in Laurel, Maryland, where he made four failed bank transactions. The file cites bank records showing that Hanjour was unable to make balance inquiries and withdraw funds from his account because he failed to enter the correct PIN number, which he evidently had forgotten. Two days later, Hanjour returned to the bank, this time accompanied by an unidentified male, and made another unsuccessful attempt to withdraw funds, in this case $4900.

It is astonishing that the FBI file was ever touted as authenticating Hanjour's flight credentials. The document falls short on that score and actually raises new questions. How likely is it that a man who was unable to remember his own PIN number, and who just weeks before 9/11 flunked a simple test for a driver's license, could have executed a difficult maneuver in a commercial airliner? The chances, I would submit, are approximately zero.

The FBI file includes one other curious entry. On August 20, 2001 Hanjour shopped at Travelocity.com for information about September 5, 2001 flights from Dulles International Airport to Los Angeles. This suggests that, as of August 20, Hanjour did not yet know the date of the planned attack, either because he had not been briefed or because the date had not yet been selected. By the end of the month, however, the die was cast.

On August 31 Hanjour and another "middle-eastern male" purchased one-way tickets for America Airlines Flight 77 from a New Jersey travel agent. The date of departure: September 11, 2001. Still, one has to wonder what Hanjour believed was supposed to happen on that fateful morning.

WHO IS EDDIE SHALEV?

The record compiled by the FBI for the purpose of authenticating Hani Hanjour's flight skills fails to convince. And it also fails to support the testimony of the "other flight instructor," Eddie Shalev, who certified Hanjour to rent a Cessna 172 from Congressional Air Charters just three days after Marcel Bernard, the chief instructor at Freeway, refused to rent Hanjour the very same type of plane.

As we know, *The 9/11 Commission Report* makes no mention of the incident at Freeway airport, nor does it discuss Eddie Shalev, other than identifying him in a brief endnote. The failure to discuss this other flight instructor was a grave omission, because it now appears that Shalev's testimony was crucial. By telling the Commission what it was predisposed to hear, Shalev gave the official investigation an excuse to ignore the preponderance of evidence, which pointed to the unthinkable.

So, who is Eddie Shalev? His identity remained unknown for more than seven years, but was finally revealed in one of the files released in January 2009 by the National Archives. The document, labeled a "Memorandum for the Record," is a summary of the April 2004 interview with Eddie Shalev conducted by commission staffer Quinn John Tamm.[39] The document confirms that Shalev went on record: "Mr Shalev stated that based on his observations Hanjour was a 'good' pilot," which is certainly consistent with the endnote in *The 9/11 Commission Report.*

It is noteworthy that Tamm also spoke with Freeway instructors Sheri Baxter and Ben Conner, as revealed by yet another recently released document.[40] Although I was unable to reach Tamm or Baxter for comment, I did contact Conner, who confirmed his conversation with Tamm.[41] Conner says he fully expected to appear before the Commission, where he would have been able to challenge Shalev's assessment. However, the call never came.

But the real news is the revelation that Eddie Shalev had previously been in the Israeli military. The file states, "Mr. Shalev served in the Israeli Defense Forces in a paratroop regiment. He was a jumpmaster on a Boeing C-130. Mr. Shalev moved to the Gaithersburg area in April 2001 and was sponsored for employment by Congressional Air Charters ... [which] has subsequently gone out of business."

The memorandum raises disturbing questions. Consider the staffer's strange choice of words in describing Shalev's employment. What did Quinn John Tamm mean when he wrote that Shalev "was sponsored for employment"? Did the Commission even bother to investigate Congressional Air Charters? It is curious that the charter service subsequently went out of business. Also, did the Commission vet Eddie Shalev? Does his military record include service in the Israeli intelligence community?

Real people have known addresses. But the whereabouts of Eddie Shalev has been unknown for years. As reported by David Griffin, a 2007 search of the national telephone directory, plus Google searches by research librarian Elizabeth Woodworth, turned up no trace of him. A LexisNexis search by Matthew Everett also came up dry.

Not satisfied, I conducted my own searches, and succeeded in turning up two possible addresses for an "Eddy Shalev" in the Gaithersburg-Rockville area. But the leads went nowhere, and his phone number was no longer in service. The 9/11 Commission memo indicates that Shalev's US visa was about to expire in July 2004, suggesting that Shalev may have returned to Israel. If he is in the US, the man needs to be found, subpoenaed and questioned under oath before a new investigation.

Quinn John Tamm and the two Freeway instructors, Sheri Baxter and Ben Conner, should also be subpoenaed. All are key witnesses, and obvious starting points for a new 9/11 investigation.

Given his background, the search for, and possible extradition of, Eddie Shalev could become controversial. But 9/11 investigators must not be turned aside. We must follow the trail of evidence, regardless. Should it lead into a dark wood, we must resolve to go there. And if it takes us to the gates of hell, so be it. For no force, certainly no lobbying group or political action committee, can be allowed to trump the search for 9/11 truth.

ENDNOTES

1	http://www.archives.gov/research/9-11-commission/.

2	Marc Fisher and Don Phillips, "On Flight 77: 'Our Plane is Being Hijacked," *Washington Post*, September 12, 2001.

3	"Hijackers 'knew what they were doing," *CNN*, September 12, 2001, posted at http://edition.cnn.com/2001/US/09/12/hijackers.skills/.

4	"'Get These Planes on the Ground': Air Traffic Controllers Recall Sept. 11, *ABC News*, October 24, 2001, posted at http://web.archive.org/web/20011025074733/http://abcnews.go.com/sections/2020/2020/2020_011024_atc_feature.html.

5	"Primary Target: 189 Dead Or Missing From Pentagon Attack", *CBS News*, September 21, 2001, posted at http://www.cbsnews.com/stories/2001/09/11/national/main310721.shtml.

6	Steve Fainaru and Alia Ibrahim, "Mysterious Trip to Flight 77 Cockpit", *Washington Post*, September 10, 2002, posted at http://www.washingtonpost.com/wp-dyn/content/article/2007/08/13/AR2007081300752_pf.html.

7	David W. Chen, "Man Traveled Across U.S. In His Quest to Be a Pilot", *New York Times*, September 18, 2001, posted at http://www.nytimes.com/2001/09/18/us/nation-challenged-suspect-man-traveled-across-us-his-quest-be-pilot.html.

8	Amy Goldstein, Lena H. Sun and George Lardner Jr., "Hanjour an Unlikely Terrorist," *Cape Cod Times*, October 21, 2001.

9	Ibid.

10	Ibid.

11	The Japanese flight instructor's testimonial is posted at http://911myths.com/images/b/b2/Team7_Box18_PilotTrainingInfo_Japanese_Instructor_Hanjour.pdf.

12	Ibid.

13	A copy of Hanjour's FAA license is posted at http://www.scribd.com/doc/13120915/Airman-Records-for-Alleged-911-Hijacker-Hani-Hanjour.

14	Kellie Lunney, "FAA contractors approved flight licenses for Sept. 11 suspect," GovernmentExecutive.com, June 13, 2002.

15	"FAA Probed, Cleared Sept. 11 Hijacker in Early 2001," *FOX News*, May 10, 2002.

16	Hani's Jet Tech evaluation and other documentation were entered as evidence during the trial of Zacarias Moussaoui: Training Records, Hani Hanjour, B-737 Initial Ground Training, Class 01-3-021, Date: 2/8/01, Jet Tech International, posted at http://www.vaed.uscourts.gov/notablecases/moussaoui/exhibits/prosecution/PX00021.pdf

17	*The 9/11 Commission Report, Final Report of the National Commission on Terrorist Attacks Upon the United States* (New York: W.W. Norton & Co., 2004), pp. 226-227.

18	"FAA Probed, Cleared Sept. 11 Hijacker in Early 2001," *FOX News*, May 10, 2002.

19	Ibid.

20	Jim Yardley, "A Trainee Noted for Incompetence," *New York Times*, May 4, 2002.

21	"Report: 9/11 Hijacker Bypassed FAA," Associated Press, June 13, 2002.

22	*The 9/11 Commission Report*, p. 242.

23	http://911myths.com/images/2/2a/PENTTBOM_About_Hanjour.pdf.

24	*The 9/11 Commission Report*, p. 242.

25	Thomas Frank, "Tracing Trail of Hijackers," *Newsday*, September 23, 2001. The story by Newsday has been confirmed in its essentials by one of the newly-released

9/11 files. See http://www.scribd.com/doc/15103091/T1A-B38-John-Tamm-Memos-Fdr-Entire-Contents-Re-FBI-Investigation-and-Hijackers-Memos-Corre-spondence-Summaries-Withdrawal-Notices-032

26   Phone conversation with Marcel Bernard, June 26, 2009.

27   Phone conversation with Ben Conner, June 28, 2009.

28   *The 9/11 Commission Report*, pp. 226-27.

29   Ibid., p. 530, note 147.

30   Ibid., p. 227.

31   Ibid., p. 531, note 170.

32   http://media.nara.gov/9-11/MFR/t-0148-911MFR-00551.pdf.

33   David Ray Griffin, *The New Pearl Harbor Revisited* (Northhampton: Olive Branch Press, 2008), p.80.

34   http://911myths.com/images/2/2a/PENTTBOM_About_Hanjour.pdf.

35   Numerous testimonials by commercial pilots, all of whom question the official story, can be found here: http://patriotsquestion911.com/pilots.html.

36   Philip Marshall, *False Flag 911*, pp. 6-7.

37   Ibid., pp. 34-37.

38   Phone conversation with Marcel Bernard, June 26, 2009.

39   http://media.nara.gov/9-11/MFR/t-0148-911MFR-00551.pdf.

40   Memo from John Tamm to Dieter Snell, April 15, 2004, posted at http://www.scribd.com/doc/15103091/T1A-B38-John-Tamm-Memos-Fdr-Entire-Contents-Re-FBI-Investigation-and-Hijackers-Memos-Correspondence-Summaries-With-drawal-Notices-032

41   Phone conversation with Ben Conner, June 28, 2009.

Susan McElwain

Chapter 13

Shoot-Down?

United Airlines Flight 93 crashed near Shanksville, Pennsylvania about a half hour after "top gun" Hani Hanjour allegedly executed his strike on the Pentagon, and a few minutes after the collapsed South Tower enveloped lower Manhattan in a swirling cloud of dust. The victims trapped in the nearby North Tower (those not compelled by heat and smoke to jump to their deaths) had less than a half-hour to live. Later, thousands of additional firemen and other first-responders would become victims of the dust itself.

Within hours of the crash of UAL 93, a swarm of FBI agents descended on Shanksville. They found wreckage scattered over several square miles, encompassing three separate debris fields, for which reason the FBI briefly entertained the possibility of a midair explosion, and also initially refused to rule out a shoot-down.

However, the day after a NORAD spokesperson announced that "NORAD-allocated forces have not engaged with weapons any aircraft [on 9/11], including Flight 93,"[1] the FBI's William Crowley told the press, "There was no military involvement."[2] As will become clear, this latter statement is considerably more dubious, though it should be remembered that other government agencies or personnel could be culpable without "military involvement."

Despite the official denials, the media coverage continued to reflect skepticism due to persistent rumors that the White House had issued a shoot-down order,[3] and because of continuing press reports that F-16s had been in hot pursuit of UAL 93, just before it went down.[4] Those reports were wrong, but given the conflicting accounts and persistent rumors, it is hardly surprising that many Americans doubted the official denials.

Public skepticism was also fueled by eyewitness accounts coming out of Shanksville. Numerous local residents reported seeing a white jet immediately after the crash. Witnesses said it had twin engines mounted at the rear, but no markings of any kind. They said it circled the crash site, then flew away. One witness, John Fleegle, who was one of the first to arrive at the crash site, watched as the white jet flew into the sun.[5] Three students also saw what they thought was a fighter fly over Shanksville's high school, reportedly within seconds of the crash, just as a mushroom cloud was rising from the crash site.[6]

Falcon 20 commuter jet

The next day, the FBI announced that two civilian aircraft had been in the area, which probably explained the eyewitness accounts. The first aircraft, a Falcon 20 commuter jet (similar to the one in the photo), had been on an approach to Johnstown Airport when air traffic controllers rerouted it to Shanksville. The pilot of the Falcon 20 circled the crash site for several minutes, before resuming his approach to Johnstown. This is confirmed by radar data.

The second plane was a single-engine Cessna, piloted by a local farmer who told the press he flew over about 45 minutes after the crash.[7] This second aircraft requires no further explanation because it was propeller-driven, hence, fails to match the description of a white jet. Also, the Cessna arrived much too late to explain the eyewitness accounts.

It is unclear whether the FBI had the RADES radar data at its disposal in the days following the 9/11 attack. But we know that the 9/11 Commission did when it began its investigation in late 2003.

Miles Kara, a former intelligence officer, handled this aspect of the investigation for the commission. He previously had served on the staff of the 2002 Joint Inquiry, the first official investigation of the September 11, 2001 attacks conducted by the Joint House/Senate Intelligence Committee. Kara developed the following composite diagram of the crash of UAL 93, based on the 9/11 radar data. The diagram was released in 2009 along with many other official commission documents. It contains information that raises new questions about the official story.

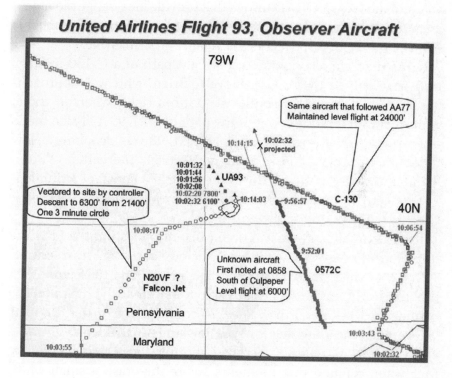

United Airlines Flight 93, Observer Aircraft

The diagram shows, for example, that the Falcon 20 commuter jet did not arrive at the crash site until 10:11 A.M., a full eight minutes after the official crash time of 10:03 A.M., which is significant, because in the context of the 9/11 attacks, *eight minutes is an eternity.* And this should have been immediately apparent to the 9/11 Commission staff.

At the time of the crash, the Falcon 20 was on an approach to Johnstown Airport. It first appears at bottom left at 10:03:55, then, makes a course change at 10:08:17, when air traffic controllers instructed the pilot to reconnoiter at the presumed crash site. Although its arrival time is not explicitly indicated by the diagram, this is non-controversial. John Farmer confirmed it when I asked him to double-check the radar data in his computer. Nor does Miles Kara dispute it.

As indicated, UAL 93 was on a south-southeastern heading when it went down. The doomed airliner was at 6100 feet when it was lost to radar at 10:02:32. The fact that UAL 93 dropped below radar at that time is explained by the local topography, the proximity of the Appalachian Mountains, and the considerable distance between Shanksville and the FAA/NORAD towers that provide long-range radar coverage for the area. Due to these combined factors, long-range radar is blind below about 6,100 feet in the vicinity of Shanksville.

Kara's diagram also includes the flight path of a C-130 military transport piloted by Lt. Col. Steve O'Brien, who was approaching Shanksville from the southeast (bottom right) when air traffic controllers vectored him out of the path of UAL 93. O'Brien made a sharp jog to the northeast, just as UAL 93 was dropping below radar, then changed course again at 10:06:54. Thereafter, O'Brien maintained a generally northwest heading at a constant altitude of 24,000 feet. The C-130 was about 17 miles away from UAL 93 when O'Brien made the zig to the northeast.

The Falcon 20's late arrival time calls into question the FBI's interpretation of events. As noted, various eyewitnesses reported seeing the white jet *moments* after the crash. And there are other problems. Although it is not possible to tell from the diagram, according to Miles Kara, the Falcon 20 commuter jet never dropped below radar, meaning that it never flew under 6,000 feet.[8]

The fact is significant, because another local resident, Susan McElwain, claimed that moments *before* the crash a small white aircraft buzzed her minivan. She said she watched as it banked and disappeared behind some trees. This strange sighting was within a mile of the crash site.[9] The Falcon 20's continuous radar track rules it out as a candidate for the aircraft in her account.

Incidentally, this also debunks a report in *Popular Mechanics* magazine that the Falcon 20 circled the crash site at 1,500 feet.[10] This was yet another false report.

In sum, the Falcon 20's late arrival time raises the possibility that the FBI conflated separate events. The reason? Probably to avoid having to seriously investigate the eyewitness accounts. In the days following the attack, the FBI no doubt came under mounting political pressure to wrap up its investigation in Shanksville as soon as possible. When NORAD officially disclaimed media reports of a shoot down, the FBI had a ready-made excuse and took the easy out. The FBI officially ended its Shanksville investigation on September 25, 2001.

When the 9/11 Commission started its work in late 2003, its staffers had the 9/11 radar data in hand and should have spotted this possible flaw in the FBI's version of events: that the eyewitness accounts are not easily explainable in terms of the Falcon 20 due to its late arrival time. On this basis, the 9/11 Commission should have gone back and done the detective work the FBI failed to do. The staffers should have interviewed all of the eyewitnesses in Shanksville. After which, they should have crosschecked the different accounts to determine what really happened. Although this is standard police protocol and the method by which detectives routinely solve crimes, incredibly, none of this was done in the case of 9/11, the most serious crime in US history.

As indicated by the diagram, Miles Kara also plotted the radar track for an "unknown aircraft," which disappears from radar at 9:56:57, a few minutes before the crash. This seemed suspicious to me. Notice, this aircraft first appears at 8:58 south of Culpeper, Virginia, and it was on a near-intercept with UAL 93 as it approached Shanksville. Kara estimated its "projected" flight path, i.e., the dotted line, based on its last known position and heading. But this was sheer conjecture.

When I asked Kara why the Commission failed to identify the "unknown aircraft" he expressed displeasure with my question, and called it a "fishing expedition."[11] Kara informed me that the aircraft was "not a plane of interest" because, in his words, it was "a slow mover," meaning that it was a prop-driven single-engine plane, probably "along the lines of a Piper Cub."[12] The unknown aircraft had a generic Mode 3 transponder, and started out squawking 1200, but changed to 0527 at 9:04 A.M.[13]

Given my suspicions, I asked John Farmer to recheck the radar data. He confirmed its low flight speed, which rules out a jet. After some more digging in the FAA database, Farmer found the aircraft's flight plan and was able to identify the plane.[14] It was indeed

179

a Piper and appears to have played no role in the crash of UAL 93. In this instance, Kara was apparently correct.

The other unidentified aircraft

Of the many remarkable stories from September 11, 2001, Shanksville resident Susan McElwain tells one of the strangest. At the time of the 9/11 attacks, she lived just down the road from the crash site. She claims that moments before UAL 93 went down, a small white aircraft buzzed her minivan. The encounter occurred as she was approaching a rural intersection several miles north of town. During my trip to Shanksville, I had no trouble locating the intersection, on Buckstown Road about a half-mile east of the crash site.

Over the years, McElwain's story has not changed. She insists that the close encounter happened before the crash and that she got a good look at the aircraft as it flew off.[15] At the time of the incident, McElwain had not yet learned about the events in New York or Washington. She says the aircraft was small and "pure white, with no markings." She saw no rivets and when asked to describe it, McElwain uses terms like "molded", "all one piece" and "fiberglass."

She says it passed so low that she ducked instinctively. For some reason, she turned off her car radio and was suddenly aware of the silence. The aircraft was surprisingly quiet: an important detail because it rules out a missile and also tends to rule out a jet.

When I learned of this detail, I immediately thought of the Predator, an unmanned aerial vehicle (UAV) developed by the US military (see the photo below). The Predator is powered by a silent-running motor that drives a single tail-mounted propeller.[16] It cruises at 100 mph, and it has a stall speed of about 50 mph.

Normally, military UAVs are equipped with both military and civilian transponders, which makes them immediately identifiable to air traffic controllers. However, an UAV could easily be rigged for stealth by outfitting it with a civilian transponder only, which might allow it to become lost in the clutter of air traffic.[17] It is possible that McElwain sighted such an aircraft.

On the afternoon of September 11, McElwain voluntarily contacted the FBI and informed them of her experience. That evening, two FBI agents showed up at her house and conducted a brief interview. However, the agents showed little interest in her story and even tried to talk her out of it. By this time, the official version of events was already being touted in the news media.

I met Susan McElwain on my Shanksville trip, and I later sent her photos of a number of UAVs, including the Predator. However, none looked like a match to her. As of now, the mystery aircraft remains unidentified.[18] Still, judging from her description it is likely she encountered some type of UAV, possibly a classified design that the US military has never formally unveiled. If this is correct, the obvious next question is: *Why was a UAV in the vicinity of the UAL 93 crash site?*

Predator UAV

The Commission staffers failed to register the significance of McElwain's story, because, like the FBI, they neglected to do the tedious detective work that police routinely do, after a crime: namely, interview all witnesses, then crosscheck the various accounts to determine what actually happened.

Commission staffer Miles Kara provided his take on the matter in several emails, in which he expressed the view that eyewitness testimony is unreliable evidence, at least when compared with primary source data, which he listed: flight data recorder, cockpit voice recorder, FAA radar data, US Air Force radar data, audiotapes of air traffic control communications, and satellite infra-red data.[19]

I agree that eyewitness accounts are inherently subjective and therefore must be treated with caution during criminal investigations. Multiple witnesses to the same event often describe what happened very differently, because each witness sees it from a different perspective. This is why it is essential to crosscheck the various accounts. Another concern is that memory fades over time. With the passage of months and years, humans have a tendency to enhance, exaggerate, and/or otherwise distort the facts; and this tendency is universal.

The problem for Miles Kara and the Commission is that none of these are an issue with the Shanksville eyewitnesses. The unanimity of multiple accounts is remarkable. Moreover, nearly all the testimony was reported within days or weeks of September 11, in some cases within hours, while memory was fresh. The sheer amount of testimony is also impressive.

Fortunately, several websites did a nice job of compiling and preserving this evidence, although I did discover several errors in the reporting.[20] By some accounts, as many as a dozen people saw the white jet. When I conducted my own review, I counted as many as eighteen possible witnesses. While in Shanksville, I looked up John Fleegle at the garage where he works. He was happy to talk and reiterated what I had read on the Internet. Later, I also interviewed Tom Spinelli, Fleegle's coworker at the marina on 9/11. Spinelli corroborated Fleegle's account. He told me that he accompanied Fleegle to the crash site and that tiny pieces of debris landed in the back of Fleegle's pickup en route. Spinelli estimates that it took 5 to 8 minutes to reach the crash site; which means that he and Fleegle probably saw the Falcon 20. Spinelli agrees with Fleegle that it was hard to gauge the white jet's altitude, because "it stayed in the sun."[21]

A careful screening of all the witnesses might have determined who saw what, but this was never done. When I sent Miles Kara a link to the McElwain interview posted at Youtube, he replied that McElwain was confused about the time and actually saw the Falcon 20. But I doubt it.

While in Shanksville, I interviewed teachers at the local elementary school, located three miles from the crash site, who told me they felt the impact like an earthquake. They not only heard the crash but felt the shock wave pass through the building. Susan McElwain was much closer, probably within a mile, so it is very unlikely that she confused "before" and "after." And, of course. the Falcon 20 was always on radar and thus never flew under 6000 feet.

Despite its potentially explosive importance (more likely, because of it), the 9/11 Commission gave short shrift to testimony of the Shanksville eyewitnesses. This should not surprise us. Dismissing eyewitnesses was the Commission's *modus operandi*, especially when the accounts failed to support the story the Commissioners wanted to tell. Before we move on, I will very briefly cite two examples that underscore my point.

One of *The 9/11 Commission Report's* conspicuous omissions is its failure to mention the 118 New York City firemen and first responders who described explosions (often in graphic detail) at the World Trade Center, even though the Commission had this testimony.[22] According to apologists for this grievous censorship, the firemen confused explosions with the sounds of the towers collapsing, or electrical transformers exploding from the intense heat of the fires, or windows blowing out, or something or other. These explanations sounded plausible, but they unraveled in 2007-08 with the discovery of both residues and actual traces of unexploded nanothermite in samples of World Trade Center dust.[23] Thus, in the end, science supported the eyewitnesses.

The 9/11 Commission also ignored government witnesses, such as the field agents from the FBI's Minneapolis office, whose efforts in August 2001 to obtain a search warrant for Zacarias Moussaoui's duffle bag were obstructed by higher-ups at FBI headquarters. The field agents included Coleen Rowley, named by *Time* magazine in 2002 as its person of the year. According to the Justice Department, the information in Moussaoui's bag was critically important and would have enabled Crowley and her cohorts to prevent 9/11. But evidently the Commission was not interested in hearing how their efforts to protect the nation were thwarted from above, as the panel never bothered to interview Crowley.[24]

Given the Commission's cavalier treatment of witnesses in general, its failure to follow up in Shanksville becomes more understandable, though no more acceptable.

FROM SURVEILLANCE TO ATTACK

Curiously, Miles Kara underscored the importance of Susan McElwain's account when, in an e-mail, he sought to discredit speculation about a shoot-down: "In order for there to be a shoot down there are two essential elements, both must be present. First, there must be a launch platform. Second, there must be a controller, air or ground. There is no evidence of either [in the case of UAL 93], therefore, the shoot down speculation does not hold water and does not even rise to the level of an actionable research statement."[25]

But the possible presence of a UAV near the crash site means that an attack platform with controller may indeed have been present. Furthermore, we know the technology existed at the time. A review of the development history of unmanned aerial vehicles shows that UAV technology matured in the years prior to 9/11. Although military drones were formerly used almost exclusively for intelligence gathering, this changed in 1994 when the US military awarded General Atomics a joint-forces contract to develop a new UAV known as the Predator.[26]

The new UAV system was specifically designed to function as an attack platform in search-and-destroy missions. Today, Predators come equipped with sophisticated sensors, synthetic aperture radar, laser spotters, and who-knows-what-else in the way of electronic gadgetry. They can deliver Hellfire missiles and probably other kinds of advanced weaponry. They are flown remotely by a controller, either directly by line-of-sight or via a satellite link.

The Predator was first deployed in the Balkans during the summer of 1995 and subsequently flew more than six hundred surveillance missions in Bosnia. In 2000 Predators were used in Afghanistan for the purpose of locating and targeting Osama bin Laden, already on the FBI's most-wanted list for his role in the 1998 bombings of the US embassies in Kenya and Tanzania, which killed hundreds. CIA Director George Tenet vociferously opposed this deployment, but he was overruled by the Clinton White House, which according to a senior Department of Defense official "had to cram this down the throat of the Agency."[27]

Jim Pavitt, head of the CIA's Directorate of Operations, was overheard complaining that "if the Predator was used against bin Laden and the responsibility for the use of lethal force was laid at the Agency's doorstep, it would endanger the lives of CIA operatives around the world."[28] Pavitt's comment seems pure hogwash, as the CIA has extensively deployed Predators on this type of mission since 9/11.[29] At last count, the CIA was utilizing attack drones in at least six foreign nations: Iraq, Afghanistan, Pakistan, Yemen, Libya and, most recently, Somalia.

According to *The 9/11 Commission Report*, the Predator's early trial missions in Afghanistan in September 2000 were successful in locating Osama bin Laden, and this generated considerable enthusiasm in the Clinton White House. Counter-terrorism czar Richard

A. Clarke was so impressed with the quality of the real-time video feed that he called it "truly astonishing."[30] However, officials suspended the search and destroy mission in October 2000 because of deteriorating weather at the onset of the harsh Afghanistan winter, with the understanding that the kill project would be revived in the spring.[31]

Although a Predator successfully launched Hellfire missiles in February 2001 during a US Air Force test flight near Nellis AFB, demonstrating the feasibility of using the Predator as an attack platform,[32] the mission did not survive the election of George W. Bush. Instead of going after bin Laden, the new administration did the reverse. After his inauguration, Bush instructed the FBI to back off its ongoing investigations of the bin Laden family.[33]

By the spring of 2001, remote control technology had come of age. In April 2001 a different type of unmanned vehicle, the Global Hawk, made history by flying from Edwards AFB in southern California to Edinburgh AFB in South Australia.[34] The nonstop 8,600-mile trip across the Pacific took just twenty-two hours and set an endurance record for a remotely operated vehicle.[35] The drone returned to California after a dozen joint exercises with the Australian military.

The previous year, the Global Hawk had made a similar transatlantic run to Europe, where it participated in NATO exercises. Like the Predator, the Global Hawk is remotely controlled either directly via line-of-sight or via satellite link. Unlike the Predator, however, it is jet-powered and soars at very high altitudes, up to 65,000 feet. It can remain aloft for up to forty-two hours and with a range of 14,000 miles, has a truly global reach. Designed primarily for intelligence gathering, the Global Hawk comes equipped with advanced radar as well as infrared and electro-optical sensors, which allow it to survey vast amounts of real estate and return up to 1,900 high-resolution images during a single flight. These are truly amazing specs, by any standard.

In June 2001, the Joint Chiefs of Staff acknowledged the newly emergent technology by issuing a new order regarding US policy in cases of aircraft piracy. The new order (CJCSI 3610.01A)[36] was signed by Vice Admiral S.A. Fry, Director of the Joint Chefs of Staff, and replaced the existing order (CJCSI 3610.01), which had been in effect since 1997.[37] Viewed side by side, the two documents are almost identical. Indeed, the passage stating the actual hijack policy did not change, and can be summarized: When hijackings occur the military's operational commanders at the Pentagon and at the North American Aerospace Command (NORAD) must contact the office of the Secretary of Defense for approval and further instruction.

At the time, of course, this was Donald Rumsfeld. The only difference in the new order was that it included an extra passage in the policy section mentioning two new kinds of airborne vehicles: "unmanned aerial vehicles (UAVs)" and "remotely operated vehicles (ROVs)." The order stated that, henceforth, both are to be regarded as "a potential threat to public safety." So, why did two new categories of airborne vehicles require the drafting of a new military order, especially since the basic policy in cases of hijackings did not appreciably change?[38] The only rational answer is what I have already indicated: In June 2001, for reasons having to do with national security, the US military deemed it necessary to acknowledge the maturation of remotely-operated-vehicle technology.

Although the average US citizen did not then and still does not know anything of these developments, surely we had a right to expect more from the 9/11 Commission, which, after all, was formally charged to investigate the 9/11 attacks, and was also blessed with a staff of technically competent individuals. However, judging from the *9/11 Commission Report*, the only "threat to public safety" the Commission recognized was the threat from foreign enemies like al-Qaeda.

The panel never considered the possibility of a domestic threat, and so, was blind to all evidence pointing in this direction. The limited scope of its official investigation reflected this bias. In fact, as discussed in my last book, the very same pattern played out in the case of the National Institute of Standards and Technology's (NIST's) investigation of the World Trade Center collapse.[39] The surest way to neuter an investigation is to limit its scope, ahead of time, thus making the truth unobtainable.

FLYING OUTSIDE THE BOX

Based on her account, the white aircraft that buzzed Susan McElwain's minivan near the UAL 93 crash site on 9/11 was no more than fifty to sixty feet off the ground, much too low to show up on radar. Still, we would expect such a craft to show up on radar somewhere that morning, either coming or going. But there is nothing.

This is curiously similar to what unfolded at Camp David, where we had multiple reports of a crash and a putative sighting of a craft, but no radar track. Elsewhere I have argued that an unexplained twenty-five-second time lag in the NEADS radar data stream on 9/11 might have enabled a covert operator to delay NORAD's response to the hijackings by momentarily interrupting the radar signal from AA 11, thus altering what military technicians were seeing in real time on their scopes at the NEADS facility near Rome, New York.[40]

But this cannot explain the total absence of a radar track, which would pose insurmountable problems for a covert operator; since multiple radar towers simultaneously track each craft. We are left with an unexplained mystery.

When radio talk show host Dr. Bill Deagle and I brainstormed this question in December 2008 during a lively on-air discussion, we gave ourselves permission to think outside the box. Taking the issue to the next level, we raised a question: Has the US military developed a heretofore undisclosed type of stealth technology, one that would enable aircraft so equipped to evade radar detection?

We did not resolve the matter, that afternoon. But we did get a lucky break. After the show a listener by the name of Steve Denoo contacted Deagle with new, significant information.[41] Denoo is a stockholder in a high-tech company, Anaren, which has supplied radar equipment to the US military for many years, and which, according to Denoo, specializes in this very type of stealth technology.

Denoo told us that while attending an Anaren stockholder's convention in the mid-1980s he witnessed an unusually forthcoming presentation by a company engineer, who explained that Anaren was then developing a new type of radar jamming technology for the Department of Defense. The engineer went on to explain the basics of how it worked.

As explained by Denoo, advanced radar jamming is simple, at least conceptually. The process of concealment involves several discrete steps. The jamming unit first must identify and store the radar signals from all of the radar towers on the ground that are within range. This also entails precisely locating each antenna. But the actual jamming occurs when the unit sends back a modulated signal essentially telling each radar tower on the ground that "I'm not here." The net effect is to make the plane invisible to radar. According to the Anaren engineer, all of this is accomplished in a microsecond. The technology is sophisticated, but it is also compact enough that jamming units can be retrofitted in a variety of aircraft.

We did some checking and were able to confirm almost everything Denoo told us. Anaren is indeed a defense contractor, and it specializes in developing radar systems for the US military. The company, based in Syracuse, New York, does research and development, but also delivers components and subsystems. Although Anaren is not a large firm it is one of the oldest and most successful defense contractors in the radar field. The company is listed at Nasdaq, and a summary of its military product line, posted by Reuters, states, "The company's products include radar countermeasure subsystems, beamformers, switch matrices and radar feed networks."[42]

The summary provides additional relevant information: "Defense radar countermeasure subsystems digitally measure, locate and counter enemy radar systems. Anaren's digital radio frequency measurement (DRFM) devices are used for storing and retrieving radio frequency signals as a part of military aircraft self protection systems. Its digital frequency discriminators (DFD) are employed in electronic warfare (EW) systems to detect and measure the radio frequency (RF) signals emitted by enemy radar systems. The company also manufactures a suite of electronic subassemblies designed to process radar signals detected by a receiver."[43]

In 1996 Anaren filed a description of its products with the Securities and Exchange Commission. The document is still posted online and is similar to the above summary, but includes a few additional details. According to the SEC document, "The company [Anaren] is a leader in subsystem products including digital frequency discriminators (DFD), digital radar frequency memory (DRFM), and other custom designed subsystems used in electronic warfare applications.... DFD products rapidly measure the frequency and other characteristics of radar signals. This information is used in electronic warfare systems to identify, classify and/or counter radar systems. DRFM products digitalize and store radar signals *and can reproduce them in real time to counter advanced radar systems. DRFM products are currently the only technology available that can replicate radar signals with sufficient fidelity to counter today's advanced coherent radar systems* [my emphasis]"[44]

A 2008 filing by Anaren with the SEC indicated that the firm has steadily expanded in recent years. Although most of Anaren's business continues to be in the civilian communications sector, in 2008, "the space and defense segment accounted for about 40% of the company's revenues." The filing includes a list of defense contractors that regularly do business with Anaren. Lockheed-Martin was at the top with 13% of the company's net sales. Other familiar names were ITT, Northrop Grumman, MCL Industries, and Raytheon.[45]

Wikipedia describes radar jamming technology as follows: "A DRFM system is designed to digitize an incoming radio frequency (RF) input signal at a frequency and bandwidth necessary to adequately represent the signal, then reconstruct that RF [radio frequency] signal when required. The most significant aspect of DRFM is that as a digital "duplicate" of the received signal, it is coherent with the source of the received signal.... A DRFM may modify the signal prior to retransmitting which can alter the signature of the false target; adjusting its apparent radar cross section range, velocity, and angle. DRFMs present a significant obstacle for radar sensors."[46]

Wikipedia continues: "The DRFM digitizes the received signal and stores a coherent copy in digital memory. As needed, the signal is replicated and retransmitted. *Being a coherent representation of the original signal, the transmitting radar will not be able to distinguish it from other legitimate signals it receives and processes as targets.*" [my emphasis]

It is clear that a decision was made at the Pentagon many years ago to pursue multiple R&D pathways in the search for the Holy Grail of radar concealment. One path utilizing deflection and absorption led to the development of the F-117 Nighthawk and the budget-busting B-2 stealth bomber.[47] However, it now appears that the US military simultaneously pursued another separate R&D pathway, reflected in Anaren's product line; which may actually be a more cost-effective way to achieve the same result. In any event, by now, it should be evident that advanced radar jamming is not science fiction. It exists, and has for many years.

An early use of radar jamming occurred during Israel's June 1982 invasion of Lebanon. Although the Israeli attack was primarily aimed at the PLO bases in and around Beirut, the Israelis also encountered and engaged Syrian forces, which had been invited into the country in 1976 by the Lebanese government to help enforce the truce after the Lebanese civil war. The Syrian positions in the Bekaa Valley included at least nineteen Soviet-supplied surface-to-air missile (SAM) batteries, which the Israeli Air Force deemed a threat to its control of Lebanese airspace.

The subsequent aerial battle was the largest since the Korean War, and it began with a ploy that involved the pioneering use of unmanned aerial vehicles in combat.[48] The Israelis flew unarmed drones toward the Syrian positions; and the Syrians, believing they were under attack, made the mistake of turning on their radars prematurely. The Syrian radars "painted" the drones, which collected the radar signals and relayed them to Israeli AWACS planes orbiting over the Mediterranean. The AWACS analyzed the data and were able to pinpoint the locations of the Syrian radar towers.

It was then a simple matter of sending in Israeli fighters to surgically take them out, along with the associated Syrian SAM batteries. Israeli drones also circled above the Syrian air bases to monitor the departures of Syrian MIG fighters, and likewise fed this data to the Israeli AWACS, which used it to coordinate the Israeli attack. The ensuing dogfight was one-sided. The Soviet-supplied Syrian MIGs were equipped with radar designed to "see" forward and backward. But the MIGs were blind laterally, a weakness the Israelis exploited. The Israeli fighters literally blind-sided the MIGs. The Israelis also disrupted Syrian communications by jamming their radio frequencies, and used radar jamming to evade the few remaining Syrian radars. During the two-hour battle the Israeli Air Force (IAF) decimated the SAMS and the Syrian Air Force.[49]

While some at the Pentagon gloated over Israel's decisive victory because it showed the superiority of US weapons, more thoughtful individuals, such as former undersecretary of state George W. Ball, were sharply critical, because the Israelis "gratuitously threw away an asset of great value not only for Israel but for America. It [Israel] provided both the Russians and the Syrians with detailed knowledge of their own tactical and technical deficiencies, which they could then correct."[50] Both pro and con viewpoints reflected the Cold War mentality of the day. In any event, the case shows that the various elements of radar jamming already existed as early as 1982, although at a more crude level of development.

Although the US and Israel have never formally unveiled cloaking technology, there have been hints that it does exist. In March 2010, according to Hungarian media, "two Israeli Gulfstream V-type jets, equipped with sophisticated intelligence gear, flew more than 1,300 miles over Turkey, Bulgaria and Romania....before flying over eastern Budapest, *and then disappearing.*"[my emphasis][51] The Hungarian Defense Minister claimed that the planes were "uninvited and unannounced," and he called for an investigation. However, an official at the Israeli embassy denied that the aircraft were spy planes and insisted they were on a legitimate diplomatic mission.

To my knowledge, no one has thus far explained why or how the two planes "disappeared" over Budapest. Although I attempted to contact the reporter who covered the story for the *New York Post*, I was unable to reach him.

Last spring, I heard about another possible instance from my colleague Bob Pinnacle. For several weeks in May and June 2010, Pinnacle personally observed several P-3 Orion AWACs planes flying off radar very low (~2,500 feet) in broad daylight over Pasadena and Los Angeles.[52] When Pinnacle loaded the radar page for the Burbank Airport, which has a "playback" option, he discovered that the P-3s dropped off radar on a number of occasions, for unexplained reasons. He informed the local *Pasadena Weekly*, and was told by someone at the news desk that "we will look into it," but the paper never printed a word about the strange "disappearance" over downtown Pasadena.

I would bet this is not a lone case. The military use of radar cloaking technology may be fairly commonplace, but passes unnoticed because most Americans simply are not paying attention. The Department of Defense has developed many black technologies about which we the people know absolutely nothing. Yet, I seriously doubt that cloaking technology is standard equipment in NORAD aircraft; or its existence would have leaked, long ago. Here is my question: was it used on 9/11?

On December 4, 2011, as this book was being readied for publication, another relevant case came to light. That evening, the world press reported that a highly classified CIA drone had been lost over Iran while on a surveillance mission deep inside the country. Days later, the Iranians displayed the captured craft on state television. Videos and photos of the drone, which has been identified as an RQ-170 Sentinel, show it to be in almost pristine condition, raising the strong possibility that it did not crash but had been forced down by the Iranians.[53]

US government officials acknowledged that Lockheed-Martin had developed the drone in a secret compartmented intelligence program. The officials spoke on condition of anonymity because the RQ-170 Sentinel has a classification rating Above Top Secret. The UAV is so advanced that the US military had never before released its photograph. Indeed, the investigation into its disappearance also remains classified.[54]

Although the US military went to great lengths to keep the RQ-170's capabilities secret, as a result of the downing, it is now known that the bat-winged surveillance vehicle has a wingspan of about 65 feet and flies at 50,000 feet. Its surveillance missions over Iran are apparently being flown out of a base in Afghanistan, although the handlers who remotely control the craft are based in the US, in Nevada.

The incident has a special relevance in the context of this discussion, because US officials have acknowledged that the CIA drone is designed to evade radar, evidently by virtue of its non-metallic structure, wing design, and skin coatings. Although the RQ-170 does not match what Susan McElwain saw near Shanksville on September 11, 2001, the incident over Iran nevertheless confirms that the CIA has a covert program to develop UAVs capable of evading radar, thus, providing indirect support for the alternative shoot-down scenario featured in this chapter.[55]

A SHOOT-DOWN?

Before returning to the eyewitness accounts, another anomaly in the record requires mention here. As noted, UAL 93's time of crash at Shanksville is officially listed as 10:03 A.M., according to *The 9/11 Commission Report*, and one might expect this to be non-controversial. But such is not the case. Our subject, after all, is 9/11, where even the most apparently mundane data can take on extraordinary significance.

Seismic instruments at various locations registered an event near Shanksville on 9/11 consistent with the crash of an airliner, but at 10:06 A.M., not at 10:03 A.M., a discrepancy that has never been explained. In 2002, an article in the *Philadelphia Daily News* quoted Terry Wallace, perhaps the leading seismologist in the nation. Said Wallace: 'The seismic signals are consistent with an impact at 10:06:05, plus or minus two seconds.'[56] At the time, Wallace headed up the Southern Arizona Seismic Observatory. He is presently an Associate Director of Science and Engineering at the Los Alamos National Laboratory.

I contacted Terry Wallace in 2010, and he stood by that estimate, though he also admitted that the data is "sparse and quite noisy." Wallace wrote with the caution one expects of a good scientist, calling the data "consistent with an impact at 10:06; however, the quality of the data do not preclude an earlier impact – there simply are not enough seismic data (number of stations, or signal-to-noise on the available stations) to reject/verify a 10:03 impact."[57]

The fact that the seismic data conflicts with the official crash time of 10:03 is a strong indicator that the actual events at Shanksville have not yet been properly understood.

Several of the Shanksville eyewitnesses reported hearing a loud screaming noise shortly before UAL 93 plunged to earth, which some think was the sound of a missile.[58] While this remains possible, in my view it is unlikely. Missiles are not only noisy, they are highly visible. Given the large number of witnesses at Shanksville, surely if a missile had been used someone would have reported seeing it. In my view, it is signifiant that no one did.

Moreover, the now confirmed absence of any NORAD fighters in the vicinity also rules out the possibility that a loyal general ordered a shoot down, as some have argued.[59] According to this view, the shoot down involved a missile but was later covered up for political reasons. But the 9/11 radar shows this did not happen.

The evidence points to a different type of shoot down scenario, possibly involving a UAV strike platform. UAVs can fire missiles, but, as noted, the use of a missile here is unlikely. Would the controller of a covert aircraft risk using a highly visible and noisy weapon like a missile? Probably not, because this would compromise stealth. More likely, he would use some type of cutting-edge technology consistent with the covert nature of the operation. The preferred technology might be some type of directed energy weapon.

There is a considerable amount of evidence that civilian aircraft, including commercial jetliners, are extremely vulnerable to electromagnetic interference. Harvard professor Elaine Scarry did an excellent job reviewing this evidence in a series of articles in the *New York Review of Books* between 1998 and 2000. In the articles Scarry explored whether the US military may have inadvertently caused several controversial airline crashes, possibly during military exercises off the Atlantic coast.[60]

Each of the flights (TWA 800 on July 17, 1996, SwissAir 111 on September 2, 1998, and EgyptAir 990 on October 31, 1999) had departed from JFK International Airport in New York City; and there was some evidence that each of the crashes involved, in Scarry's words, "an electrical catastrophe." In her articles Scarry opined that much of the pertinent research was locked up in classified studies. She urged the military to release this information so that the threat to airline safety could be better evaluated.

From the open literature, however, it was already clear that high intensity radiated fields (HIRF) can cause fatal airline crashes. Electromagnetic interference can produce sparking, fires and even explosions, resulting in the failure or shut down of key components, such as engines and autopilot, causing a plane to go into a steep uncontrolled dive. All of this is consistent with the crash of UAL 93.

Although key components in military aircraft are usually shielded from radiation, even so, the Pentagon has also had its share of problems. Electromagnetic interference was responsible for a number of Black Hawk helicopter crashes between 1982 and 1988. As a senior Army aviator put it: "EMI is causing these aircraft to flip upside down and crash and kill everyone on board."[61] The military solved the problem by spending $175 million to retrofit the Black Hawk's flight control computers with additional shielding.[62]

The Navy also had a serious problem with its F-111 fighter. Seven of the planes were disabled in 1986 during naval operations off the coast of Libya. An eighth F-111 crashed into the ocean, killing two airmen, after exploding in a fireball.[63] The Navy concluded that EMI was likely responsible.

Even before Scarry's first article appeared in 1998, military experts were expressing concern on Capitol Hill that if terrorists ever got their hands on a new type of radio frequency weapon known as a Transient Microwave Device (TED) they might wreak havoc on "financial institutions, aircraft....and other critical equipment."[64] TEDs use simple spark-gap switches to release a single powerful pulse or spike of energy that is comparable to an electrostatic discharge. The phenomenon will be familiar to anyone who has rubbed his stocking feet on a carpet before touching a doorknob.

Whereas other types of high powered microwave (HPM) devices deliver a smooth sine wave at a specific frequency, TEDs send an extremely transient spike across a very broad spectrum, which makes this type of weapon especially dangerous to computers and other electrical equipment, because the spike will impact any weak link in the system. A TED only requires a relatively small power source, such as a battery, and can be made compact enough to fit into an attache case.

The level of the Pentagon's concern was reflected in a 70-page Quadrennial Defense Review that included almost one hundred references to this new type of threat.[65] The actual reason for the US military's concern, however, had nothing to do with Islamic terrorists, but with the fact that, for many years, Soviet scientists had led the world in the development of radio frequency weapons.[66]

It is noteworthy (and also perhaps deeply ironic, given the theme of this chapter) that in August 2001, just weeks before 9/11, a computer scientist at the University of Rhode Island, Michael Hayden (no relation to the former head of the NSA), posted an article in which he showed mathematically that the actual threat of a successful terrorist strike involving TEDs was vanishingly small.[67] His assessment was undoubtedly correct. After all, such advanced technologies are not developed in caves half-way around the planet but in well-endowed government laboratories. Incidentally, the same argument holds for the nanothermite residues discovered in the WTC dust, and also in the case of the October 2001 anthrax attacks.

EVIDENCE FOR A HIGH-TECH SHOOT DOWN

Is there evidence that such a weapon was used on September 11, 2001? Perhaps. That morning, there were reports of power outages in the vicinity of Shanksville. According to one source, the mayor of the nearby community of Indian Lake notified the utility company about a disruption of electrical service.[68] Local residents also said their lights flickered just before the crash of UAL 93.[69] Phone service was also down, and stayed down for many hours.[70]

One of the reasons I went to Shanksville was to check out these reports. It did not take me long to confirm them. John Fleegle told me his TV flickered, moments before the crash. At the time, Fleegle was employed at the Indian Lake marina, about a mile and a half from the crash site. He said he was watching the TV coverage of 9/11 when the screen flickered. Moments later, he heard the loud scream of engines, then, the horrendous crash.[71]

Tom Spinelli was also at the marina and confirmed Fleegle's account. He added more details, explaining that the television at the marina actually went out, briefly, then came back on.[72] Another local resident, Korri Walker, had a similar experience. At the time, Walker lived off Highway 160, also east of Shanksville. She told me she was on the phone (an electric plug-in phone) while simultaneously watching the television coverage of 9/11, when suddenly both the TV and phone went dead.[73] The power stayed off for some time.

There were also indications that an electrical failure had crippled UAL 93. The radar data shows that UAL 93's transponder, which earlier had been turned off, came back on just moments before the crash.[74] From the standpoint of the hijackers, this makes absolutely no sense, and could be evidence of an electrical malfunction. It is also conceivable that the unresolved controversy over the crash time has a similar electrical origin.

While this is conjecture, as noted, questions persist about UAL 93's recovered flight data recorder and its Cockpit Voice Recorder. In 2002, the FBI allowed family members of the deceased to listen to the approximately-thirty-minute tape from UAL 93's recovered cockpit voice recorder. According to the *Philadelphia Daily News,* the "relatives later reported they heard sounds of an on-board struggle beginning at 9:59 A. M., but there was a final 'rushing sound' at 10:03, and the tape fell silent."[75] There was no sound of an impact at 10:03 A.M., the official crash time, only this "rushing noise," like the sound of air whistling through the plane.

This suggests that an explosion may have breached UAL 93's fuselage. Which could also explain why debris was so widely scattered, and why, for instance, the residents of Indian Lake reported seeing letters (i.e., mail) falling "like confetti." In fact, the third debris-field at New Baltimore, eight miles from the crash site, is hard to explain unless the fuselage was breached *before* the crash, when UAL 93 was still airborne.

The last phone message from UAL 93 may also support such a conclusion. Passenger Ed Felt supposedly placed a call from UAL 93's rear washroom at 9:58 A.M. Understandably distraught, the man reported an explosion and also white smoke. The last thing he said was that the plane was going down. At that moment, the line went dead. The Felt call is one of only two cell phone calls from UAL 93 that the FBI defended at the 2005 trial of Zacarias Moussaoui.

Many have cited the call as evidence that a fighter downed UAL 93 with a missile. But we know this did not happen for the simple reason that no NORAD fighters were anywhere near UAL 93. Nor is it likely that any of the NORAD fighters were equipped for stealth. If radar cloaking had been standard equipment, its existence would have leaked, long ago. In conclusion, the hypothetical use of a high-powered microwave weapon, mounted on a UAV strike platform, is consistent with all of the known facts, including a possible explosion.

Endnotes

1   Richard Gazarik and Robin Acton, "Black box recovered at Shanksville site," *Pittsburgh Tribune-Review*, September 14, 2001, posted at http://www.pittsburghlive.com/x/pittsburghtrib/s_12969.html.

2   Ibid.

3   The rumors continued to be reflected in media reports long after 9/11. USA Today, September 16, 2001; *Washington Post*, January 27, 2002; ABC News and CBS News, September 11, 2002. The rumors also circulated on the Internet. In 2002 the University of St. Thomas posted a story about an alum, Lt. Col. Anthony Kuczynski, who, according to the story, piloted an USAF E-3 Sentry AWACS plane over Pennsylvania on 9/11. Kuczynski claimed that two F-16s "were given direct orders to shoot down an airliner." Dave Foster, "UST Grad Guides Bombers in War," *Aquin*, December 4, 2002. The story was posted on the UST website, but has since disappeared from cyberspace. A similar report appeared in author James Bamford's 2005 book, *Pretext for War* (New York: Anchor Books, 2005), pp. 65-66.

4   Deputy Defense Secretary Paul Wolfowitz told the *Boston Herald* that "that the Air Force was tracking the hijacked plane that crashed in Pennsylvania on Tuesday after other airliners slammed into the Pentagon and World Trade Center and had been in a position to bring it down if necessary." *Boston Herald*, September 15, 2001. The *New York Times* also repeated the report. See

     http://www.attackonamerica.net/pentagontrackeddeadlyjet.html

     Rumors of hot pursuit were repeated in many press reports. For example, see http://www.post-gazette.com/headlines/20011028flt93mainstoryp7.asp

5   http://www.archive.org/details/GNN_Flight93_Pt2

6   http://www.archive.org/details/GNN_Flight93_Pt2

7   http://www.thepittsburghchannel.com/news/961654/detail.html

8   Email from Miles Kara, October 31, 2010.

9   http://www.youtube.com/watch?v=An_nXpr5K0A&feature=related

10 *Popular Mechanics* falsely reported, as follows: "According to David Newell, VF's director of aviation and travel, the FAA's Cleveland Center contacted copilot Yates Gladwell when the Falcon was at an altitude 'in the neighborhood of 3000 to 4000 ft.'—not 34,000 ft. 'They were in a descent already going into Johnstown,' Newell adds. 'The FAA asked them to investigate and they did. They got down within 1500 ft. of the ground when they circled. They saw a hole in the ground with smoke coming out of it. They pinpointed the location and then continued on.'" None of which was true! *Popular Mechanics* also falsely reported that the Falcon 20 commuter jet was "owned by the VF Corp. of Greensboro, N.C., an apparel company that markets Wrangler jeans and other brands."

http://www.popularmechanics.com/technology/military/news/debunking-911-myths-flight-93#whitejet

Not so. According to an Associated Press story in August 2002, the FBI briefed US District Judge Leonie Brinkema about evidence it would present at the trial of Zacharias Moussaoui. The evidence was to include the cockpit voice recorder tape from the Falcon 20 commuter jet owned by NetJets, a company that was itself owned by multi-billionaire entrepreneur Warren Buffet.

http://legacy.signonsandiego.com/news/nation/terror/20020808-1446-moussaoui-pictures.html

11 Email from Miles Kara, October 27, 2010.

12 Ibid.

13 Email from John Farmer, October 28, 2010.

14 Mark,

The only thing I noted is that you are calling the small plane a 1200. It started out squawking 1200, but changed to 0527 for M3 at 13:04:06.170. Here are the two flight plans I found for it.

```
|122238.5|N95AP  702|FSP 06F  |O ENR  |          IHD    02        AML  D95 3859/7655 CGS         |
|        |          |          |       | N95AP    067   13     90  349                   0527    |
|        |          |          |       |          033              040                           |
|        |          |          |       | FA32/G   1244                               DIA  IA+    |
|        |          |          |       | T155 G173                                  BWI  BA+    |
|        |          |          |       |      06                                     WHA  DC+    |
|        |          |          |       | 702    01      HGR 231/002        IL/L CGS              |
```

```
|125435.6|N95AP  702|FSP 06F  |O ENR  |          1 BUSTR  59        MRB  D95./.BUSTR MRB         |
|        |          |          |       | N95AP         12      90        MRB183 V4 AML CGS  0527  |
|        |          |          |       | FA32/G   1255                                           |
|        |          |          |       | T155 G170                                  DIA  IA+    |
|        |          |          |       |      06                                     WHA  DC+    |
|        |          |          |       | 702    02      HGR 256/006        IL/L CGS   WHA  AD+    |
```

Here is the FAA N-registration info. Looks like a Piper single engine.

Aircraft Description

Serial Number	32-46012	Type Registration	Corporation
Manufacturer Name	PIPER	Certificate Issue Date	11/14/2000
Model	PA-32R-301	Expiration Date	03/31/2013
Type Aircraft	Fixed Wing Single-Engine	Status	Valid
Pending Number Change	None	Type Engine	Reciprocating
Date Change Authorized	None	Dealer	No
MFR Year	1995	Mode S Code	53231134
		Fractional Owner	NO

Registered Owner

Name	ARLAN LLC		
Street	1662 CREE CT		
City	OXFORD	State	MICHIGAN
County	OAKLAND	Zip Code	48371-6620
Country	UNITED STATES		

Airworthiness

Engine Manufacturer	LYCOMING	Classification	Standard
Engine Model	IO-540 SER	Category	Normal
		A/W Date	11/16/2000

15   http://www.youtube.com/watch?v=_gliHOhXYFQ&feature=related

16   Steve Coll, *Ghost Wars* (New York: Penguin, 2005), pp. 527–8 and 658 note 5.

17   Email from Robin Hordon, November 26, 2010.

18   Reports on the Internet that McElwain saw an A-10 Warthog are mistaken.

19   Email from Miles Kara, October 21, 2010.

20   I discovered at least two errors at the site known as "Killtown." According to this site, John Fleegle said he arrived at the crash site within a minute. But Fleegle told me it was more like five minutes. When I spoke with Tom Spinelli, who was with Fleegle, he estimated the time at 5-8 minutes. Spinelli also told me that he never saw the white jet before the crash, only after. Here is the Killtown compilation:

      http://killtown.911review.org/flight93/mystery-aircraft.html

      History Commons has another compilation. Remember to scroll down:

      http://www.historycommons.org/context.jsp?item=a1007businessjetasked#a1007 businessjetasked

21   Conversation with Tom Spinelli, March 25, 2011.

22   The New York Fire Department (NYFD) had gathered these interviews between October 2001- January 2002 at the order of then-New York Fire Commissioner Thomas Van Essen, who later told the *New York Times* he wanted to preserve the accounts for historical reasons, "before they became reshaped by a collective memory." The department also made transcripts of the tapes: all told, some 12,000 pages of written testimony. The city had withheld all of this material for several years because, as Nicholas Scoppetta, Van Essen's successor, told the *New York Times*, federal prosecutors advised him that its publication might impede the ongoing prosecution of alleged al Qaeda terrorist Zacarias Moussaoui. Jim Dwyer, "City to Release Thousands of Oral Histories of 9/11 Today," *New York Times*, August 12, 2005.

      The reason was flimflam. The histories obviously had no bearing on the Moussaoui trial. At any rate, this was the opinion of the NY state Court of Appeals, which ordered most of the material to be released, the result of a lawsuit filed by the *New York Times* and joined by the families of the victims. The oral histories were eventually made public in August 2005, and they are currently posted on the *New York Times* web site. The FDNY testimonials are posted as pdf files at http://graphics8.nytimes.com/packages/html/nyregion/20050812_WTC_GRAPHIC/met_WTC_histories_full_01.html For a convenient look at some of them go to http://www.911review.com/coverup/oralhistories.html

      Although the oral histories were only made public in August 2005, according to the *New York Times* the 9/11 Commission gained access to the material long before this by bringing legal threats against the city of New York. Jim Dwyer, op. cit.

      The 9/11 Commission actually drew upon the histories while drafting chapter nine of its final report, which covers the plane impacts and WTC collapse. Chapter nine makes reference to "our review of 500 internal FDNY interview transcripts." A reader, however, will search the chapter in vain for any mention of the 118 responders who saw, felt and heard explosions. In fact, in the entire 567-page *9/11 Commission Report* there is only one reference to explosions. The lone case was drawn from interviews that the panel conducted in 2004 and is presented not as part of a discussion of an alternative collapse scenario (i.e., a demolition caused by explosions), but rather, for the purpose of discrediting the witness for even thinking such thoughts. For an good analysis see http://www.journalof911studies.com/articles/Article_5_118Witnesses_WorldTradeCenter.pdf

23   http://www.bentham.org/open/tocpj/articles/V002/7TOCPJ.htm?TOCPJ/2009/0 0000002/00000001/7TOCPJ.SGM

      Also see: http://www.springerlink.com/content/f67q6272583h86n4/

24   Robert Schopmeyer, *Prior Knowledge of 9/11*, (Palo Alto Publishing, Los Altos, CA, 2006), p. 368. Author Schopmeyer explained to me that he learned this firsthand from Coleen Rowley and her boss Joseph Rivers, whom he interviewed in July 2004 at the Minneapolis FBI field office. Schopmeyer says that during the two-hour sit-down interview Rowley and Joseph told him that no one from the commission had ever contacted them at any time prior to the release of *The 9/11 Commission Report*. Email from Robert Schopmeyer, November 28, 2010.

25   Email from Miles Kara, October 20, 2010.

26   http://www.fas.org/irp/program/collect/predator.htm

27   Dan Benjamin and Steve Simon, *The Age of Sacred Terror*, cited in Richard A. Clarke, *Against All Enemies* (New York: Free Press, 2004), pp. 220-222.

28   Ibid.

29   In 2007, CIA Director Michael Hayden resorted to the same dodge when he attempted to explain why the CIA had destroyed hundreds of hours of videotapes of the early CIA interrogations of captured al-Qaeda operatives Abu Zubaydah and Ramsi Binalshibh, during which the CIA used "enhanced interrogation techniques," the agency euphemism for torture. The methods included waterboarding, which induces a sensation of drowning in the unfortunate individual. Hayden told the press that the tapes posed "a serious security risk." Hayden's statement was agency newspeak for: The CIA destroyed evidence to shield its own officials from legal prosecution, given that torture is a felony offense. This was the view of Tom Malinowski, Washington director of Human Rights Watch. Mark Mazetti, "CIA Destroyed Two Tapes Showing Interrogations," *New York Times*, December 7, 2007.

      Hayden served up more nonsense when he added that the agency had followed the letter of the law by notifying the appropriate committee heads in Congress before destroying the tapes. The claim was immediately disputed by Senator Jay Rockefeller (D-WV) and Representative Peter Hoekstra (R-MI), the respective chairmen of the Senate and House Intelligence Committees. A spokesman for Hoekstra said that he "was never briefed or advised" that the tapes even existed, let alone "that they were going to be destroyed." "CIA destroyed terrorism suspect videotapes," *NBC News*, December 7, 2007.

      Hayden's statement also prompted the former co-chairs of the 9/11 Commission, Thomas Kean and Lee Hamilton, to fire off an angry op-ed in the *New York Times* charging that the CIA had obstructed their official investigation of the 9/11 attacks. Kean and Hamilton made it clear that they had never been told about the existence, let alone the destruction, of the tapes, even though the commission had formally requested the agency to hand over all relevant documents and records pertaining to the captives. This was long after then-CIA Director George Tenet denied Kean and Hamilton permission to interview the al-Qaeda captives, access which Kean and Hamilton correctly believed was essential for its official investigation. In the end, the commission had to base its mandated investigation on third-hand CIA intelligence reports, many of which were "poorly written and incomplete summaries" which "raised almost as many questions as they answered." Thomas H. Kean and Lee H. Hamilton, "Stonewalled by the CIA," *The New York Times*, January 2008.

30   *9/11 Commission Report*, pp. 189-190.

31   Richard A. Clarke, *Against All Enemies*, p. 221.

32   http://www.fas.org/irp/program/collect/docs/man-ipc-predator-010228.htm

33   http://www.guardian.co.uk/world/2001/nov/07/afghanistan.september11
      Also see: http://news.bbc.co.uk/2/hi/events/newsnight/1645527.stm

34   http://www.fas.org/irp/program/collect/global_hawk.htm

ø - A "best face" supposition. More realistically, they may have revealed who was really running them on the tapes.

35   "Robot plane flies Pacific unmanned," *ITN News*, posted at http://web.archive.org/ web/20010707000937/http://itn.co.uk/news/20010424/world/05robotplane.shtm

36   The June 1, 2001 order can be downloaded at www.dtic.mil/doctrine/jel/cjcsd/ cjcsi/3610_01a.pdf

37   The July 1997 order can be downloaded at www.dtic.mil/doctrine/jel/cjcsd/cjc-si/3610_01.pdf

38   I should mention that some do not entirely agree with this assessment, Former air traffic controller Robin Hordon, for instance, believes that a significant change in policy did occur in June 2001, even though this was not reflected in the new order issued by the Joint Chiefs. Hordon thinks a change was introduced operationally and required the FAA, henceforth, to notify the Pentagon before declaring an air emergency. This, in his view, helps to explains the slow response time on 9/11.

39   The NIST study is discussed at length in my previous book about 9/11: Mark H. Gaffney, *The 9/11 Mystery Plane and the Vanishing of America* (Walterville, OR: TrineDay, 2008), pp. 129-193.

40   *The 9/11 Mystery Plane and the Vanishing of America*, p. 101.

41   Email from Dr. Deagle, January 3, 2009; emails from Steve DeNoo, January 3, 4, 2009.

42   http://www.reuters.com/finance/stocks/companyProfile?symbol=ANEN.O&rpc= 66

43   Ibid.

44   http://www.secinfo.com/dr66r.95r.htm#2cq

45   http://files.shareholder.com/downloads/ANEN/644246062x0xS891092%2D08%2 D4543/6314/filing.pdf

46   http://en.wikipedia.org/wiki/Digital_radio_frequency_memory

47   http://www.fas.org/irp/mystery/history.htm

48   http://wapedia.mobi/en/Operation_Mole_Cricket_19#1.

49   Pollack, Kenneth M., *Arabs at War: Military Effectiveness, 1948-1991* (Lincoln, NE: Bison Books, 2004), p. 533.

50   George W. Ball, *Error and Betrayal in Lebanon* (Washington DC: Foundation for Middle East Peace, 1984), pp. 42-43.

51   Andy Soltis, "2nd Mystery 'hit' Israeli jet flyover amid Hungary slay," *New York Post*, March 189, 2010. Posted at http://www.nypost.com/p/news/international/ nd_mystery_hit_9oQse5yfi46JbHUmXrSy2N

52   Emails from Bob Pinnacle, May 19, 20, 21, 24, June 16, 20, 2010.

53   The Iranians may have exploited a weakness in the RQ-170's navigational system. The drone is known to utilize GPS. But apparently the GPS signal was not encrypt-ed, raising the possibility that the Iranians spoofed the system, uploaded different coordinates, and "fooled" the drone into landing inside Iran. Scott Peterson, "Ex-clusive: Iran hijacked US drone, says Iranian Engineer," *Christian Science Monitor*, December 15, 2011.

54   John Walcott, "Iran Shows Downed Spy Drone as US Assesses Technology Loss," *Bloomberg Business Week*, December 12, 2011.

55   Email from Susan McElwain, December 19, 2011.

56   William Bunch, "Three-minute discrepancy in tape" *Philadelphia Daily News*, Sep-tember 16, 2002, archived at http://www.911omissionreport.com/three-minute_ discrepancy.html.

57   Email from Terry Wallace, November 1, 2010.

58 "Witness Joe Wilt, 63, said he heard a whistling like a missile, then a loud boom as he stood in the doorway of his Shanksville home across the road from the site. His view was blocked by a group of trees, but he said he saw a fireball rise 800 feet into the air, then give way to black smoke." Anne Michaud, "Frantic 911 call preceded crash outside Pittsburgh," *Boston Globe*, September 12, 2001, posted at http://www.boston.com/news/packages/underattack/globe_stories/0912/Frantic_911_call_preceded_crash_outside_Pittsburgh+.shtml

59 Former fighter pilot Robert Bowman (Lt. Col. USAF, ret.) articulated such a view. Email from Robert Bowman, November 13, 2010

60 Elaine Scarry, "The Fall of TWA 800," *New York Review of Books*, March 24, 1998; Elaine Scarry, "The Fall of EgyptAir 990," *New York Review of Books*, October 5, 2000.

61 "Ordinary radio waves Allegedly Can Knock Down Combat Copter," *Los Angeles Times*, November 9, 1987, p. A4.

62 Mark Thompson, "Mixed Signals May Have Misguided US Weapons: Pentagon Probing Electronic Interference Also Suspected in F-111 Crash During Libya Strike," The *Washington Post*, January 1989.

63 *Washington Post*, April 16, 1986; April 20, 1986.

64 Statement of Mr. David Schriner to the Joint Economic Committee, US Congress, February 25, 1998.

  http://cryptome.org/rfw-jec.htm

65 Statement of Lt. General Robert Schweitzer, US Army, (Ret) before the Joint Economic Committee, US Congress, June 17, 1997. http://cryptome.org/rfw-jec.htm

66 Statement of Dr. Ira W. Merritt before the Joint Economic Committee, US Congress, February 25, 1998.

  http://cryptome.org/rfw-jec.htm

67 Michael B. Hayden, "Electromagnetic Attack: Is Your Infrastructure and Data at Risk?", August 10, 2001, posted at http://www.lib.iup.edu/comscisec/SANSpapers/hayden.htm

68 Ibid.

69 http://www.archive.org/details/GNN_Flight93_Pt2

70 http://www.abovetopsecret.com/forum/thread282938/pg1

71 Conversation with John "Toe Head" Fleegle, Shanksville, March 3, 2011.

72 Phone conversation with Tom Spinelli, March 24, 2011.

73 Phone conversation with Korri Walker, Shanksville, March 3, 2011.

74 Email from John Farmer, March 19, 2011.

75 William Bunch, "Three-minute discrepancy in tape," *Philadelphia Daily News*, September 16, 2002.

Chapter 14

Correcting the Record

In the period since 9/11, numerous false accounts of the events at Shanksville have sprouted, especially on the Internet. This should not surprise us given the many conflicting reports both on and after September 11 2001, the dubious treatment in official reports and by the media, not to mention the fact that various interest groups insist on viewing 9/11 history through their own agendas

Fortunately, the RADES radar data recorded during the 9/11 attacks provide a powerful tool that can help us to weed some of these out, provided we exercise the appropriate caution in interpreting the data.

As we have seen, the radar data from 9/11 has already proved its usefulness, and there are other examples. Recently, John Farmer showed that the radar data for American Airlines Flight 77 (AA 77) accords perfectly with the timeline of AA 77's approach to Washington as recounted by former Secretary of Transportation Norman Mineta during his testimony before the 9/11 Commission in 2004.

The issue is important because Mineta's account of what happened in the White House bunker tends to incriminate then-Vice President Dick Cheney, and no doubt, this is why Mineta's testimony was excluded from the official report. Curious readers are encouraged to check out Farmer's post, on line.[1]

One can find numerous stories on the Internet that one of the F-16s scrambled from Langley Air Force Base, brought down UAL 93 with a sidewinder missile.[2] According to another report, it was an F-16 from Andrews AFB.[3] These reports have circulated widely and some are quite detailed. One source actually names the fighter pilot who supposedly pulled the trigger on UAL 93.[4] Another unnamed source claims to be the individual who administered the shoot down order.[5] The 9/11 radar data plainly shows, however, that all of these reports are mistaken. Consider the following diagram, based on the 9/11 radar data. It shows the flight path of the three Langley fighters scrambled on September 11, 2001.

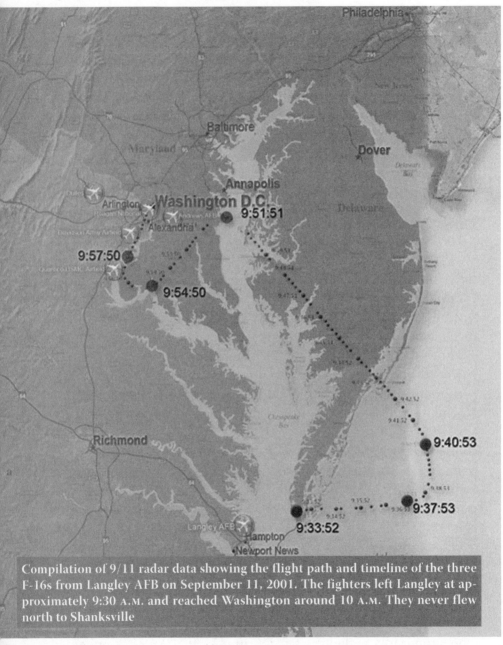

Compilation of 9/11 radar data showing the flight path and timeline of the three F-16s from Langley AFB on September 11, 2001. The fighters left Langley at approximately 9:30 A.M. and reached Washington around 10 A.M. They never flew north to Shanksville

As indicated, the F-16s from Langley AFB were airborne by roughly 9:30 A.M. but failed to reach Washington until 10 A.M.

The pilots were delayed after being sent on three consecutive wild goose chases, a fact so embarrassing to the US military that for years the Pentagon covered up the actual flight path of the Langley fighters. The 9/11 Commission revealed the first and second wild goose chases in its final report, published in 2004, but perpetuated the cover-up regarding the third.

However, after an honest bureaucrat released the 9/11 RADES radar data in October 2007, in compliance with the Freedom of Information Act (FOIA), the cat was out of the bag and an official acknowledgment of some kind was inevitable. The US military finally disclosed the rest of the story to Lynne Spencer, who was the first to document the Langley fighters' wildly erratic third leg south of Washington in a 2008 book, *Touching History*.[6]

You will notice that the F-16s from Langley reached Washington just three minutes before the official crash time of UAL 93 (10:03 A.M.), whereupon, the pilots established a defensive cap over the capital. They did not cover the 127 miles to Shanksville in three minutes. Nor could they have done so had they tried.

Even if one accepts the alternative view that the crash occurred at 10:06 A.M., there was still insufficient time to reach Shanksville.[7] In any event, the issue is mooted by the radar data, which shows it never happened. Although one of the Langley pilots flew up the Potomac River to Great Falls, he never got close to Pennsylvania. End of story.

According to another Internet report, "one of the four Langley pilots" returned to base on 9/11 minus his full complement of Sidewinders. On this basis, we are evidently supposed to conclude that the pilot used one to shoot down UAL 93.[8] But this report is also wrong, and again Spencer helped set it straight.

In the first place, only two F-16 pilots were on alert at Langley AFB on the morning of September 11, not four. At the last minute, a third F-16 pilot, Capt. Craig Borgstrom, was ordered to join the scramble. His third aircraft (call sign = Quit 27) was not fully armed: Borgstrom returned to base without missiles because he had none when he took off.[9]

THE FIGHTERS FROM ANDREWS AFB

The next diagram is a composite based on the 9/11 radar data, and shows the flight paths of the F-16s from Andrews AFB on

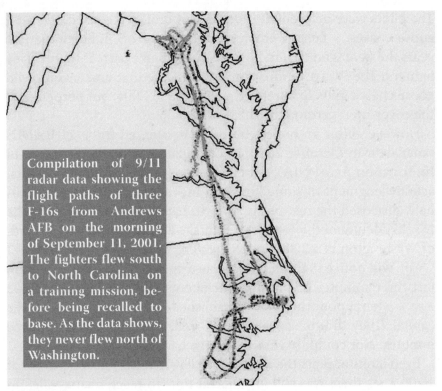

Compilation of 9/11 radar data showing the flight paths of three F-16s from Andrews AFB on the morning of September 11, 2001. The fighters flew south to North Carolina on a training mission, before being recalled to base. As the data shows, they never flew north of Washington.

September 11, 2001.[10] As it plainly shows, the fighters never flew north of Washington DC, which rules out any possibility that they were involved in a shoot-down of UAL 93.

Although this is self-evident from the data, I will briefly re-cap their story. On the morning of 9/11, three F-16s departed Andrews at 8:35 A.M. on a training mission to North Carolina. The fighters were not armed with Sidewinders. Shortly after Andrews AFB went on alert (sometime between 9:30-9:35 A.M.), the three pilots were recalled to base. The first of the F-16s returned to Andrews at 10:14 A.M., which was already well *after* the crash of UAL 93.

The Andrews pilots were low on fuel by this time, but one of them, Major Billy Hutchison, evidently still had enough for a short flight over Washington. Hutchison took off again and was the first F-16 pilot scrambled from Andrews AFB on 9/11 in defense of the nation's capital. By then of course, as noted, the fighters from Langley had already established a defensive cap over the city.

According to 9/11 Commission staffer Miles Kara, who posted a radar diagram of Hutchinson's flight path on his web site, Andrews personnel did not finally succeed in getting fully armed F-16s in the air until after 11 A.M.[11] I have seen no evidence disputing this.

Though the US Air Force's slow reaction time on September 11 may justify both outrage and suspicion, the radar data nevertheless plainly show that the fighters from Langley AFB and Andrews AFB played no role in the crash of UAL 93.

Perhaps you are wondering, OK, but what about a NORAD fighter from some other base? To check this out, I asked John Farmer to consult the radar data for Shanksville. When he did he determined that no NORAD fighters were anywhere near UAL 93 at the time of the crash.[12] No fighters were on patrol over southwestern Pennsylvania during the relevant time frame. [See the following composite diagram showing the flight paths of all NORAD aircraft on 9/11.]

Thus, the assertion on the Internet by a self-proclaimed E-3 AWACS crew member that he gave the order for NORAD fighters to shoot down UAL 93 cannot be correct. The testimony, by the way, is anonymous, which ought to make us skeptical.[13]

But the account is also dubious for other reasons. The individual states that his E-3 was based at Andrews AFB; which cannot be correct since the home base for all US Air Force E-3s is Tinker Air Force Base in Oklahoma City, not Andrews. The individual, moreover, asserts that after 8 a.m. his pilot received an order "to loiter between Washington and Pittsburgh." But, again, the 9/11 radar data shows that no E-3 was in the vicinity during the relevant timeframe. We must conclude that the testimonial is mistaken and may even be a deliberate attempt to muddy the waters.

There were E-3 AWACS planes on patrol that morning, but not over Pennsylvania. After a thorough search of the radar data, John Farmer located one E-3 northwest of Memphis, Tennessee. Another was in a stationary orbit over the Atlantic, off the Virginia coast.[14]

A second Internet account seems more credible, although to the best of my knowledge it has never been confirmed. In 2002 *The Aquin*, the student newspaper of the University of St. Thomas (located in St. Paul, Minnesota) posted a story about one of its graduates, Lt. Anthony Kuczynski, who, it asserts, piloted an E-3 on 9/11. The article later disappeared from cyberspace, though a portion was archived.[15]

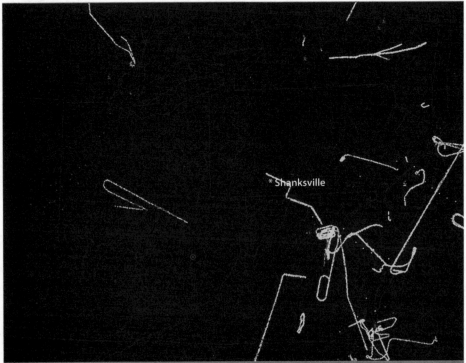

Compilation of 9/11 radar data showing the flight paths of all NORAD aircraft in the Northeastern Air Defense Sector (NEADS) on September 11, 2001, between 9:45 - 10:15 A.M. The data confirms that the only NORAD plane in the vicinity of UAL93 at the time of the crash was a C-130H transport (call sign: GOPHER06) piloted by Lt. Col. Steve O'Brien, who was en route to his Air National Guard base in Minnesota.

According to the story, on the morning of 9/11 Lt. Kuczynski received an order to shoot down United Flight 93; however, the associated fighters were unable to carry out the order before UAL 93 crashed at Shanksville. Although the account is sketchy, it might have some basis in fact.

In sum, the 9/11 radar data confirm that the NORAD spokesman was telling the truth on September 13, 2001, when he announced, "NORAD-allocated forces have not engaged with weapons any aircraft [on 9/11], including Flight 93."[16]

The radar data show that the lone military aircraft in the vicinity of Shanksville during the relevant time period was a C-130H transport (call sign = Gopher 06).[17] Curiously, this was the same C-130H, piloted by Lt. Col. Steve O'Brien which earlier had tailed the aircraft (presumably AA 77) that struck the Pentagon. Although this bizarre coincidence is very suspicious, I have seen no evidence

why is Michigan account omitted?

that O'Brien was somehow involved with the downing of either aircraft. As noted, the C-130H never approached closer than about 17 miles to UAL 93.

But even if NORAD was not involved, this does not rule out the possibility of a shoot-down, as I have already shown.

ABSENCE OF EVIDENCE AS EVIDENCE OF ABSENT OVERSIGHT

There is another serious ramification. The absence of any NORAD fighters near Shanksville also means that acting Chairman of the Joint Chiefs Richard Myers exhibited a shocking level of ignorant bravura two days after the attack, when he told the Senate Armed Services Committee, "We had launched on the one that eventually crashed in Pennsylvania. I mean, we had gotten somebody close to it."[18]

Moments later, Myers backpedaled, essentially admitting to the senators that he was clueless about the total breakdown of US air defenses. One would think that the acting commander of all US military forces would have arrived at his own Senate confirmation hearing fully briefed about the force structure under his command, and ready to explain how and why it had failed to perform on 9/11. But no such thing happened.

The gross ignorance Myers displayed is so shocking that I believe we must view it as suspicious. Instead of ratifying his promotion to Chairman, the Senate committee should have urged the president to relieve Myers of his command, effective immediately, and replace him with someone who could answer the obvious questions.

LAST THOUGHTS

We are left with many loose ends. One of the most intriguing questions is the one I raised in Chapter One: was there a connection between the events at Shanksville and the reported crash at Camp David at 10:38 A.M.? In other words, was the white aircraft that Susan McEwain observed near the UAL 93 crash site the same object that crashed or exploded near Camp David? Assuming there was an incident at Camp David, we can rule out the crash of a commercial airliner, which would have been impossible to hush up because of the large number of fatalities.

In this, the *Baltimore Daily Record* may have been technically accurate on September 12 in its correction of the record, as noted in Chapter One, that no *airliner* had crashed near Camp David. Did the incident involve a much smaller plane?

The chronology of both events lines up rather well. The crash at Shanksville occurred at 10:03-06, the incident at Camp David roughly a half-hour later. Given that Camp David is about 90 miles east of Shanksville, this would imply a cruising speed of about 180 mph. Which eliminates the Predator, with a cruising speed of only 100 mph, as a candidate for my hypothetical UAV.

The bigger question, of course, is Why? Allow me to speculate. Assuming a covert aircraft had been outfitted with radar cloaking technology, it is unlikely that security staff at Camp David (or site "R," located about six miles north of Camp David) brought it down with a missile, even assuming they were on heightened alert, for the simple reason that they would not have seen it on radar. But there is another possibility. Did a ground controller make a decision to terminate the covert mission for some reason with on-board explosives, before the attack platform could return to base?

Again, this is conjecture. But if the evidence and reasoning I have presented are valid, it is likely there are potential witnesses, even today: people who have crucial information about the incident. They could be firemen or other emergency responders who were warned to silence for "reasons having to do with national security," the same old canard that has served, time and again, to undermine the US Constitution.

If there *are* such witnesses, they are probably unaware just how important their testimony might be to the restoration of our democratic institutions. Let us hope they see this paper and come forward. The confirmed crash/explosion of a covert aircraft on 9/11 might presage the unraveling of the plot against America, and lead to the exposure and, let us hope, the swift prosecution of the guilty. In which case, justice delayed will not be justice denied.

There is no statute of limitations for the crime of murder.

ENDNOTES
1   http://forums.randi.org/showpost.php?p=6959886&postcount=131
2   http://piratenews.org/flight93.html

3   http://onlinejournal.com/artman/publish/article_3568.shtml

4   In an Alex Jones radio interview Col. Don de Grand-pre identified the pilot as Maj. Rick Gibney, of the 119th Fighter Wing.

       http://infowars.com/print/Sept11/93_shootdown.htm

       Staff at *Popular Mechanics* magazine later did some checking, however, and discovered that Lt Col. Gibney was in Bozeman, Montana on the morning of September 11, 2001, and so could not possibly have flown one of the Langley fighters. In this case *Popular Mechanics* may have gotten it right.

       http://www.popularmechanics.com/technology/military/news/debunking-911-myths-flight-93#f16pilot

5   http://ishotdown93.blogspot.com/2008/04/my-role-in-shooting-down-flight-93.html

6   Lynn Spencer, *Touching History* (New York: Free Press, 2008), p. 181.

7   According to the *Philadelphia Daily News*: "The seismic signals are consistent with impact at 10:06:05," plus or minus two seconds, said Terry Wallace, who heads the Southern Arizona Seismic Observatory and is considered the leading expert on the seismology of man-made events. "I don't know where the 10:03 time comes from." William Bunch, "Three-minute discrepancy in tape," *Philadelphia Daily News*, September 16, 2002. Posted at http://www.911omissionreport.com/three-minute_discrepancy.html

8   http://georgewashington.blogspot.com/2008/04/us-air-force-shot-down-flight-93.html

9   *Touching History*, p. 119.

10   John Farmer produced this diagram from the RADES radar data in March 2008. The times are geared to universal or Greenwich time. He sent it to me with the following note: Mark: The image below is the history of the Andrews fighters. Three took off from Andrews AFB at around 12:35 (GMT) and headed south. I think some of the confusion may be coming from tracking them by M3 codes which can change as they are handed off from one ARTCC to the next. The M2 codes (military) for these three aircraft are: 6413,1212 and 6402.

       What is interesting to me is that at 12:50 they drop to below 2,000 feet and off radar until just after 13:00 (approximately 10 minutes). They then enter the North Carolina bombing range area and remain there until around 13:37. At that time, one (M2 = 1212) heads in a direct line back towards Andrews AFB, landing there at approximately 14:13. That fighter takes off again from Andrews AFB at 14:41 and takes up a holding pattern over DC. The remaining two fighters head back at approximately 14:12 from the NC area, with M2 = 6402 landing at Andrews AFB at approximately 14:30 followed by M2 = 6413 at 14:45.

       I've attached an Excel file that has the raw data for the Andrews Fighters and an extra tab for all M2 bit traffic in the DC and Langley area from 12:15 until 14:40. All military aircraft may or may not have an M2 code (like the infamous C-130), but they all have the M2 bit. Let me know if I can assist further. John. Email from John Farmer, March 31, 2008.

11   http://www.oredigger61.org/?cat=14

12   I received this reply from Farmer: Mark, I double checked. I ran the data through 11:30 A.M. and there are no military aircraft in the area except GOFER 06 (according to NEADS radar). John

       Email from John Farmer, October 23, 2010.

13   http://ishotdown93.blogspot.com/2008/04/my-role-in-shooting-down-flight-93.html

14   Email from John Farmer, April 6, 2012. For the online discussion about Farmer's discovery of the E-3s go to http://forums.randi.org/showthread.php?t=203707

15   http://www.dcdave.com/article5/060704.htm

16   Richard Gazarik and Robin Acton, "Black box recovered at Shanksville site," *Tribune-Review*, September 14, 2001. Posted at http://www.pittsburghlive.com/x/pittsburghtrib/s_12969.html

17   Email from John Farmer, October 23, 2010.

18   Myers was the acting Chairman of the Joint Chiefs on September 11, 2001 because the Chairman General Hugh Shelton was on a flight to Europe. http://www.cogsci.uci.edu/~ddhoff/Myers.html

Epilogue

The Future is Up For Grabs...

O n the afternoon of 9/11, even as the smoke from the Pentagon fires drifted across the Potomac, Secretary of Defense Donald Rumsfeld showed up on Capitol Hill to hector Carl Levin and other senators for a blank check to wage the "war on terrorism." The shakedown strategy worked like a charm. Congress complied with a windfall of cash.

Over the next ten years, the Department of Defense budget steadily expanded, until, in 2011, the total approached $800 billion. But even this obscene number may be too low. Christopher Hellman, a former policy analyst at the Center for Arms Control and Non-Proliferation, has argued that the actual figure is a staggering $1.2 trillion per year, *if* we also factor in military aid to foreign countries, international peacekeeping operations, veteran's benefits, military pensions, and the military component of the interest we pay on the national debt.[1]

As I write, the Congressional spigot flows unchecked into Pentagon coffers. Untold billions of taxpayer dollars continue to disappear down numerous rabbit holes into a black world lost to our sight. The flow of cash feeds hundreds of Top Secret projects, many involving next generation weapons and military technologies that have never been unveiled. Some of them have probably been under development in government labs for many years. The American people know nothing of this classified world, which has been kept shrouded in secrecy.

I have argued that some of these cutting-edge technologies were used on 9/11. If I am even partly correct, it means the vast increase in US military spending after 9/11 was not the start of our troubles but the inevitable outcome of many years of failed democratic oversight. In that case, the September 11 attacks were not only more complex than we have been led to think, they were stranger than most of us have guessed in our wildest nightmares. If the full story is ever told, it will mock our complacency like the gods of the ancient world.

I believe the issue of secrecy is paramount. The technologies I have discussed certainly were not on my radar screen before I began to investigate 9/11. Like most Americans, I was blithely unaware that technological advances were altering our world, almost beyond recognition. While it is certainly true that new technologies hold amazing potentials to free us from drudgery and improve the quality of our lives, make no mistake, technology can just as easily enslave us. Nor is it likely that its most hopeful possibilities will be realized so long as the cutting edge remains shrouded in secrecy.

But I would go even further: If ordinary citizens do not soon awaken to the insidious dangers that black technologies pose to our freedoms, the shameless puppeteers who command them from the shadows may ultimately succeed in imposing their new world order upon us. In that case, the experiment in self-government that began with the drafting of the US Constitution more than 200 years ago will come to an inglorious end, just another of history's failed experiments.

Even as a majority of Americans continue to shrink from the pivotal significance of 9/11, fortunately, an international consensus is emerging on the issue. This is reflected by a January 2011 poll in Germany, arguably home to the world's most informed and best educated public. The poll showed that 89% of Germans have rejected the US government's official story about 9/11.[2]

The figure represents a startling defeat for US propagandists. Nor is it likely that the political reality it reflects will be reversed, any time soon. Credibility being a precious commodity, once lost, it is extremely difficult to recoup. Germany's recent withdrawal of support for the NATO-backed conflict in Libya shows that the tide of opinion is already being reflected in the policy decisions of the German government.[3] Moreover, the same trend may soon be repeated in Japan, in part due to the ongoing nuclear disaster in Fukushima prefecture.

As I write, the multiple melt-downs at the Daiichi nuclear plant have the potential to be worse than Chernobyl. But even if the worst does not happen, and let us hope for the sake of the Japanese it does not, Daiichi has already exposed the self-interested poverty of US policymakers. In the aftermath of World War II, the US government pressured a prostrate Japanese nation to purchase US nuclear technology. The reactors at Daiichi were designed by General Electric.

That decision was an unconscionable blunder given that Japan is situated atop several active tectonic fault lines and has a long history of major earthquakes and tsunamis. As the Japanese people struggle to recover, they will likely become more nationalistic and independent of the United States. For many years, the Japanese supported US deficit spending by loyally purchasing US government bonds. But this will probably change, as all available capital will be urgently needed at home. Even before Daiichi, the Japanese media was more open to opposing viewpoints about 9/11 than its US counterpart. In post-Daiichi Japan, skepticism about the US and especially 9/11 is likely to increase and could even develop into open hostility.

The German poll and the nuclear disaster in Japan together represent a stunning reversal for the United States, which since the end of World War II has stood at the pinnacle of world power. Incredible as it seems, in a mere sixty years the US has squandered the rare opportunity bequeathed to it after World War II: to lead the world into an era of unprecedented peace and prosperity. Instead, US elites have demonstrated that they are unworthy to lead.

History's rare opportunity will not be repeated. The reins of world leadership seem destined to pass eventually into other hands, but not, let us hope, into the hands of the international bankers, though this appears to be the plan.

As a global shift in economic power occurs that is less friendly to US interests, possibly led by the BRIC nations (i.e., Brazil, Russia, India and China), we should expect that Washington will increasingly resort to the use of raw military force to maintain US strategic advantages, much as the Crown did in the twilight of the British empire. In that case, US and NATO-sponsored wars will likely continue and escalate until they trigger another world conflagration, just as waning British power led to World War I. Except, this time, there will be a crucial difference: today, any global conflict will probably involve the use of nuclear weapons.

This is why, in 2012, there can be no rest for honest men.

Truly, there has never been a time like the present, not in all of human history. Even as powerful anti-democratic forces gain strength in the US and abroad, new conflicts are impelling us into a dangerous future. Humanity stands poised on the brink of a very uncertain tomorrow. We are quite literally dancing on the edge...

But of what kind of future? Will we witness a peaceful flowering of global culture, or a vanishing?

One thing is clear. We will not succeed in our efforts to demobilize the US war machine and restore the US Constitution unless we open our eyes, full wide. *Because our only chance to exert a positive influence on events will be through right action, and that means we must understand our world as it actually is, not as we would like it to be, or as some would have us believe.*

The facts are stark, as I have attempted to show. Our nation is presently in the grip of diabolically evil forces that have betrayed and subverted our democratic values. But who are these individuals? I would argue: they are the same people who keep telling us that unregulated, i.e., predatory, capitalism is divinely ordained, and not to be questioned. They and their allies presently dominate Wall Street, both political parties, the courts, Congress (which they have bought), not to mention the White House (also bought) and the major US corporate media outlets (which they own); and by which means they have put many of our countrymen to sleep.

No mistake, mass hypnosis and denial will continue to be the greatest obstacles to a democratic renaissance here at home. The uncompromising search for truth cuts against the grain of US exceptionalism, instant gratification, reality and celeb TV, consumerism, cheap thrills, sports-on-demand, infotainment and every other readily available form of escapism in our mass culture. As Orwell wrote, "in a time of universal deceit, speaking the truth becomes a revolutionary act."

Sometimes, in order to see the light, it is necessary to wake up and face the darkness. Time may be short, but there is still a chance that our fellow citizens can be aroused, before it is too late. We must never give up, for so long as the Spirit dwells in the hearts of men and women, the future will be up for grabs ... and ours to win.

ENDNOTES

1   Christopher Hellman, "The Real National Security Budget," *Counterpunch*, March 1, 2011. Posted at http://www.counterpunch.org/hellman03012011.html

2   http://911blogger.com/news/2011-01-21/poll-germany-895-doubt-official-version-911

3   "Who's in charge? Germans pull forces out of NATO as Libyan coalition falls apart," *Daily Mail* (UK), March 23, 2011. Posted at http://www.dailymail.co.uk/news/article-1368693/Libya-war-Germans-pull-forces-NATO-Libyan-coalition-falls-apart.html

Afterword

Plausibility of 9/11 Aircraft Attacks Generated by GPS-Guided Aircraft Autopilot Systems Part Two

by Aidan Monaghan (B.Sc., EET)

COMMON PERFORMANCE CHARACTERISTICS

Descending constant radius turns are another feature of GPS guided navigation systems involving both Required Navigation Performance (RNP) approach procedures and the Wide Area Augmentation System (WAAS) signal. Such turns, also known as Radius-to-Fix (RF) turns, [1] are similar to the 330-degree descending right turn that American Airlines Flight 77 performed over Alexandria, Virginia on 9/11, immediately before its final approach and impact with the Pentagon.[2] The point at which AA 77's 330-degree descending right turn terminated is also comparable to a Final Approach Fix (FAF), the point from which a straight final runway approach segment would commence. Such autopilot-controlled turns were possible on 9/11. As noted, the WAAS signal became available one year before the attacks.

The Department of Aeronautics and Astronautics at Stanford University described experimental RF turns, similar to the 330-degree descending turn performed by AA 77, following 1998 test flights in Alaska involving a WAAS prototype: "The Wide Area Augmentation System ... allows pilots to fly ... approaches that cannot necessarily be flown with current instrumentation... including ap-

proaches turning to a short (less than one mile) final [approach]....
Pathways were constructed from....climbing, or descending constant radius arcs....Autopilots could use WAAS position and velocity to fly curved trajectories."[3]

The flight paths of the attack aircraft observed on September 11, 2001 would apparently be reproducible by RNP-like segments used in combination and performed by specialized aircraft avionics systems available, and certified prior to September 11, 2001, for use in Boeing 757 and 767 aircraft.

DESCENDING IN-FLIGHT TURNS SUGGEST SUPERIOR CONTROL OF 9/11 WTC AIRCRAFT

Both aircraft that struck the WTC also performed descending turns prior to impact. The approximately 20-degree banked constant radius turn executed by UAL 175 from about 1.5 miles away, eight seconds before impact, was especially challenging from the standpoint of hands-on pilot control. Before the turn, UAL 175 was wings-level and on a sharply descending trajectory. A precisely timed and properly banked turn was critical to offset crosswinds that otherwise would have caused the aircraft to drift laterally an estimated 122 to 134 feet.[4] In which case, UAL 175 would probably have missed the South Tower altogether.

Two factors were required for successful impact. The first was selection of the correct banking angle, which also had to be uniformly maintained throughout the final approach. The second was the correct start-time of the banking turn. If UAL 175 had started the turn just one second sooner, or later, (assuming a speed of 799 feet per second), the aircraft would probably have missed the tower.

If the banking angle had been just 5 degrees more, or 5 less, than observed, a difference indiscernible to a casual observer, UA 175's flight path would have been displaced approximately 100 feet to the left or right, respectively. In this case, the plane's fuselage would have come close to missing the tower. The stability of UAL 175's banking turn during the final approach suggests that the aircraft was under autopilot control.

It is also curious that just 2.5 seconds before impact, UAL 175 increased its banking angle substantially by another 18 degrees.[5]

Because this additional bank angle was so dramatic and not necessary for a well centered impact, it raises the possibility that it was performed under autopilot control, in order to simply create an impression of active human control for the numerous cameras by then focused on the towers. Would a pilot have jeopardized an otherwise inevitable impact with such a reckless and unnecessary maneuver?

Analysis of UAL 175's final approach shows that the small margins for error in the constant radius banking turn required to impact WTC-2 from approximately 1.5 miles distant would have posed a substantial challenge to an inexperienced pilot. The uniformity and accuracy of the initial bank in achieving impact indicates that the initial angle selection was very nearly correct to achieve a perfectly centered impact. AA 11's impact via its descending banked turn was in fact perfectly centered.

All of this weighs against human control. Documents show that this type of descending constant radius autopilot controlled turn was specifically supported by augmented GPS service made available just one year prior to September 11, 2001. As noted, this type of turn was also supported by Boeing 767 Flight Management Systems (FMS) as early as 1998.[6]

NECESSARY AVIONICS SYSTEMS

On September 6, 1996 Rockwell-Collins Commercial Avionics announced plans by Boeing and other major commercial airlines to install Rockwell-Collins Multi-Mode Receiver (MMR) landing systems within their Boeing 757 and 767 aircraft.[7] The MMR system can utilize the WAAS signal as well as the basic GPS signal, Very High Frequency (VHF), Ultra High Frequency (UHF), Very High Frequency Omnirange (VOR) navigation signals and eventually the Local Area Augmentation System (LAAS) navigation signal.[8] LAAS is an application of WAAS technology designed for local use at major airports.

On September 7, 1998 Honeywell International announced plans by American Airlines and United Airlines to install the RNP-capable Pegasus Flight Management System (FMS) within their Boeing 757 and 767 aircraft, with a 150-waypoint route capacity.[9]

A Boeing document circa 1999 describes this technology: "Operators of 757s and 767s may also choose to upgrade to the recently certified Future Air Navigation System (FANS) FMC (Pegasus), which is Y2K-ready and available. Service bulletins for the 757 and 767 FANS retrofit will be issued upon operator request."[10]

Aviation and popular publications describe a 2006 test flight involving a commercial Boeing 757 airliner outfitted with this technology. During the test, the Air China flight snaked along a narrow river valley in Tibet between towering Himalayan peaks, then descended "on a precisely plotted highway in the sky" through heavy clouds to a remote airstrip. The destination was the brand new runway at Linzhi, one of the world's most difficult-to-reach towns.

En route, the 757 passed through the planet's most challenging terrain. The mountainous region has no radar coverage, no ground-based navaids, and no air traffic controllers to provide assistance. The plane was guided entirely by autopilot using global-positioning satellites and on-board instruments. The test was so successful that Air China subsequently announced that it would start regular commercial air service into Linzhi.

Capt. Chen Dong Cheng, an Air China pilot who rode as an observer on the inaugural flight, explained that commercial service into Linzhi would never have been feasible without the precise, automated navigation system which was custom-designed for that particular plane and airfield.[11] According to *Aviation Week*, the Boeing 757 that made the historic flight was equipped "with dual GPS receivers, [dual] flight path computers and [dual] inertial reference systems so that no single failure could cause a loss of navigation capability."

The approach to the 9,700 foot-elevation runway at Linzhi airport is difficult, but according to Steve Fulton, the technical officer at Naverus, which developed the technology, "RNP is very precise and the aircraft ... [was] equipped with Honeywell Pegasus flight management systems and Rockwell Collins multi-mode receivers." The GPS-based system was accurate to within 3-4 meters (10-13 ft).

Although the test occurred in 2006, according to Fulton, "this type of accuracy has been routinely possible since 2000."[12] By 1999, Boeing 757 and 767 aircraft like those involved in the 9/11 terrorist attacks contained digital flight control systems that could "automatically fly the airplanes on pre-selected routes, headings, speed or altitude maneuvers."[13]

SYSTEMS ACCURACY ACHIEVED PRIOR TO 9/11

Records show that between 1994 and 2002, the FAA, US Air Force and NASA sponsored numerous runway approach and touchdown test flights. These tests of augmented GPS and the auto-land systems of Boeing 757, 767 and other Boeing 700 series aircraft routinely achieved horizontal and vertical positional accuracies of several meters or less. Nearly all of these tests occurred prior to 9/11.

It is noteworthy that the four planes involved in the September 11, 2001 terrorist attacks were virtually the very same aircraft models used in these tests: the Boeing 757-200 and 767-300.

Also significant is the fact that the parameters of the "highways in the sky," as well as the runways at major US airports like JFK International, Chicago-O'Hare International and Los Angeles International, closely match the physical dimensions of the World Trade Center towers. The major runways are between 150 and 200 feet wide.[14] The WTC towers were each 208 feet wide.[15]

In October 1994, the FAA sponsored a series of test flights which demonstrated the amazing accuracy of augmented GPS. The tests involved a United Airlines Boeing 737 and occurred at NASA's Crows Landing Flight Facility in California. During 110 autopilot approaches and touchdowns, the Boeing 737 consistently achieved "accuracies on the order of a few centimeters."[16]

During October 1994, the FAA sponsored another series of automated landings in cooperation with Ohio University. In this case the augmented GPS was integrated into the Flight Management System (FMS) of a donated United Parcel Service Boeing 757-200 aircraft. During 50 automated approaches and touchdowns, the augmented GPS system performed at least as well as the standard Instrument Landing Systems (ILS) technology then in use at US airports.[17]

During July and August 1995, Honeywell, Boeing and NASA sponsored tests at NASA's Wallops Island, Virginia flight test facility using NASA's Boeing 757-200 test aircraft. GPS was used in the tests to provide guidance for 75 autopilot approaches and touchdowns. Preliminary performance data showed that the augmented GPS landing system achieved the predicted positional accuracy of 1-2 meters.[18]

During October-December 1998, WAAS signal en route navigation and Category I precision instrument aircraft runway approaches were conducted over the North Atlantic Ocean and in the nation of Chile, using FAA-owned Boeing 727 test aircraft. Overall positional accuracies of 3-4 meters were successfully achieved.[19]

During August 1999, the FAA sponsored multiple augmented GPS signal autopilot approach and touchdown tests using a donated United Parcel Service 767 aircraft. The tests involved the prototype GPS-based Local Area Augmentation System (LAAS), which is intended to compliment the FAA's WAAS service. The LAAS signal can provide aircraft positional accuracy of less than one meter vertically and laterally.[20] This is even better than the 3-4 meter accuracy achieved by WAAS.

During the summer of 2001, the US Air Force and Raytheon jointly sponsored test flights at Holloman AF Base, New Mexico of a new automated GPS-based landing system for the Department of Defense. The new system, known as the Joint Precision Approach and Landings System (JPALS), was designed to be fully interoperable with similar planned civilian systems also under development. On August 25, 2001, a Fed-Ex 727-200 aircraft equipped with a Rockwell-Collins GNLU-930 Multi-Mode Receiver, achieved the first precision approach and touchdown using JPALS, which is the military counterpart of the civilian LAAS system.[21]

TRANSFERRING PILOT CONTROL

On October 9, 2001, a company named Cubic Defense Systems, Inc. applied for a US patent for a system that transfers pilot control of an aircraft to the autopilot during an emergency, which then implements an uninterruptible programmed flight plan and navigates the aircraft to a given destination. This would be accomplished through the use of electronic or mechanical relays to be activated by pilot operation of an aircraft hijack notification system: a so-called panic button.

As we know, none of the four aircraft destroyed on September 11, 2001 "squawked" the unique transponder hijack code—"7500"—which is the standard FAA protocol for notifying air traffic controllers that a hijacking is in progress. The omission was highly conspicuous, and pointed to either modified function or insufficient activation time.

Another optional feature of the Cubic system would terminate the pilot's capacity to communicate from the cockpit. This feature is also relevant to our discussion, for as we know, in two instances on 9/11, alleged hijacker communications apparently intended for passengers aboard AA 11 and UAL 93 were instead heard by air traffic controllers. This points to possible modified functionality of on-board communications. No flight deck transmissions intended for ground controllers were ever broadcast from the 9/11 attack aircraft.

The Cubic patent makes reference to Honeywell's research and development in 1995 of augmented GPS flight navigation, apparently as a signal navigation aid. It is also noteworthy that the Cubic system envisions a remote access capability. New flight instructions transmitted by a remote sender would be uploaded for the purpose of overriding and redirecting the autopilot system and would then navigate the aircraft to a predetermined destination.[22]

An operable system equivalent to the one described in Cubic Defense Systems' patent application filed October 9, 2001 could have been in place on September 11, 2001. There is evidence that similar systems were already operational by that time.

AUTOMATIC AUTOPILOT OVERRIDE TECHNOLOGY OF PILOT CONTROL OF BOEING AIRCRAFT

In a 2003 *Aviation Week* report, Honeywell described an already existing capability of a GPS-guided aircraft autopilot system to take control of an aircraft away from a pilot during an emergency: "Assisted recovery builds on existing enhanced ground proximity warning systems (EGPWS), autopilot or fly-by-wire technologies to prevent an aircraft from crashing into terrain or buildings.... If pilots don't respond to warnings within a certain amount of time, assisted recovery directs autopilot or fly-by-wire control systems to steer aircraft away from a crash.... A Honeywell spokesman said an override option does exist in its assisted recovery system through a secret disabling code." [23]

Honeywell's state-of-the-art Flight Management Systems were in use on September 11, 2001 by all four allegedly hijacked aircraft. The development of collision avoidance control override capability within a Boeing 757 is also documented, as early as 1999: "Ultimately, if required, the system could initiate an automatically flown evasive maneuver. Validation flights were completed at the NASA Wallops Flight Facility and in-flight demonstrations of the system were completed at Minneapolis-St. Paul International Airport in November 1999 for FAA officials and other Government and industry representatives. The NASA B-757 ARIES and a Honeywell Gulfstream IV (G-IV) were used in the flight test effort."[24]

A 2005 report on ground proximity warning systems also indicates that the Boeing 767s that crashed into the World Trade Center (WTC) relied on navigation databases that included the locations of the WTC towers. According to the report, "The hijacked passenger jets that hit the World Trade Center buildings were equipped with EGPWS.... The twin towers were in the database."[25]

REMOTE FLIGHT TRANSMISSION

Documents also show that the capability to remotely transmit altered aircraft flight plan data via remote data link transmissions directly into Boeing 757 and 767 aircraft Flight Management Computers (FMCs) for use by the autopilot, was available circa 2001.

During the early 1990s, the airlines introduced a new data link interface between ground controllers and aircraft. The new link utilized the pre-existing Aircraft Communication Addressing and Reporting System (ACARS), which had already been in use for many years. The new uplink feature made it possible to digitally upload a new flight plan into an aircraft's Flight Management System, which includes the autopilot, while in mid-flight.[26]

Thus, on 9/11 someone not associated with the airlines could have hacked into ACARS and uploaded alternative flight plans.

Another technology to remotely transmit altered flight plan data directly into an aircraft's Flight Management Computer (FMC) for autopilot use was also available circa 2001. It is known as Dynamic Airborne Reroute Procedure (DARP), and was first developed in 1999 to facilitate the rerouting of transoceanic flights when necessary for safety reasons to avoid storms, or simply to make routing more timely and fuel-efficient. DARP enables aircraft course changes via modified flight plan waypoints that are remotely transmitted and installed into an aircraft's FMC by VHF or satellite communications transmission uplinks. The technology works in conjunction with ACARS. By 2000, the DARP system was supported by the Honeywell Pegasus Flight Management System used in Boeing 757s and 767s.

A March 2003 article in *Aviation Week* describes the new system: "Dynamic Rerouting [is the] the ability of controllers ... to change a filed routing once the flight is in progress.... The new flight plan with all new waypoints goes into the data link to the comm satellite and is then downlinked into the FMS of the individual aircraft.... And 'Wow,' say all the old pilots, 'Untouched by human hands!... Our [dispatch] computer uplinks a route into the FMS that is identified as 'Route 2.' You're already flying 'Route 1.'"[27]

A January 2002 Boeing document describes the uplink capability of the Pegasus Flight Management System used in Boeing 757s and 767s: "[the] AOC (airline operations center) data link is an optional feature of the Pegasus Flight Management Computer (FMC).... This feature provides data link communication of ... route modifications ... directly into the FMC."[28]

Another Boeing document, of May 2000, mentions two different ways of entering route modifications into the Pegasus Flight Management System for Boeing 757s and 767s. One involves a remote uplink: "A route request may either be a route modified by the crew, or a route which has been sent to the airplane from the Airline Data System."[29]

This document provides further relevant information on the Pegasus Flight Management System for Boeing 757s and 767s:

- "Three independent VHF systems (radios and antennas) are installed on the airplane to provide line-of-sight voice and data communication."[30]
- "Satellite communications (SATCOM) may be provided for remote communications where terrestrial contact is unavailable, or by airline policy regardless of the state of other communication capabilities."[31]
- "The FMC has the capability to store 2 routes, designated as route 1 and route 2. The route which defines the flight plan along which the airplane is to be flown is the active route."[32]

QUALITY OF GPS SERVICE DURING ATTACKS

After the Clinton administration made GPS available for civilian use, the geometric strength of GPS satellites became the single factor most affecting the quality of the GPS signal. Its technical name is Geometric Dilution of Precision (GDOP), and is expressed as a numerical measure. According to Wikipedia, "GDOP is a GPS term used in geomatics engineering to describe the geometric strength of satellite configuration on GPS accuracy...the greater the number of satellites, the better the value of GDOP."[33]

Curiously, according to estimates generated in 2011 by a leading GPS computer planning program, at the time of UAL 175's impact with World Trade Center 2, twelve out of twelve GPS/WAAS satellites were visible from the latitude/longitude coordinates of the WTC (40° 42° 42° N; 74° 0° 45° W). At the time of AA 11's impact with WTC 1, eleven out of twelve GPS/WAAS satellites were visible from those coordinates. So we see that the WTC attacks occurred during a window of maximum or near-maximum GPS satellite visibility.[34]

This period of maximum occupied only twelve percent, i.e., less than one and one half hours, of the daylight period on September 11, 2001. Similar GPS conditions also existed at the Pentagon during AA 77's impact. Indeed, graphs generated by the aforementioned planning program reveal that the AA 11 and AA 77 impacts occurred within only minutes of maximum satellite visibility periods.

The GPS planning software cited above utilizes GPS almanac data transmitted daily by GPS satellites and is published by the US Coast Guard. The data contains course orbital parameters from all global navigation satellites utilized by the GPS planning software. The GPS almanac data would have made it possible to predict the quality of both GPS satellite visibility and GDOP days or weeks in advance of 9/11.

The numerical values for GDOP are expressed on a scale of 1-10. During the time period when both aircraft struck the towers, the value of GDOP at the WTC was between 2 and 2.5. The maximum GDOP value between sunrise and sunset on September 11, 2001 was approximately 1.8. Wikipedia describes these GDOP values, as follows: "1-2 Excellent: At this confidence level, positional measurements are considered accurate enough to meet all but the most sensitive applications; 2-5 Good: Represents a level that marks the minimum appropriate for making business decisions. Positional measurements could be used to make reliable in-route navigation suggestions to the user."[35]

HIGHER SPEEDS LIMIT LATERAL DRIFT AND DEFLECTION ANGLES

The observed speeds of both aircraft were extreme in comparison to the speeds that are typical of descending commercial aircraft. AA 11 struck the North Tower at an estimated 466 mph. UAL 175 was moving even faster: it struck the South Tower at an estimated 545 mph.

These high speeds are problematic from the standpoint of pilot control, because they significantly reduce the response time for making hands-on course corrections. However, they are preferable from the standpoint of autopilot control, because they have the effect of minimizing the deflection angles and ground track displacements created by crosswinds and any wind shear.

On the morning of September 11, 2001, wind speed and direction for the altitude of the aircraft impacts with each WTC tower were reported to be between 11 mph and 22 mph, and from the direction of true north.[36] Although this wind speed can be characterized as moderate, it was nonetheless a factor and would have posed a substantial challenge even to a skilled pilot.

Achieving a desired course under crosswind conditions requires consideration of the relationship between an aircraft's direction and speed and the wind's direction and speed. Such relationships are represented trigonometrically by a "wind triangle," which is typically calculated by aircraft Flight Management Systems: "On aircraft equipped with advanced navigation equipment, the wind triangle is often solved within the flight management system, (FMS) using inputs from the air data computer (ADC), inertial navigation system (INS), global positioning system (GPS), and other instruments."[37]

Comparison of observed (higher) and hypothesized (lower) aircraft speeds demonstrates that the greater observed speed of UA 175 reduced potential wind-induced drift angles and distances while en route toward WTC-2.

In conclusion, there is compelling evidence that the technology already existed at the time of the September 11, 2001 attacks to remotely control Boeing 757 and 767 aircraft by accessing their state-of-the-art Flight Management Systems and utilizing altered flight paths uploaded through existing data links.

ENDNOTES

1   "United States Standard For Required Navigation Performance (RNP) Approach Procedures With Special Aircraft And Aircrew Authorization Required (SAAAR)," Federal Aviation Administration, June 3, 2005, p. 13, posted at http://www.faa.gov/documentLibrary/media/Order/ND/8260_52.pdf.

2   "Flight Path Study - American Airlines Flight 77," National Transportation Safety Board, February 19, 2002, posted at http://www.gwu.edu/~nsarchiv/NSAEBB/NSAEBB196/doc02.pdf.

3   Keith W. Alter et al., "Inflight Demonstrations of Curved Approaches. and Missed Approaches in Mountainous Terrain," Department of Aeronautics and Astronautics, Stanford University, 1998, p. 1-7, posted at http://waas.stanford.edu/~wwu/jennings/publications/ION98/iongps98.pdf.

4   Aidan Monaghan, "Review of Analysis of Observed and Measured In-Flight Turns Suggests Superior Control of 9/11 WTC Aircraft," Journal of 9/11 Studies, February 16, 2011, p. 1, posted at http://www.journalof911studies.com/volume/2010/Monaghan_Analysis.pdf.

5   "UA 175's Mile Long 20 Degree Banked Turn On 9/11," Youtube, September 11, 2001, posted at http://www.youtube.com/watch?v=FZi7TiXWcC4.

6   Keith W. Alter et al., "Inflight Demonstrations of Curved Approaches. and Missed Approaches in Mountainous Terrain," Department of Aeronautics and Astronautics Stanford University, 1998, p. 7, posted at http://waas.stanford.edu/~wwu/jennings/publications/ION98/iongps98.pdf.

7   "Rockwell Collins' Landing System Picked for Both Airbus and Boeing Planes; Lead Announcement at Farnborough Air Show," PRNewswire, September 6, 1996, posted at http://www.highbeam.com/doc/1G1-18652301.html.

8   "GNSS - Frequently Asked Questions – WAAS," Federal Aviation Administration, posted at http://www.faa.gov/about/office_org/headquarters_offices/ato/service_units/techops/navservices/gnss/faq/waas/index.cfm.

9   "Honeywell Announces Orders For New-Generation "Pegasus" Flight Management System," Aviation Week, September 7, 1998, posted at http://www.aviation-now.com/shownews/farnday1/pressr15.htm; "Boeing 757/767 State of the Art Upgrade," Honeywell Aerospace, posted at http://www.honeywell.com/sites/aero/Flight_Management_Systems3_C1997B88E-FCF9-72B5-3A26-801F48F156BD_H79C28D81-B679-A247-C0CE-32B08C84BC08.htm.

10 "Year 2000 Readiness Disclosure," Boeing, posted at http://www.boeing.com/commercial/aeromagazine/aero_03/sy/sy01/story.html.

11 Dominic Gates, "Kent company bringing a navigation revolution," Seattle Times, October 22, 2006, posted at http://seattletimes.nwsource.com/html/businesstechnology/2003316294_naverus22.html.

12 David Hughes, "Air China's First RNP Approach Into Linzhi Airport, Tibet," Aviation Week, September 24, 2006, posted at http://www.aviationweek.com/aw/generic/story_channel.jsp?channel=comm&id=news/aw092506p1.xml.

13 "Rockwell Collins To Provide Autoland System for Boeing Next-Generation 737," Business Wire, October 5, 1999, posted at http://www.highbeam.com/

doc/1G1-55993162.html.

14   "JFK International Airport," Wikipedia, http://upload.wikimedia.org/wikipedia/commons/b/b0/JFK_airport_map.gif; "Chicago-O'Hare International Airport," Wikipedia, http://upload.wikimedia.org/wikipedia/commons/3/30/ORD_airport_map.PNG; "Los Angeles International Airport," Wikipedia, http://upload.wikimedia.org/wikipedia/en/a/a3/LaxAirportDiagram2.jpg.

15   "The World Trade Center," Wikipedia, http://en.wikipedia.org/wiki/File:World_Trade_Center_Building_Design_with_Floor_and_Elevator_Arrangment.svg.

16   "GETTING TO THE POINT IN PINPOINT LANDING," NASA, 1998, posted at http://www.sti.nasa.gov/tto/spinoff1998/t2.htm.

17   Judy Huggard-Gallagher, "FAA/Ohio University Avionics Engineering Center Partnership," Federal Aviation Administration, December 1998, posted at http://www.tc.faa.gov/logistics/grants/success/OU.pdf.

18   George Lewison, "Honeywell's Differential GPS Satellite Landing System," *Avionics News Magazine*, September, 1996, p. 2, posted at http://www.bluecoat.org/reports/Lewison_96_DGPS.pdf;

     "ARIES: NASA's 'Flying Lab' Takes Wing," NASA, December, 1999, posted at http://www.nasa.gov/centers/langley/news/factsheets/757.html.

19   "FAA Performs Successful Satellite-Based Flight Tests Over the North Atlantic," Federal Aviation Administration, October 16, 1998, posted at http://www.faa.gov/news/press_releases/news_story.cfm?newsId=4868; "FAA Completes Successful WAAS Flight Trials in the Republic of Chile," Federal Aviation Administration, December 16, 1998, posted at http://www.faa.gov/news/press_releases/news_story.cfm?newsId=4898.

20   "FAA, ATA, UPS Test New Satellite Technology," Federal Aviation Administration, August 13, 1999, http://www.faa.gov/news/press_releases/news_story.cfm?newsId=5052.

21   "Civil-Military Interoperability For GPS Assisted Aircraft Landings Demonstrated," *Space Daily*, October 1, 2001, posted at http://www.spacedaily.com/news/gps-01k.html.

22   Cubic Defense Systems, Inc. et al., "Anti-hijacking system operable in emergencies to deactivate on-board flight controls and remotely pilot aircraft utilizing autopilot," United States Patent, October 9, 2001, posted at http://patft.uspto.gov/netacgi/nph-Parser?Sect2=PTO1&Sect2=HITOFF&p=1&u=%2Fnetahtml%2FPTO%2Fsearch-bool.html&r=1&f=G&l=50&d=PALL&RefSrch=yes&Query=PN%2F6641087.

23   Lori Ranson, "Honeywell Aims To Test Crash-Evading System On Larger Planes," *Aviation Week*, August 13, 2003, posted at http://www.aviationweek.com/aw/generic/story_generic.jsp?channel=aviationdaily&id=news/eva08133.xml.

24   Michael S. Wusk, "ARIES: NASA Langley's Airborne Research Facility," American Institute of Aeronautics and Astronautics, posted at http://www.cs.odu.edu/~mln/ltrs-pdfs/NASA-aiaa-2002-5822.pdf.

25   David Hughes, "Airbus Shows Interest in Honeywell's Auto Pull-Up Software," *Aviation Week*, September 25, 2005, posted at http://www.aviationweek.com/aw/generic/story_generic.jsp?channel=awst&id=news/09265p08.xml&headline=Airbus.

26   "Aircraft Communication Addressing and Reporting System," Wikipedia, http://en.wikipedia.org/wiki/ACARS.

27   David Esler, "FANS: Where Is It for Business Aviation?" *Aviation Week*, March 4, 2003, posted at http://www.aviationweek.com/aw/generic/story_generic.jsp?channel=bca&id=news/FANS033.xml.

28   "767 Flight Deck and Avionics," Boeing, January, 2002, p. 123, posted at http://www.smartcockpit.com/pdf/plane/boeing/B767/misc/0001/.

29   "757/767: Air Traffic Services Systems Requirements and Objectives - Generation 2," Boeing, May 12, 2000, p. 41, posted at http://www.boeing.com/commercial/caft/cwg/ats_dl/757-767_ATS_SRO.pdf.

30   Ibid., p. 49.

31   Ibid., p. 50.

32   Ibid.

33   "Dilution of Precision (GPS)," Wikipedia, http://en.wikipedia.org/wiki/Dilution_of_precision_(GPS).

34   Aidan Monaghan, "Official GPS Data Reveal Superior Aviation GPS Service Provided To WTC & Pentagon During 9/11 Attacks," 9/11 Blogger, May 31, 2011, posted at http://911blogger.com/news/2011-05-31/official-gps-data-reveal-superior-aviation-gps-service-provided-wtc-pentagon-during-911-attacks.

35   "Dilution of Precision (GPS)," Wikipedia, http://en.wikipedia.org/wiki/Dilution_of_precision_(GPS).

36   William M. Pitts et al., "Federal Building and Fire Safety Investigation of the World Trade Center Disaster Passive Fire Protection," NIST NCSTAR 1-5A, p. 24, posted at http://wtc.nist.gov/NCSTAR1/PDF/NCSTAR%201-5A%20Ch%201-8.pdf.

37   Wind Triangle," Wikipedia, http://en.wikipedia.org/wiki/Wind_triangl.

Appendices

DIRECT TRANSLATION ONLY OF DECLARATION BY SUSPECT.

FULL NAME: ROELOF IGNATUIS JOHANNES VAN ROOYEN

ADRES: BOTHAUSHOF 11A, HILDEN D40723, SOLINGERSTRASSE 186 D40764, LANGEVELD, RHEINLAND GERMANY.

1.

On Monday the 13th of February 1995 I was approached by Andreas Feller of the German Police a Langeveld, Germany. He informed me of my rights in accordance with German law and that the Soull African Police were investigating certain criminal charges against me. My rights regarding the making o statements were also explained to me. After thus been warned I made a statement to Adreas Feller as prescribed by German law. This statement was translated from English to German in which language was taken down.

2.

I also took note of the fact that certain questions could be put to me resultant from my statement. I an quite prepared that further questions be put to me resultant from my statement in order to finalise the matter. I am also quite satisfied that questions be put to me by members of the South-African police services in the absence of a German translator or the German Police.

3.

I wish to continue with answers to questions put to me and I am also aware of the fact that these answers may be used as evidence in a court of law.

4.

At 09:15 on 1995/02/14 in my hotel room number 1610, Rheinstern Hotel, Rheinstern, Düsseldorf the following questions were put to Mr. Roelof Ignatuis van Rooyen, South-African identify number 570429 5021 08 5 suspect in Pretoria North MAS 57/08/92 in the presence of Lieutenant-Colonel A.E. Botha.

4.1

QUESTION: What is your full name and surname?
ANSWER: Roelof Ignatius van Rooyen as indicated in my identity document.

4.2

QUESTION: Where and when were you born?
ANSWER: 29 April 1959, Kroonstad, South-Africa.

4.3

QUESTION: What is your South-african identy number?
ANSWER: 570429 5021 08 5.

4.4

QUESTION: Who are the Directors of Eastcorp and when was Eastcorp established?
ANSWER: The Directors are myself, Riaan Stander as well as Fanie Smith, the latter being the Secretary of the Company. The date of establishment was ± November/December 1991

4.5

QUESTION: Do you have any code names or make use of aliases?
ANSWER: No.

Three pages from deposition of Roelof Ignatius Van Rooyen

(6)

4.31

QUESTION: Who presented the "Letter of Credit" to Compushop?

ANSWER: No "Letter of Credit" was presented to Compushop. We ordered a computer. The company would have delivered and install the computer according to contract. As this was a reasonably large order, the company (Compushop), wanted a credit reference. I referred them to our auditor. The computers were delivered but there were enormous problems. It never worked. The scanners did not work. There were numerous defective functions in the computer system that was installed. There was a civil lawsuit regarding the computers which was ruled in favour of my company. Wim Cornelius appeared in the case and it was concluded in Pretoria court. I was prepared to personally pay for the computers that were installed at Ou Wapadweg, Ifafi.

4.32

QUESTION: Were all certificates of deposits held by Fanie Smith?

ANSWER: Yes.

4.33

QUESTION: Was the "Letter of Credit" completed at the company in question at the time of presentation?

ANSWER: Only one "Letter of Credit" was presented at Mc Carthy's for verification, but was completed at the auditors offices of Fanie Smith. I just want to mention that when Potnak was in hospital myself and Riaan seized blank certificates and stamps in Potnaks office which was locked. I then placed them in a place of safety. We immediately informed the Reserve Bank of the position. Riaan wrote a letter to Christo Wiese and Wim Cornelius to inform them as well as Fanie Smith. The police people that we have in the office were also informed of the developments.

4.34

QUESTION: What is Curtis/Maudin/Ouster's share in Eastech/Eastcorp/Oceantec and Intercol?

ANSWER: Eastech - No involvement by Eastech.

Eastcorp - There was no involvement by Eastcorp.

Oceantec and Intercol were involved in the same investigation here. Myself (Oceantec) and Intercol were asked to do an investigation for a group of people in which Curtis/Maudin and Oster were involved. I must mention, however, that I heard of the name Curtis for the first time in the year 1991. I did not know that he was part of the group of people with whom I was doing business. The investigation was in connection with allegations that large sums of money was owing resulting from a financial transaction. I only began his (curtise's) inquiries on behalf of the sydicate. Within the first day we realised that it was a direct state matter and that the U.S.A., the C.I.A. and several other groups in the secret service were involved, as well as very,very high-coupled people in the American Goverment. Secondly we realised that a large group of the So-called brokers who were involved in the transaction, requested or tried to obtain the amount. I explain:- One of the members of the group had access to a financial bank computers. The man's name is Paul Grey. According to our information they extracted a "Security Display" from the computor/C.M.B. 10 (Reuters) - as far as I know. These groups of people coupled the documents to a so - called transaction which they tried to intercept. Curtis/Maudlin/Oster is involved in completely different transactions long before Eastach with Oceantec and Intercol.. They paid us an amount of money for the work that was done and the work is not even complete. It is interesting that Grobler also commenced with a civil action in Virginia, U.S.A. I hear he knows that he has taken on the American State. I also do not know how Curtis and Grobler got acquainted. To me it is a mystery.

4.45

QUESTION: Who is Jean Rutz of Saudi Finance?
ANSWER: A person who lives in France. I was involved in Saudi Finance.

4.46

QUESTION: Who is Robert De Chayney?
ANSWER: This is the money power behind Eastech Bank or a portion of the finance provided. He is a director of the bank in Mexico. There was no involvement with Eastech/Eastcorp by all the abovementioned individuals with the exception of Robert de Cheyney.

4.47

QUESTION: What was Bank Pribar?
ANSWER: A bank in Uruguay and had nothing to do with Eastcorp.

4.48

QUESTION: What is the meaning of the word **REMAH**?
ANSWER: I have no idea. REMAH is REMAH.

4.49

QUESTION: What is the meaning of the word **HAMER?**
ANSWER: If you are refering to operation HAMER it is an extremely large, very delicate operation in co-operation with the authorities of various countries in which Oceantec is involved, but has nothing to do with Eastcorp or Eastech Bank. America, England, Germany, France, Italy although part of the investigation was against individuals who live in South-Africa. The South-Afrcan police service by name C1 or C10 was not involved with Oceantec.

4.50

QUESTION: There was mention of funding by the Government of Eastcorp from time to time. Who was it and what was the amount?
ANSWER: That was wrongly understood and had nothing to do with Eastcorp. There is a group of people that were appointed under BOSS appointed by state security.

4.51

QUESTION: Were you an officer in any military power in South-Africa?
ANSWER: No, never.

4.52

QUESTION: What was Riaan Stander's duties as director of the company Eastcorp/Intercol?
ANSWER: Riaan was director of security. The duties that he would perform would have been to physically ensure the security of the bank, to scrutinise the truthfulness of all documents that involved the bank. Do the necessary investigation as background on possible investors. Riaan liased directly with the people of C1 or C10, namely Eugene de Kock, Pieter Botha Chaples Klopper and Willie Nortjè. These people asked us to assist them in certain operations i.e. infiltration of far right groups in Pietersburg with the purpose to establish the movement of large quantities of weaponary. Pieter Botha brought weapons for Riaan.

PLAINTIFFS' EXHIBIT 7

Thirty-three pages from deposition of Erle Cocke, Jr.

1

UNITED STATES DISTRICT COURT
SOUTHERN DISTRICT OF NEW YORK

- - - - - - - - - - - - - - - - - -x
                            :

STEVEN A. CURTIS, DAVID LEE MAUDLIN, :
DAVID WAYNE OSTER,   :

                            :

                Plaintiffs :

      -against-   : 95 CIVIL 0031 (JES)

                            :

ADRIAAN BAREND STANDER, ROELF   :
IGNATIUS JOHANNES VAN ROOYEN,
INTERCOL (PTY) LTD., OCEANTEC   :
GROUP/SYNDICATE,   :

                            :

                Defendants :
- - - - - - - - - - - - - - - - - -x

                 Chevy Chase, Maryland

                 Thursday, April 13, 2000

Deposition of

           ERLE COCKE, JR.

a witness, called for examination by counsel for the

plaintiffs, pursuant to notice, taken at 5610 Wisconsin

Avenue, Building 2, Apartment 403, beginning at 1:50 o'clock

p.m., before Thomas C. Melo, a Notary Public in and for the

State of Maryland, when were present on behalf of the

respective parties:

THOMAS C. MELO
REGISTERED PROFESSIONAL REPORTER
8223 TUCKERMAN LANE
POTOMAC, MARYLAND 20854-3745
PHONE (301) 299-9076

239

1   For the Plaintiffs:

2   JOSEPH J. D'ERASMO, ESQ.
          103 North Adams Street
3   Rockville, MD 20850-2217

4   For the Defendants:

5   (No appearance)

6 <u>DEPOSITION OF</u>   <u>EXAMINATION BY COUNSEL</u>   <u>PAGE</u>

7 Erle Cocke, Jr.   Mr. D'Erasmo   4

8

9   <u>E X H I B I T S</u>

10 <u>DEPOSITION NUMBER</u>   <u>PAGE</u>

11 1   36

12 2   66

13

14   –   –   –

15

16

17

18

19

20

21

22

3

1   P R O C E E D I N G S

2   MR. D'ERASMO: Preliminarily, before we begin

3 this deposition, I want to note for the record that I have

4 contacted by telephone Mr. William Cornelius who is the

5 attorney for Adriaan Barent Stander and his company, PTY

6 Limited, and Interpol PTY Limited, to be here. He did not

7 ask for a postponement of the deposition so he could be here.

8 I told him I would take whatever instructions he felt he

9 wanted to give me in connection with the deposition. He

10 represents the other parties in this matter.

11   He indicated to me he waived the right to be here

12 today, this just being a deposition in aid of the enforcement

13 of the judgment under the Federal rules, and stated the only

14 things he requested was that I leave the record open for a

15 reasonable period of time for the purpose of having him

16 submit additional questions as the client would ask.

17   I explained I would not keep the record open

18 indefinitely, but I would give him a couple weeks to talk

19 to his client and provide us with any questions appropriate.

20   So, we can proceed.

21 Thereupon

22   ERLE COCKE, JR.

1 a witness, called for examination by counsel for the

2 plaintiffs and, after having been first duly sworn by the

3 Notary Public, was examined and testified as follows:

4   EXAMINATION BY COUNSEL FOR THE PLAINTIFFS

5   BY MR. D'ERASMO:

6   Q   General, would you please state your full name?

7   A   Erle, E-R-L-E, Cocke, C-O-C-K-E, Jr.

8   Q   And your current business address?

9   A   1629 K Street, Northwest, Suite 1250, Washington,

10 D. C. 20006. I am President of Cocke and Phillips, with

11 two L's.

12   Q   All right. And can you tell us briefly what

13 your duties are in that occupation?

14   A   I am Chief Executive Officer and have been since

15 1962.

16   Q   I will have a few questions a little later. But

17 could you give me a brief resume of your background and your

18 education, training and experience beginning with your

19 educational backgriund?

20   A   Graduate of the University of Georgia with an

21 AB. I have an MBA from Harvard Business School, and a

22 number of honorary degrees, making speeches. I am in Who's

1 Who in America for the last 48 years.

2 Q   All right.   Do you also have a law degree?

3 A   Actually, I have an LLB degree.   But even when

4 I was in law school I was not interested in the judicial side

5 of the law.   I have always been a legislator, not a judicial

6 type.   So, I have written thousands of pages of legislation

7 both in Georgia, UN, Geneva.

8   I am recognized as an international lawyer, but

9 I am not recognized as a member of the bar in the United

10 States.

11 Q   I know you had an outstanding military career.

12 Could you tell us briefly your background?

13 A   I came on active duty as soon as I was eligible

14 and 21 years old, in 1942, and throughout the entire second

15 war.   And I was called back for Korea and called back for

16 Vietnam.   I am a retired Brigadier General of the Georgia

17 National Guard.   The retirement they were giving is a little

18 different because any time they want you, so they send for

19 you anyway.   So, you go back to work when they send for you.

20   So, although my service was broken up a number

21 of times, I did serve in all three wars.

22   Actually, most of the decorations, medals, and

6

1 so forth, are all covered in the biographical information.

2   Q   Just for the purpose of briefly describing those

3 in what appears to be your Who's Who entry, you were

4 decorated with a Silver Star, Bronze Star and cluster,

5 Purple Heart with three clusters, Croix de Guerre, Chevalier

6 Legion of Honor in France, Medal of Honor from the

7 Republic of the Philippines, is that correct?

8   That is correct.

9   Q   Star of Solidarity. I understand you also were

10 a Commander in the Knight of Malta?

11   A   Yes, I am a Grand Commander in the Knight of

12 Malta, the first Protestant in about 1200 years so honored.

13   Q   You were connected with the American Legion?

14   A   I am a former National Commander of the American

15 Legion. I am the youngest National Commander. I am now

16 the oldest National Commander and the book ends have met.

17   Q   Also, I understand you received a Diploma and

18 Medal Cruz Roja from the Red Cross?

19   A   Yes, that is correct.

20   Q   And Honorable Comrade of the Nationalist Chinese

21 Air Force in 1951.

22   A   Yes, that is correct.

1   Q   You were associated with the Masons?

2   A   Yes, I am a Mason, I am a Shriner.

3   Q   And I believe you held a special position with

4 the Masons?

5   A   Well, semi-official might be a better word

6 because I never was on the paid staff. I was just a

7 member in the true sense of volunteerism professionally.

8   Q   When did you leave the military, officially

9 retired?

10   A   Well, I retired in 1947 the first time.

11   Q   Okay.

12   A   And then I was called back for 1951, and then

13 I was called back for '66.

14   Q   Is it possible to sum up the kind of assignments

15 you had in the military?

16   A   Well, in the second war I was an artillery

17 officer and division staff officer.

18   And the Korean war I worked as a liaison from

19 General Marshall's staff to General MacArthur's staff.

20 MacArthur's people were very good. They always put me out

21 front so if I failed, and Marshall's staff failed, MacArthur's

22 staff didn't fail.

1 Q   And in 1966?

2 A   1966 Westmoreland was commanding and he sent for

3 me. I didn't know whether I was going to meet him for

4 10 days, or 10 months, and I stood out 10 months.

5 Q   What were your duties?

6 A   I had been a prisoner of the Germans in the

7 second war. I had Americans that were captured by the

8 Koreans and brainwashed and didn't come home. And once

9 that Westmoreland saw that he was going to have prisoners

10 of war problems, he started to send for people that already

11 had them. That's when I got there. And I did all kinds

12 of little things for him. He broke his arm while I was

13 there. He sent me out to dedicate this and meet this guy.

14 I did a lot of chores in that sense because, as he once

15 said, you probably are the only general officer that had

16 theater experience.

17 Q   All right. Now, you had some, what I have

18 described as post-military assignments with the U. S.

19 Government.

20 A   Yes. I was on the U. S. delegation to the 14th

21 and 15th General Assemblies of the United Nations, which

22 was '59 and '60, which is when -- I was actually a Democrat

1   in the Eisenhower Administration. Out of 10 places, the

2   White House gets 7 and the opposition gets 3. I was one

3   of the three.

4   Q   What was your position?

5   A   I was a delegate to the UN, with the rank of

6   Ambassdaor, pay of Ambassador, and it worked out very well.

7   One thing is I could speak. So, every time they needed a

8   pinch hitter, I was used quite frequently from time to time

9   on that score.

10   After the UN, I was the first full time U. S.

11   representative at the World Bank for the U. S.. At that

12   time I owned 28 percent of the stock and, of course, I had

13   all kinds of people in the Treasury tell me what to do.

14   Don't get me wrong, I made all the decisions. But I was

15   the executor, I was the delivery.

16   Q   Did you not have an office in the World Bank

17   at one time?

18   A   Oh, yes, I spent ' 6l through 3 and 4 there.

19   Q   What was your position at the World Bank?

20   A   I was alternate Executive Director by title, but

21   a full time employee. My boss came one time in four years.

22   So, he had the title of -- what do you call it -- Executive

1   Director. You understand what I am saying?

2   Q   Yes.

3   A   When you don't show up once in four years.

4   Q   He didn't direct?

5   A   He didn't direct much.

6   Q   What was your position at that time?

7   A   I was the U. S. representative at the World Bank.

8   Q   And you worked for more than one President,

9 aside from Eisenhower?

10   A   Well, really, from Truman to date. At some

11 stage of the game I worked for all of them. I have to

12 admit some of them were very minor chores and others were

13 important.

14   Q   Any major chores that you are able to talk about?

15   A   Well, your relationship with presidents change.

16 Each one gives you a different mission. And each one gives

17 you a different way of reporting. And therefore -- yes, I

18 can talk about whatever you want to. But I think that's

19 really immaterial. Why should I tell you this kind of

20 thing with this President, and that conversation with that

21 President? And no relationship to what you are talking about.

22   Q   All right. You also were employed by some

1 significant private organizations, for example, Delta Air

2 Lines. What was your position there?

3   A   Yes, I spent about 11 years with Delta. I

4 came in as Assistant to the President, and then 32-year old

5 Vice President. And actually it was the whole operation

6 because C. E. Woolman was President, and he had a heart attack

7 in of all places New Delhi, and for about six weeks they

8 couldn't even bring him home. And during that period of time,

9 which was 1958, I was operating it. I was small enough to

10 bring all the vice presidents in and be sure they could do it.

11 I didn't get it completely, but they finally got around to

12 say, should we buy it back or sell it or do this. So, I

13 was the decision man for six weeks.

14   Q   Any other private organizations, leaving out

15 Cocke and Phillips for the moment?

16   A   Well, I have been in and out of numerous

17 businesses. I don't think any of them really get involved

18 here.

19   Q   You have a background in finance and banking?

20   A   Well, do you want to go to family banking and

21 bring that up?

22   Q   Yes.

        A   I had a great grandfather that put a bank

1 together in 1867, which was the only bank in Georgia. I

2 had a grandfather that put one in about 1890. And then my

3 father was a commercial banker in the truest sense. He

4 was President of Fulton National Bank, which is now Bank

5 of America, for years. And he later was President of the

6 American Bankers Association. And then Chairman of FDIC.

7 Always a lot of confusion because he was the commercial

8 banker, and I was the international banker. So, we had

9 ways that we came together. My banking experience has been

10 mostly at the other side of the table. Not the banking

11 side of the table, but the person coming to the bank to do

12 business with.

13   Q   I am getting the impression that your banking

14 knowledge came not only from the family, but you had --

15   A   I took all the normal banking courses.

16   Q   That's what I wondered.

17   A   I understand banking. I can teach banking -

18 you understand what I am saying - at the college level.

19   Q   Yes. Now, could you tell me a little bit about

20 Cocke and Phillips?

21   A   Yes. It has been around since '66. One thing

22 about being in and out of the military, and in and out of

1   Washington is you can reorganize and get started quicker

2   than any other things because you just come back and get

3   on the telephone and tell them you are back and you go to

4   work.

5   Phillips is a retired general officer also. And

6   he and I are old friends from the University of Georgia

7   back in the thirties. He is now retired back in Georgia.

8   But we keep the name on it. And he still writes for me

9   occasionally. And he is a fantastic editor. He put all of

10   the Richard B. Russell papers together. He put the Dean

11   Rusk papers together. Names are not on them because they

12   all are about 25, 28 miles from his own farm, and they all

13   were in Georgia. But he is a great editor is what I am

14   trying to say. So, we keep in touch.

15   Q   That company was engaged in some kind of

16   international consulting. Could you describe that?

17   A   We started out as a normal American firm, lobbying

18   firm here in Washington, and we grew into banking particularly.

19   The UN contacts, and the World Bank contacts, sometimes they

20   help those people for 10 years. They call you up one day

21   and say, "I am an ex-finance minister in such and such a

22   republic. What do I do? All of a sudden you had a whole

1   program to put into effect, a whole business plan. And a

2   business plan for a nation is not like a business plan for

3   acompany.

4   Q   You would have had occasion, I imagine, to

5   review and analyze such plans when you were at the World

6   Bank?

7   A   I had to read them every day.

8   Q   Were there any projects at Cocke and Phillips

9   to give us an idea of the kind of things they were doing?

10   A   We changed a lot oflegislation. One I got no

11   credit out of. We had to go into 19 states and change the

12   law to make a copy press, copying machine came along, an

13   acceptable document because it was all written, it had to

14   be certified, it had to be in six copies on a typewriter,

15   it had to be a Chinese copy and so that it all came out

16   together. So, we went into 19 states and changed state

17   laws. 17 of them didn't take any real amendment. They

18   were almost public notice statements, and the Judge said

19   I will accept, and once he accepted, then it became pretty

20   much custom. But these other states, you had to go through

21   the legislator to make a copy a legal document.

22   That's the kind of thing that we did.

15

1   Q   Were you engaged in assisting, for example,

2   international companies with their banking operations with

3   banking contacts?

4   A   Oh, yes, they always call on you for all kinds

5   of odd chores.

6   Q   Would that be true also of some of the government

7   intelligence agencies?

8   A   Oh, yes. One thing is if they trusted you, they

9   practically came in and said, what do I do? I mean, you

10   didn't argue with them. You sort of proceeded with the

11   program and gave them a few choices, of course. But

12   practically always followed what we did. I was administrator,

13   arbitrator. I was a moderator, bringing people together.

14   Q   And would that be true in the financial and

15   banking world in particular?

16   A   Oh, yes. I have been able to close things that

17   other people can't close.

18   Q   You may note that I have asked you whether or

19   not you have had occasion to work with some of the

20   government intelligence agencies.

21   A   I have never been paid for activity. Most of the

22   time they followed me in the sense that the FBI stayed with

     me all the time I was in

1 New York. When I was at the World Bank, I had a CIA man

2 that moved his office across the street from me. And he

3 came by at least weekly anyway. We had a lot of contacts,

4 yes. But to say that I was an employee in strictly the

5 intelligence level, the answer is no.

6   Q   Were you ever a contract employee?

7   A   No. I got to the point where I never made a

8 trip outside of the country before I got back here, we will

9 talk to you, what did you find out, where did you go, who

10 did you see. And a Christmas card--I get two or three

11 Christmas cards from China. And the 5th or 6th of January

12 they were over here, what is this, who are they. And I

13 gave them all the expected answers. Most of them wanted

14 to make a picture.

15   Q   It sounds like you have been actively engaged

16 in business and government as well in the Washington, D. C.

17 area since like 1947?

18   A   '61 when I went to the bank. But even at Delta,

19 I expect I spent several days a week here. But 11 years

20 practically. So, I had an office here. But I didn't

21 literally -- when the oldest daughter had to go to school

22 that put me living here.

1   Q   That was 1961?

2   A   '61.

3   Q   Now, you know that we have talked endlessly

4 about a project transaction called Project Hammer.

5   A   Yes.

6   Q   You, obviously, are familiar with that name?

7   A   Yes. It is a nondescript name of something

8 that's awful hard to define.

9   Q   Can you tell us in a general way -- do you

10 understand it now?

11   A   Uh-huh.

12   Q   --what the overall objectives of Project Hammer

13 were?

14   A   Well, it was mainly to bring monies back to

15 the United States from all types of activities, both

16 legitimately and illegitimately. Not that they were in

17 the smuggling bueiness per se, but they were all in the

18 arms business, they were all retracing dollars of one

19 description or another that had accumulated all through the

20 forties and fifties really. And that probably is as

21 broad a definition as I can give you. And all kinds of

22 nationalities were involved, all kinds of people were

1   involved, and I got a real legitimate claim, I don't know.

2   Q   Now, do you have any idea who created it to

3   begin with, Hammer?

4   A   No, I would be reluctant to even make a guess.

5   Obviously, it had to have somebody at a pretty high level

6   to start the initial structure, but it obviously got way

7   out of proportion as time went on.

8   Q   Well, if you are repatriating all kinds of funds,

9   that's what it sounds like you are saying.

10   A   Yes.

11   Q   That would involve it sounds to me, please

12   correct me, I am naive about some of these things, it

13   involved various agencies of the U. S. Government?

14   A   Yes. Obviously, the CIA, the FBI, the National

15   Security Agencies of all types, Pentagon in the broad sense

16   of it and as such, and the Treasury, Federal Reserve. Nobody

17   got out of the act, everybody wanted to get in the act.

18   Q   And let's call it, if you know loosely for the

19   moment, were these funds directly to a country, or were they

20   all kinds and counter activities?

21   A   I think you will find that they have everything

22   in it. Everybody figured out a way to get that plum in, get

1   that plug in, and hoping to get more out.

2   Q   Who was it, the best you can recall, who was a

3   dominant participant in terms of running this project, this

4   vast project?

5   A   Well, the President originally brought me in

6   was Shelley Smith Rhoades, and we went through all the

7   South Africans that obviously will come up later here,

8   and I think from my own investigation rhat they were

9   parallel accounts in the Citibank of New York, in both

10 their Athens, Greece office and in their New York City

11 office.

12   Q   This was an ongoing long term kind of project?

13   A   Completely.

14   Q   It sounds like it would involve many different

15 commercial or financial banking institutions over the

16 years. Would that be true?

17   A   No question about it. Everybody got into the

18 act that could.

19   Q   Since you mentioned Citibank, when do you tihink

20 Citibank got into the act, roughly?

21   A   I don't know when they actually got in. Take

22 your coat off.

1   Q   Thank you, sir.

2   Q   To my knowledge, I am pretty sure they were in

3   about '88 anyway in a big way.

4   Q   And what were they supposed to do? What was the

5   function they had?

6   A   They were going to be the trustees. They were

7   going to be running the program. They were going to be

8   the disbursing agency. They were the cheese.

9   Q   Would it be fair to say that Citibank's role was

10   that of coordinator of the whole process of taking these

11   funds in, accounting for them, and distributing them?

12   A   If they want, they set themselves up as if they

13   were.

14   Q   While we are on that subject, who was the

15   principal bank officer at Citibank that dealt with this?

16   A   From all records, communications and contacts,

17   John Reed was then Vice President, but he was the lone

18   coordinator, for a better word. And then he was

19   President and Chairman, if you want to go through his career.

20   Q   Well, if you know it, briefly, sure.

21   A   Basically that's what happened, yes. That's

22   public knowledge. He retires 1 May 2000.

1 tell you when he was coming to New York.

2   Q   He has been described as a trust officer with

3 respect to Citibank accounts. But from what you have just

4 said --

5   A   I have never seen that on the record. Now, he

6 may have said it, yes. I wouldn't doubt that a bit.

7   Q   But would it be more accurate to say in fact

8 the true trust officer was John Reed?

9   A   From Day 1, regardless of what his job was in

10 his bank later.

11   Q   This is an aside that I have chosen. for a while

12 he dealt with a bank called Pan Islamic American Bank. Have

13 you ever heard of that bank?

14   A   Not really. I am sure that's probably up on the

15 third floor of the building, but he certainly has no

16 permanent location.

17   Q   He is purported to be an officer in Srur, S-R-U-R,

18 an officer in the bank.

19   A   I never talked to him, no.

20   Q   Now, I have been advised, and I want to know if

21 you have knowledge or understanding if that Project Hammer

22 also included the raising of funds and the transferring of

1 funds for the purpose of providing money for military

2 operations in Southern Africa?

3   A   Sudan, the Sahara, yes, that's been mentioned.

4 Mentioned, I don't think that was the main purpose, no.

5   Q   I understand. Do you know any of the facts

6 surrounding that kind of operation?

7   A   No, except broad statements.

8   Q   What would you say is a broad statement?

9   A   Well, they wanted to take credit for almost

10 everything that was done, and therefore they stretched it

11 instead and extending the exact facts.

12   Hold it one minute.

13   (Short recess taken.)

14   BY MR. D'ERASMO:

15   Q   I have been advised, and I am wondering if you

16 have any knowledge of the fact that Mr. Van Rooyen and

17 Stander were acting as agents of U. S. arms dealers who were

18 shipping arms to Angola and Mozambique?

19   A   They certainly took credit. Whether they ever

20 closed a great deal or not, I don't know. But they would

21 always say, on my last trip to Alexandria, we didn't see you.

22 Why were you in Alexandria? Well, that's where the arms

1 year, and so forth. So, when you use the word collateral

2 that's as basic as anything in the loan business, whether

3 you are talking about buying and selling an automobile, or

4 buying and selling a nation.

5   Q   The way the word has been used in some of the

6 transactions that you and I talked about seems to be used

7 to describe the purchase and sale of commercial banking

8 instruments. And the instruments are commonly referred to

9 as collateral.

10   A   That is correct.

11   Q   But that's a slightly different version.

12   A   That's obvious. I made the simplest answer to

13 you for the automobile.

14   Q   When it is used in the way I just described, the

15 collateral, usually described as I have said, a very large

16 amount of banking instruments with a certain face value

17 that are discounted and then resold.

18   A   It is about 35. You sign it all and you sell

19 it simultaneously.

20   Q   At a discount?

21   A   Everything is at a discount.

22   Q   Now, are instruments actually issued, or

1   Q   All right. With respect to that exhibit, and

2   the question I asked earlier about the size of some of those

3   Hammer transactions, do you see a number on the bottom of

4   the page?

5   A   Yes.

6   Q   First of all, can you tell us what that number

7   means?

8   A   That on this date they thought this was the

9   value.

10   MR. D'ERASMO: And, Tom, if I may take a moment,

11   I have identified it as Exhibit 1, and I would like to

12   mark it as Exhibit 1 in the deposition, okay?

13   (Hammer Project schematic, 1 pg,
                                was marked Exhibit No. 1 and is
14   attached to the original.)

15   BY MR. D'ERASMO:

16   Q   Okay. What was the number as of whatever date

17   that is?

18   A   This number, and I am going to read it properly,

19   $223,104,000,008.03.

20   Q   And that purports to be the balance in account,

21   $223,104,000.008.03.

22   A   That is correct.

1   Q   Now, do you know how this number was obtained?

2   A   Technically, it was put in all 30 some odd

3 accounts together.

4   Q   Where were these 30 odd accounts?

5   A   Almost in one solid block at Citibank.

6   Q   Would they have been in the control of Mr. Reed?

7   A   Probably not all because there were so many

8 different participants involved, and different locations,

9 countries, that I would say no, he did not have complete

10 control, but everybody recognized it wouldn't be settled

11 until it got to him.

12   Q   And these were, you say, accounts for various

13 people around the world?

14   A   Yes.

15   Q   Produced as a result of what?

16   A   Well, most of them figured that the greed

17 in particular were mighty high. And, if I put up this

18 amount of money, then I am going to get this kind of money

19 coming back. That's the way practically all of it was.

20 I hate to use the word sole, but present might be a better

21 word.

22   Q   Were these accounts for the benefit of people

1 law schools I am talking about, passed the Bar, and so

2 forth. I am sure he got several of them. So, he had

3 inside relationships. Obviously, they didn't start, but he

4 could call them up and say, "Joe, can you do so and so?"

5 And I confirmed that. That's the kind of conversations you

6 had. You never knew who Joe was. I really didn't know what

7 he asked, and I didn't know whether I got the answer back.

8 He was thorough.

9   Q   Did you yourself contact people inside the bank

10 about this?

11   A   We did our best to make the normal approaches,

12 but I can see the President of the United States with no

13 trouble. I cannot see Reed.

14   Q   Did you communicate with anyone, other than

15 Reed, in your effort to try to free up thedse commissions,

16 or profit?

17   A   Certainly We made several trips to New York,

18 and a lot of telephone calls.

19   Q   Did you meet people from Citibank?

20   A   For a better word indirectly in the sense that

21 as soon as you got got telephone contact with one, then all

22 of a sudden he was on leave, and I picked up his assistant.

He had to go back through it. Two weeks later to approve
it. And then he goes on vacation. So, you got a run
around type of thing. You never could get the same lawyer
back is about the easiest way to say it.

Q   All right. Besides the lawyers at the bank, was
there anyone at the bank that you would talk to from time
to time about this that you feel --

A   Paul Green said, "I know all of the directors,
and when it is time to talk to the directors, I will."
Whether he did, how much he did, he did not include me in.
And, quite frankly, I didn't push too hard at this stage of
the game because my whole role was to keep 30 people happy
and thought then he was going to break the road jam and
accept the responsibility, and so forth.

Q   Now, these 30 people, would they be some of
them on this?

A   That's basically what this is. Now, where all
the 30 are, I do not know it, but they have always been
referred to as the 30 brokers.

Q   We talked a moment ago about the balance in
this account and such past account numbers listed on
Exhibit 1.

1   A   An off ledger account means that if we took out

2   a big sum of money from the bank it wouldn't change the

3   basic banking balance sheet for that day. And therefore

4   off ledger. When it is off ledger, it doesn't affect the

5   bank. That's one reason I couldn't see why they didn't

6   go ahead and complete some of them.

7   Q   And put it into the bank?

8   A   Yes.

9   Q   Now, are those off ledger accounts inspected?

10 A   They are reset is about the same way to say it.

11 You get your balance sheet - this is running a small bank

12 now -- you get your balance sheet at the end of the day, and

13 then you come back and take the second balance sheet, which

14 is off there, and then you find the boss slipped a little

15 paper his two figures, and you can go home. The

16 responsibility is --

17 Q   The bank examiners come in, do they examine these

18 off ledger accounts?

19 A   Yes.

20 Q   Excuse me, straighten me out, would these kind

21 of accounts, these off ledger accounts, be handled by the

22 private banking department of the bank?

1   A   Generally, you have a ledger account, off ledger

2   account. Now, they may give it some other fancy name for

3   putting it on the door of the building, but yes, every big

4   bank has got an off ledger balance. And they pull it every

5   day. This is not something you do monthly, you do it the

6   close of every business day.

7   Q   You believe that's where --

8   A   --that's where you hide money.

9   Q   Would that be where the Hammer operation would go?

10   A   I am sure it is.

11   Q   Now, again referring to Exhibit 1, you see the

12   words transaction continued until November or December of

13   '91? Do you see that?

14   A   I think he is very accurate .

15   Q   Do you see the name of the banks mentioned here?

16   A   Yes.

17   Q   Specifically, Bank of America, Canadian Imperial

18   Bank of Commerce, and then, of course, Citibank?

19   A   They are all corresponding banks.

20   Q   Did you ever have any discussions with any of

21   the people at any of these banks with respect to this

22   transaction?

1 put 5 years, older countries put 10 years.

2   Q   It sounds like those dormant accounts become

3 not property of the bank but the U. S. Government, or what?

4   A   There is an interim period there to where the

5 banks ought to get this money out, and then when they have

6 gotten their money out and a profit, then all of a sudden

7 they begin saying it is now time to pay the government what

8 we owe them.

9   Q   I have been advised that a chunk of the Hammer

10 Project funds that were used to trade, to invest and reinvest,

11 came from a large block of assets that CIA put in the bank.

12   A   And they pulled that several times from several

13 sources. Nobody is going to confirm it.

14   Q   Are those sources reliable?

15   A   Certainly they are educated guesses.

16   Q   If I understand it correctly, assuming that that

17 kind of statement is correct, would you regard that as

18 being only a part of the monies that were involved in

19 Hammer, or assets involved in Hammer, or was it primarily --

20   A   I don't have any idea. Hammer today, it could

21 be tremendous because if somebody has been trading it for

22 12 years they have made a lot of money.

1   Q   Do you think the traders involved in handling

2 these funds, the funds you have been describing, would be

3 government traders, or private banking traders, or a

4 combination thereof?

5   A   They were probably like IRS, they learned how

6 to do the IRS from the government side, and then retired

7 or quit, they walked across the street and open up a CPA

8 shop, and all of a sudden they are on the other side doing

9 exactly what they were collecting across the street. Now

10 they are back on this side of the street making a profit.

11   Q   I have also marked as a deposition exhibit

12 the affidavit of Mr. Hughes.

13   A   I have to admit at the outset I didn't have time

14 to read it all. I did give it a good evaluation in my

15 mind. Hughes came into this, as far as I was concerned,

16 fairly late. I really did not meet him until January 15,

17 this year, 2000. And he came in with such demands that I

18 really didn't try to work with him. And I told him, I said,

19 "Look, I don't see where if you want to pay me early, you

20 think you got something coming, and you want me to make a

21 trip to Columbus, Ohio, and that's the only place we can

22 meet." and the man is a little bit stronger than I am ready

1   A   No, I never met him.

2   Q   With respect to this transaction that he

3 discussed with you, do you have any special knowledge or

4 information about that transaction?

5   A   No, I really do not. And actually it was one

6 of the very early transactions as far as I am concerned

7 with Hammer. I think he is the one that expanded Hammer

8 in the sense that we moved from one hundred million to

9 a billion type of movement, and now we are doubling, about

10 a trillion. He is the one that enhanced it is the best way

11 of saying.

12   Q   When you say enhanced, he enhanced the demand,

13 or actual activity?

14   A   Both.

15   Q   By virtue of his financial --

16   A   Look, if he put up this kind of money, he had

17 some clout.

18   Q   Have you ever heard the name Gary Patterson

19 before?

20   A   Only as a lawyer, and he had represented Hughes.

21   Q   How about Jerry Pyers, another trader, collateral

22 trader?

Index